A Critical History of Poverty Finance

T0307971

'Nick Bernards has crafted the definitive account of the history of poverty finance, skilfully revealing its entanglements with the uneven development of capitalism.'

—Susanne Soederberg, Professor of Global Political Economy,
Queen's University, Canada

'In this outstanding history of poverty finance, Nick Bernards tackles the belief that if only markets could be designed more imaginatively, or the latest financial technology be applied, then it is only a matter of time before the poor are able to be productively included in the financial system. As Bernards points out, financial exclusion persists not because of a lack of design or fancy technology but because the problem of uneven development is persistent and structural; addressing this will require more effort than simply pinning one's hopes on yet another round of financial innovation.'

—Andrew Leyshon, Emeritus Professor of Economic Geography at the
University of Nottingham, author of *Reformatted: Code, Networks and
the Transformation of the Music Industry* and co-editor of *Money
and Finance after the Crisis: Critical Thinking for Uncertain Times*

A Critical History of Poverty Finance

Colonial Roots and Neoliberal Failures

Nick Bernards

First published 2022 by Pluto Press
New Wing, Somerset House, Strand, London WC2R 1LA

www.plutobooks.com

British Library Cataloguing in Publication Data
A catalogue record for this book is available from the British Library

ISBN 978 0 7453 4483 6   Hardback
ISBN 978 0 7453 4482 9   Paperback
ISBN 978 0 7453 4486 7   PDF
ISBN 978 0 7453 4484 3   EPUB

This book is printed on paper suitable for recycling and made from fully managed and sustained forest sources. Logging, pulping and manufacturing processes are expected to conform to the environmental standards of the country of origin.

Typeset by Stanford DTP Services, Northampton, England

Simultaneously printed in the United Kingdom and United States of America

For Laura and Max, again

Contents

Acknowledgements

I started working on what would eventually become this book as part of a Social Science and Humanities Research Council of Canada (SSHRC) Postdoctoral Fellowship at Queen's University, Canada. Thanks are due to SSHRC for financial support, to the Departments of Political Studies and Global Development Studies at Queen's for giving me space to start working on it, and, especially, to Susanne Soederberg for her support as supervisor.

I've since moved to the University of Warwick, where I've benefited a great deal from working with brilliant colleagues in the School for Cross-Faculty Studies and the Department of Politics and International Studies. I've also had the good fortune at Warwick of being able to teach several cohorts of very good students on topics very closely related to my research. I'm especially grateful to the students on GD 309 (Debt, Money and Global Sustainable Development), who have engaged with lectures and seminars in which I've worked through some of the ideas presented in this book with enthusiasm and insight.

The book draws in places on archival research funded by the British International Studies Association, through their Early Career Small Research Grants scheme. I'm grateful to BISA for this support.

Parts of this project have been presented in seminars at the University of Warwick, the University of Nottingham, and University College Dublin; at workshops hosted at the University of Durham, the University of Sussex, and the Balsillie School of International Affairs; and at various British International Studies Association and International Studies Association annual conferences. Participants and hosts at all of these events have helped a good deal in getting together the ideas presented below.

A number of people have helped refine various elements of this project as it has come together slowly over the last five years or so. Thanks are due to (alphabetically) Rob Aitken, Ali Bhagat, Malcolm Campbell-Verduyn, Chris Clarke, Ben Clift, Florence Dafe, Martin Danyluk, Juanita Elias, Shaun French, Ingrid Kvangraven, Andrew Leyshon, Laura Mahrenbach, Stephen McBride, Johannes Petry, Tony Porter, Shirin Rai, Daivi Rodima-Taylor, Leon Sealey-Huggins, Alastair Smith, Susanne Soederberg,

Celine Tan, Mat Watson (and surely to many others I've neglected to mention) for reading or discussing various parts of the project as it has come together. Special thanks are due to Malcolm, Tony, and Susanne for reading over the full manuscript in draft form. This book is much better for their input. Of course, any remaining errors are my own.

Thanks to all at Pluto for their work bringing this book into production. I'm especially indebted to Jakob Horstman for his excellent editorial work, his close reading of the manuscript, and generally for his support throughout the development of this book. Thanks also to Miri Davidson for copy-editing the finished manuscript. I'm equally grateful to the four anonymous reviewers who provided very helpful comments at proposal stage which helped to give the project a much clearer direction.

I did most of the work of writing this book during what turned out to be a very strange year. I owe an enormous debt to Laura and Max. Both were around for much more of the writing process than any of us anticipated. Both provided (usually) welcome distractions, to which, in retrospect, I owe the fact I finished writing the book (mostly) sane. Max has been a nearly endless source of joy. I could not ask for a better friend or partner than Laura. This book is dedicated to them both.

Acronyms

A2ii	Access to Insurance Initiative
ADBP	Agricultural Development Bank of Pakistan
AFI	Alliance for Financial Inclusion
ARDC	Agriculture Rediscount and Development Corporation (India)
ASA	Association for Social Advancement
BGC	Bank of the Gold Coast
BFA	Bali Fintech Agenda
BKB	Bangladesh Krishi Bank
BRAC	Bangladesh Rural Advancement Committee
CBK	Central Bank of Kenya
CCCAM	Caisse Centrale de Crédit Agricole Mutuel
CDO	collateralised debt obligation
CFAO	Compagnie Française de l'Afrique Occidentale
CGAP	Consultative Group to Assist the Poor
CNCA	Caisse Nationale de Credit Agricôle
CPK	Colony and Protectorate of Kenya
CRA	credit rating agencies
EFL	Entrepreneurial Finance Lab
FFP	*fondo financiero privado*
FMO	Financierings-Maatschappij voor Ontwikkelingslanden (Netherlands)
FMT	FinMark Trust
FOMIN	Multilateral Investment Fund
GIZ	Deutsche Gesellschaft für Internationale Zusammenarbeit
GPFI	Global Partnership for Financial Inclusion
HIGF	Housing Investment Guaranty Fund
HLPs	High-Level Principles for Digital Financial Inclusion
IAA	International Actuarial Association
IADB	Inter-American Development Bank
IAIS	International Association of Insurance Supervisors
ICPs	Insurance Core Principles
IFAD	International Fund for Agricultural Development

IFC	International Finance Corporation
IFI	international financial institution
ILO	International Labour Organization
IMF	International Monetary Fund
IPO	initial public offering
JFS	Janalakshmi Financial Services
LAB	Land and Agricultural Bank (Kenya)
LMICs	Low- and Middle-Income Countries
M-CRIL	MicroCredit Ratings International
MCRA	microcredit rating agency
MFI	microfinance institution
MIC	Microinsurance Centre
MIV	microfinance investment vehicle
NGO	Non-Governmental Organisation
RBI	Reserve Bank of India
RCT	randomised control trial
SHG	self-help group
SIDBI	Small Industries Development Bank of India
SIPs	Sociétés Indigènes de Prévoyance
S&P	Standard and Poor's
STS	science and technology studies
UKAP	UK Actuarial Profession
UNDP	United Nations Development Programme
USAID	United States Agency for International Development
USGAO	United States Government Accountability Office

Introduction

A World Bank official interviewed by the *Financial Times* in early 2019 rhapsodised the virtues of emerging financial technology (fintech):

> It reduces costs, it's much more efficient, it can be scaled up... It does come with risks as well because, you know, you really don't want to hurt those that are most vulnerable, so we have to be careful. But I think it is really remarkable. (Politi 2019)

Media outlets including the *Guardian* and *The Economist* have run glowing reports about the promise of fintech (e.g. Gould 2015; Noonan 2019). These have included breathless accounts of financial 'innovations' ranging from psychometric credit scoring methods (*The Economist* 2016) to MobiLife, a South African life insurer offering a (truly dystopian) product called 'FoodSurance' – which pays out in weekly grocery vouchers sent to beneficiaries' mobile phones if a family breadwinner dies (Noonan 2019) – to index-based livestock insurance schemes using satellite imagery to assess the extent of drought (*The Economist* 2014). Even a more cautionary piece run in *The Economist* in early 2020 opened with the assertion that 'For those seeking to help the worst-off in poor countries, the mobile phone has been a magic wand' (*The Economist* 2020). There is a growing army of consultancies, think tanks, and philanthropic organisations similarly promoting fintech applications (e.g. McKinsey & Co. 2016; Insight2Impact 2016; Hoder *et al.* 2016; PwC 2016).

This optimistic consensus about fintech is rather fragile, however, if we look any closer. There are an increasing number of critical studies looking at the development of fintech in relation to 'financial inclusion' (see Aitken 2017; Bernards 2019a; Clarke 2019; Frimpong Boahmah and Murshid 2019; Gabor and Brooks 2017; Jain and Gabor 2020; Langevin 2019; Langley and Leyshon 2020; Natile 2020). These studies have provided badly-needed critical perspectives on the rise of fintech – criticising the developmental claims of fintech advocates (Bernards 2019b; Langevin 2019), highlighting tendencies towards pervasive surveillance and discipline enacted through new modes of credit scoring

(Aitken 2017; Gabor and Brooks 2017), and analysing the dynamics of consolidation and monopolisation in emergent platforms (Clarke 2019; Langley and Leyshon 2020). Critics have equally noted a disconnect between what can be measured through, for example, mobile phone data or psychometric tests and the underlying patterns of economic activity necessary to repay loans. Big data credit scoring, Langevin (2019) notes, is 'dangerously hermetic' to real productive activity. And, again, while fintech is being touted by the G20, the World Bank, and the IMF as a solution to many of the practical challenges encountered in promoting financial inclusion, evidence is emerging that claims about the power of fintech to achieve greater 'access' to financial services, and more importantly to reduce poverty in doing so, are suspect (see Bateman *et al.* 2019; Bernards 2019a; 2019b).

Yet there is little about this story – a story of 'innovative' financial miracle cures for poverty which have turned out not to work – that is new. The claim that providing access to finance will be a 'win-win', benefiting the poorest and allowing the financial sector to open up new sources of profits, is surprisingly mutable and durable despite accumulating evidence of the inability of finance, in and of itself, to deliver actual reductions in poverty. Fintech hype promises new, digitally-enabled means of extending access to finance. But this basic objective itself is an old one. The embrace of fintech echoes both recent interventions and a much longer history of efforts at resolving relations of poverty and dispossession through the development of new financial tools. At its core, this book is an attempt to place the current vogue in global development for fintech in this longer history.

I do so by drawing together an analysis of a range of activities that can usefully be grouped under the heading of 'poverty finance', running from the early twentieth century to the present. I've adopted the term 'poverty finance' from Rankin (2013). She uses it to refer to 'the business of extending financial services to those traditionally excluded from the mainstream financial system' (2013:547). For Rankin, the general term 'poverty finance' is a means of drawing out the connections between projects in the Global North and South – showing how both microcredit and subprime mortgage markets depend on a kind of 'socio-spatial fix.' That is, Rankin emphasises how poverty finance creates new avenues for the redeployment of over-accumulated capital, both by reconfiguring spatial relations (as in Harvey's [2006] 'spatial fix') and by configuring the survival of racialised and gendered marginal populations in ways that are amenable to financial accumulation. For the purposes of this book, the general rubric of poverty finance – designating activities aimed at extending finance to those 'outside' the mainstream financial system – is also a useful way of grouping together a range of activities across time.

The history of poverty finance, understood in this sense, can be traced backward through a series of (mostly failed) interventions dating to the colonial era. Fintech has gained prominence precisely as efforts to promote 'financial inclusion' by other means have run into difficulty. Since the 2008 global financial crisis, 'financial inclusion' has become increasingly central to global and national development agendas. Enhanced access to financial services for the poorest has been widely embraced as a policy goal by major development agencies, and is increasingly seen as a necessary condition for 'inclusive' and sustainable growth, financial stability, and poverty reduction (AFI 2010). Yet there has, thus far, been little clear evidence of benefits for target populations. Critics have, from the start, highlighted the exploitative character of financial markets being developed under the rubric of 'financial inclusion' (e.g. Soederberg 2013), and called into question the 'win-win' narratives underlying them (Mader 2018). For that matter, there is, at best, limited evidence that such policy efforts have even led to wider access to financial services. Borrowing from formal financial institutions continues to be heavily outweighed by borrowing from family and friends or informal lenders in most developing regions. The growth of 'access' to formal credit has been slow, uneven, and even prone to reversals in particular cases. Indeed, the slow progress of financial inclusion has arguably been a major driver of the embrace of fintech by global policymakers (see Bernards 2019b).

The rise and fall of financial inclusion itself echoed and responded to debates on microfinance in the 2000s and 2010s. Microfinance was initially seen as a silver bullet for poverty reduction, reaching its apogee in 2006 when Grameen Bank founder and microcredit evangelist Mohammad Yunus was awarded the Nobel Peace Prize. Microfinance promised a win-win whereby poor people (primarily women), recast as 'entrepreneurs', would get access to credit in order ostensibly to build businesses and lift themselves out of poverty, all while group lending structures would mobilise local community solidarities to make sure that money was repaid and secure profits for lenders. But grand claims about the benefits of microcredit were never matched by evidence in practice (see Duvendack et al. 2011). Claims about the mechanisms through which microfinance was meant to benefit the poor were downgraded from facilitating entrepreneurial growth to 'consumption smoothing' – enabling people to manage fluctuations in income by borrowing (e.g. Rosenberg 2010; Roodman 2012). Microcredit was reframed as a means of helping people cope with poverty rather than lifting people out of it. Even sympathetic authors started highlighting 'trade-offs' implicit in the development of commercial microcredit (Cull *et al.* 2009). Alongside these reassessments, serious critiques of microcredit accumulated, increasingly coming from insiders (e.g. Sinclair 2012). This growing scepticism coincided with a series of catastrophic microcredit crises, the most notable of which took place in Andhra Pradesh, India, where dozens of over-indebted farmers committed suicide between 2009 and 2010.

As we'll see in the subsequent chapters, the story is even older than this. Microcredit itself, as a development fad, very much had its origins in some of the responses to the failures of previous rounds of financial reforms. Early neoliberals in the 1970s and the early 1980s saw financial deregulation as a means of ensuring small farmers in marginalised communities had access to credit (needless to say, this is not how it worked out). And while contemporary solutions are unquestionably different, this basic approach of framing development interventions around providing access to credit is older still. Colonial officials in the first half of the twentieth century identified the lack of access to affordable credit, savings, and insurance as a problem. And they identified many of the same underlying obstacles to solving this problem. Concerns about the comparatively high cost of making small transactions and the lack of appropriate collateral on the part of poor farmers and others lacking formal property rights in land are rampant in colonial-era documents, just as they are in contemporary invocations of fintech.

This long, dubious pedigree suggests that recent so-called 'innovations' are in fact efforts to wrestle with more deeply-rooted problems. It also suggests that we need critical analyses that work to place present-day experiments with fintech and financial inclusion in this longer history. Such an analysis is worthwhile because it holds the potential both to tell us something useful about the underlying tangle of contradictions at the intersection of finance and poverty and, more generally, about the limits of neoliberalism. Critics of microfinance (e.g. Bateman 2010; Rankin 2001) and financial inclusion (e.g. Soederberg 2014; Price 2019) have often noted that these projects are paradigmatically neoliberal. They have a point. The assumption that enabling greater access to formal savings, credit, and insurance will lead to reductions in poverty does, indeed, epitomise neoliberal logics. These successive projects imagine the solution to poverty is to be found in incorporating the poor into new forms of markets, and that poverty reduction can be achieved primarily through the creation of new spheres of private profit. Less common, though, have been efforts to step back and ask what the development of microfinance, financial inclusion, fintech, and the like can tell us about neoliberalism – a task for which the longer historical view offered in this book is very useful.

In what follows, I show how the longer history of poverty finance reflects efforts to grapple with a fundamental paradox. The reason the poor have often been seen to need access to finance – namely, their low and unpredictable incomes – is also a key reason why alleviating poverty by providing financial services to the poorest on a commercial basis has typically proven to be little more than a politically-driven fantasy. It's risky and not particularly profitable, under most circumstances, to lend money to, insure, or provide other financial services to people with small and irregular incomes. Finance capital is inherently profit-oriented. Banks and other asset holders are unlikely to invest money in anything from which they don't expect to make high returns. Moreover, while we often associate high finance with speculation and high-stakes gambling, it is often risk-averse – not least when it comes to putting money into new and uncertain environments. Mainstream financial institutions have thus been interested in providing services to poorer borrowers only on occasion, often requiring direct or indirect subsidies. The key point is that financial markets simply can't, in and of themselves, change the underlying structures of power and exploitation that create poverty. Nor, it must be said, are financiers typically much interested in doing so. While contemporary poverty finance interventions are often read as incidences of 'financialisation', the frequent reluctance of finance capital to actually engage with them should give us pause on this front. Poverty finance interventions very often seek to prepare the ground for the profitable deployment of finance capital, but are typically driven not so much by the dictates of finance itself, but by fraught efforts to coax it into serving developmental ends. Unambiguous success stories are exceedingly rare. At times, poverty finance interventions have caused real harm – as in the Andhra Pradesh crisis noted above. More often, though, the problem is that they've failed to confront and transform the wider structures of exploitation underlying relations of poverty, and have often explicitly sought to forestall wider structural changes or redistributive policies. Poverty finance, in short, fails because it works through and reinforces existing patterns of uneven development.

These fundamental dynamics manifest themselves in a recurrent tension between logics of inclusion and stratification. Soederberg (2014:22–3) argues, helpfully, that invocations of 'inclusion' and 'access' to credit and financial markets for previously marginalised groups – the extension of membership in the 'community of money', in Marx's phrase – are powerful *political* interventions. They simultaneously invoke the right to participate in certain liberal freedoms (private property, enterprise, and contractual rights) while obscuring the underlying relations of exploitation on which financial transactions ultimately rest. Yet, actually-existing poverty finance interventions have frequently operated precisely by promising new ways of enabling financial institutions to reliably sort good from bad credit risks, insurable from non-insurable risks, productive farmers and incipient entrepreneurs from their (implicitly more deservingly poor) peers. Historically, we can trace out different responses to this tension, but it is a critical one, rooted in the fundamental contradiction between profit logics on one hand and precarious livelihoods on the other.

In tracing this tension through the longer history covered below, this book makes two related arguments. First, the distinctive form of the paradox identified above in actually-existing global capitalism is a product of colonial histories. This is true, firstly, in the widely accepted sense that global patterns of poverty and uneven development are colonial in their origins. But it is also true in the less obvious sense that the organisation of production and accumulation in colonial territories has had enduring effects on the development and organisation of postcolonial financial systems. Colonial economic systems varied, but they were broadly designed to transfer profits back to the metropole, and to transfer the costs and risks of productive activities onto racialised working classes (broadly understood) in colonised territories. Colonial banks, in this context, specialised in lucrative, low-risk activities like facilitating funds transfers between colonised and metropolitan territories. They made comparatively few loans in general, almost entirely to colonial governments and large merchant firms, and to expatriate plantations, farms, or mines where these were present. These systems have often persisted in important respects long after the end of formal colonial rule. The second argument this book makes is that the story of poverty finance since the 1970s can usefully be read as a succession of failures to grapple with limits posed by these underlying patterns of uneven development. Neoliberal efforts to engineer reductions in poverty through the creation of new financial markets in such contexts are likely doomed from the start. But neoliberal modes of governance appear incapable of recognising or addressing the deep-rooted limits posed by (neo)colonial forms of capitalism.

MAKING MARKETS

While the aims of this book are primarily empirical, it is useful to outline a few key conceptual elements of the discussion to follow here. My perspective is primarily rooted in historical materialist political economy, but draws on engagements with science and technology studies (STS) approaches as well. As I'll argue further in the following pages, both of these approaches usefully enjoin us to lift the lid on the social, historical, and material relations underlying acts of market exchange, in different but complementary ways.[1]

I understand neoliberalism as, above all, a tendency towards failure-prone efforts at solving social problems by building markets (see Mirowski 2009; Peck 2010). Understanding the uneven and failure-prone unfolding of neoliberal projects, including poverty finance, thus means engaging with problems of marketisation – the conjoined processes by which markets are constructed and through which social processes are rendered subject to markets. Processes of marketisation are rarely easy or straightforward, as the long series of failed efforts at developing markets for poverty finance shows particularly clearly. Marketisation often founders on the messy confrontation between neoliberal fantasies of efficient, socially beneficial markets and the contradictory spatial, material and social conditions of actually-existing capital accumulation. Markets depend on underlying configurations of labour and property relations articulated across space which enable commodities to reach 'the market', processes which acts of exchange can fetishise and obscure (cf. Christophers 2014; Cahill 2020). They also depend on the presence of particular infrastructures – backgrounded and often mundane systems of devices, material objects, and social routines through which acts of exchange can be carried out across time and space (see Bernards and Campbell-Verduyn 2019). Over the next four subsections, I develop these arguments further. First, I outline the book's conception of neoliberalism as a set of politically-driven processes of marketisation. In the next two subsections, I discuss two crucial limits to processes of marketisation: the uneven development of financial infrastructures and the enduring centrality of labour to financial accumulation. Finally, I differentiate this perspective from previous analyses drawing on the concept of financialisation.

Neoliberalism as marketisation

'Neoliberalism' can, admittedly, be a slippery concept. It's useful, I think, to view neoliberalism as a set of logics unfolding (unevenly) through particular regulatory projects. As Mirowski (2009) and others have noted, the core organising logic of neoliberal politics is an epistemic faith in the 'market' as the most efficient means of processing information and allocating resources. Insofar as there is a core 'neoliberal' belief, then, it is that 'prices in an efficient market "contain all relevant information" and therefore cannot be predicted by mere mortals' (Mirowski 2009:435), coupled with a growing recognition that markets themselves need to be produced and engineered into being (see Nik-Khah and Mirowski 2019). By extension, collective problems are seen as best resolved by expanding the scope of existing markets, by making new ones, or by approximating market-like mechanisms in cases where neither of these is possible (Frankel *et al.* 2019).

Neoliberalism, in this sense, represents a political logic which is only ever realised in part and with great difficulty – neoliberalism tends to 'fail and flail forward', in Peck's (2010:7) phrase. Brenner *et al.* helpfully insist that, rather than an epochal 'end state', neoliberalism is better understood as a series of dispersed and variegated 'neoliberalizing processes', dating roughly to the 1970s, which have 'facilitated marketization and commodification while simultaneously *intensifying* the uneven development of regulatory forms across places, territories and scales' (Brenner *et al.* 2010a:184; see also Brenner *et al.* 2010b; Peck 2010; 2013a). While longer-run processes of marketisation and commodification are endemic in capitalism, neoliberalism is distinguished first of all by the emphasis on the market as a mechanism for collective decision-making and resource allocation, and increasingly also by the emphasis on *engineering* or *designing* markets. Failure and troubleshooting, in short, are integral aspects of the history of neoliberalism (see Best 2013; 2020). What is critical for the moment is that the existing history of *responses* to these failures is dominated by a tendency to resort to markets 'suitably reengineered and promoted' to 'provide solutions to the problems seemingly caused by the market in the first place' (Mirowski 2009:439).

In short, neoliberalism should be understood as a political project seeking to expand the scope of markets in governing social life, particularly by dispersed processes of market design and engineering. Neoliberal views often treat the market as a kind of 'default setting' for human interaction. A number of recent Marxist critics have rightly cautioned against critiques of neoliberalism that fall into the same trap of fetishising 'the market' as a social form (Cahill 2020; Knafo 2020; Copley and Moraitis 2021). Markets are not a default setting on economic activity that can be 'disembedded' from (or re-embedded in) social regulation. Markets need to be constructed, often imperfectly, out of concrete social and spatial relations (and mediated by a variety of devices, routines, and standards). Indeed, much of the history traced out in what follows is precisely a series of efforts to prepare the ground for the development of new markets, only for financial capital to fail to turn up. If we want to get to grips with the tendency of neoliberalism to 'fail and flail forward' (Peck 2010:7), we need to think in concrete terms about how markets are *made*, and about the limits to such processes of construction posed by existing patterns of uneven development. I argue in what follows that we need to understand two underlying conditions for such processes of marketisation, in order to grasp the troubled progress of neoliberal projects in global development: first, the uneven materiality of the 'infrastructures' needed to enable market activity and, second, the centrality of labour to capitalist accumulation. I take up each of these points in turn.

Infrastructures and uneven development

To an extent, the uneven development of markets for poverty finance is a manifestation of a more general tendency: namely, that capitalist accumulation tends to produce spatial differentiation across different (but interlinked) scales. Smith (1990) usefully attributes uneven development under capitalism to a 'see-saw' pattern of spatial development. Capitalism requires the transformation of physical space – for example, the construction of roads and power grids, local or regional concentrations of certain activities, or the production of new natures involved in agriculture or mining. As a result, mobile capital tends to cluster activities in particular places. Over time this results in rising labour and other costs, undermining the profitability of such 'developed' areas while creating the conditions for higher profitability in the 'underdeveloped' spaces previously skipped over. 'See-saw' movements of capital, 'from a developed to an underdeveloped area, then at a later point back to the first area which is by now underdeveloped' – ranging in scale from global movements of capital to relatively 'local' dynamics of gentrification – emerge as a result (Smith 1990:150). In practice, though, these see-saw movements are deeply constrained by the physical configurations of space created through capitalist accumulation in the first place: 'there is no omnipotence to capital, and what it can do in reality – albeit a reality of its own making – is much more limited' (Smith 1990:150).

Such production of space also generates important contradictions. Firstly, there is a tendency for localised rates of profitability to fall over time – as, for instance, wages and rents rise with increasing concentration of activity and competition for spatially proximate labour and land, or as infrastructures wear down and become less efficient. Secondly, there is a tendency towards overaccumulation, as accumulated capital lacks profitable avenues for reinvestment. These tendencies together lead, in Harvey's (2006) influential argument, to a perpetual search for 'spatial fixes' – ways to reconfigure new spaces to enable renewed accumulation. The search for a spatial fix in this sense has been a prominent interpretation of the (relatively) recent rise of microfinance and financial inclusion generally (see Soederberg 2013; Rankin 2013) and for the development of fintech in particular (Frimpong Boahmah and Murshid 2019).

But the critical point is that existing configurations of physical space have durable impacts on how and where capital can be redeployed. Even once they've ceased being functional, previous constructions of space can constrain the redeployment of capital in important ways. In Harvey's useful summation, 'The development of the space economy of capitalism is beset by counterposed and contradictory tendencies' (2006:417). There is a growing literature reflecting on how such dynamics of uneven development are reflected in past and present patterns of colonialism, particularly through the development of large-scale infrastructures (see Cowen 2020; Enns and Bersaglio 2020; Kimari and Ernestson 2020). Where considerations of finance have entered into these analyses, though, what has often been explored is how finance capital was circulated through infrastructure projects in colonised territories (e.g. Cowen 2020) or how financial capital has acted as an agent of uneven development (e.g. Bond 1998). Given that our present task is rather to explain the uneven development of *finance itself*, we need some slightly different tools.

It is useful here to draw on emerging debates about 'financial infrastructures' (see Aitken 2017; Bernards and Campbell-Verduyn 2019; de Goede 2021). I follow Bowker and Star (1996) in understanding 'infrastructures' here in the broader sense of backgrounded technical systems allowing basic functions and circulations to be carried out (cf. Star 1999; Edwards 2003; Karasti *et al.* 2016). The principal claim is that circulations of money, credit, and capital are material flows that move through durable, concrete sociotechnical systems and durable repertoires of social practices. Financial infrastructures in this sense include, for instance, physical buildings, record-keeping systems, means of communication, and the embedded systems of standards, metrics, and social practices used to evaluate credit risk. Finance is, in short, subject to the same patterns of uneven spatial and material development as other forms of capital.

We can make three key observations about the character of financial infrastructures which are especially pertinent here. First, (financial) infrastructures are durable. As Star notes of infrastructures more generally, efforts to change infrastructures continually 'wrestl[e] with the inertia of the installed base and inheri[t] strengths and limitations from that base' (1999:382). The material infrastructures of the global financial system embody and render durable deep-rooted patterns of uneven development. Second, infrastructures are spatial. They exist in particular places and enable (or disable) links across space in particular ways. Finally, infrastructures are shaped by and embody broader patterns of power relations and accumulation. Simply put, finance capital does not float in some ethereal market plane, but rather circulates through durable material infrastructures, which shape and constrain future patterns of accumulation. Efforts to build new markets for poverty finance rely in part on the construction of new financial infrastructures, but more often than not these processes of construction play out through complex patterns of 'wrestling' with the inertia of existing systems and with wider contradictory patterns of production and accumulation. It is easier for financial capital to carve out new spaces for accumulation in places where there is already a more elaborated 'base' in place to begin with. Or, precisely because financial infrastructures are durable, they condition subsequent patterns of uneven development.

There are two crucial points here. First, the infrastructures underlying (financial) markets and enabling exchange to take place are durable, material, and exist in space. This is one key mechanism by which colonial histories have continued to shape the uneven development of global finance. Indeed, there are good reasons to think that contemporary infrastructures remain heavily influenced by the geographies of colonial financial systems. De Goede (2021) notes, for instance, that the vast majority of the North-South transfers carried out through the SWIFT international payments system are made between former colonisers and their colonised territories. Second, the centrality of infrastructures to the operation of financial markets gives us an important degree of leverage in understanding how neoliberal poverty finance interventions have taken place. As I'll argue in greater detail in the latter chapters of this book, efforts to promote the spread of poverty finance increasingly take the form of failure-prone efforts to tinker with underlying material infrastructures aiming to smooth the flow of finance capital into poverty finance applications – a dynamic I describe as the 'anticipatory spatial fix'. Yet, as I'll argue further in the following subsection, the troubled history of poverty finance suggests that there are more fundamental limits that neoliberal projects of 're-engineering' markets run up against. Infrastructures enable some kinds of financial circulation and disable others, but financial accumulation nonetheless depends on the contradictory underlying configurations of labour and livelihoods (see Bernards 2020a).

Centring labour in financial markets

A key reason why the poor are held to need efficient financial markets is to enable more effective management of fluctuating incomes. The G20 Principles for Innovative Financial Inclusion (discussed further in Chapter 5), for instance, note that 'a crucial problem for poor people is that their incomes are not only low, but also irregular and unreliable … an annual average income of $2 a day may in actuality range from a high of $5 to low days when no income is earned' (AFI 2010:4). Access to financial services, then, is needed so that the poor can 'manage this low, irregular and unreliable income to ensure regular cash flow and to accumulate sufficient amounts to cover lump sum payments' (AFI 2010:4). Yet, it is for precisely due to irregular incomes that creating new financial markets for the poor has proven consistently difficult.

Here a number of recent Marxian contributions to studies of marketisation are useful insofar as they highlight the necessary interplay of
productive activity and 'fetishised' market relations (e.g. Christophers
2014; Cahill 2020). We can usefully follow Marx in emphasising the
constant tension between the abstract values embodied in the exchange
of money, capital, and commodities and the concrete labour performed in
particular places and times. Harvey observes that a key paradox interro-
gated across Marx's work is 'how the freedom and transitoriness of living
labour as a process is *objectified* in a *fixity* of both things and exchange
ratios between things' (2006:37). Through its embodiment in circulating commodities, for Marx, 'concrete labour becomes the form of the
manifestation of its opposite, abstract human labour' (Marx 1990:150).
Notably, Marx later observes that this dynamic of abstraction reaches its
logical conclusion in circulations of money in financial markets. Here,
'all that we see is the giving out and the repayment' and 'everything
that happens in between' – namely concrete productive activities that
enable the repayment of debts and interest – is 'obliterated' (1991:471).
Importantly, though, this 'obliteration' is only ever partially achieved.
As Harvey notes, financial capital remains dependent on a 'process of
realization within the continual flow of production and consumption'
(2006:95). Insofar as financial profits appear to be 'decoupled' from productive activities, or purely speculative, then, they represent 'the capital
mystification in its most flagrant form' (Marx 1991:516, emphasis added).

Marx's injunction here is to include in our analysis the productive activity that must 'happen in between' payment and repayment
to enable financial accumulation to take place. As Bryan and Rafferty
(2010:216) argue, for instance, the exponential growth in derivatives
markets has required that 'the conditions of working-class life – the need
for multiple-income households; the needs of education, old-age, and
others – are reconfigured so as to privilege the payments that will form
the basis of securities'. The (accordingly) troublesome and failure-prone
character of neoliberal interventions has not often been given sufficient
attention. There have been a number of important contributions which
have sought to locate the sources of financial crises in the overexten-
sion of credit and the inability of financial capital to realise returns in
the 'real' economy – as per Harvey's oft-cited aphorism, 'no matter how
far afield a privately contracted bill of exchange may circulate, it must
always return to its place of origin for redemption' (2006:246). Froud
et al. (2010), for instance, point to the inability of pre-crisis financial

innovations in the US to overcome the 'tyranny of earned income'. Soederberg (2014) somewhat similarly highlights the ways in which 'debtfare' policies seeking to govern poverty and social reproduction through the extension of new forms of credit have created systemic contradictions in the US and Mexico.

Yet there is another vital corollary here: financial markets can't be conjured easily without underlying patterns of production and reproduction enabling the realisation of interest (see Bernards 2019a; 2019b; 2020a). As we'll see very clearly in the following chapters, constructing financial markets in the first place is liable to be difficult in the absence of underlying configurations of labour and social reproduction that enable regular payments of, for example, interest, premia, and savings. The point here is that Marx's reflections on markets and fetishism offer a useful way of thinking through a set of fundamental limits against which neoliberal projects aiming to conjure and re-engineer financial markets are likely to continually run up. Again, it is both difficult for the poor to participate in markets and unprofitable to construct new markets for them, for precisely the reason why the poor are often held to *need* the construction of new markets – namely, low and unpredictable incomes. Here again, as I'll show in the following chapter, patterns of uneven development engendered by colonial patterns of dispossession and extractive development have rendered the construction of new financial markets in postcolonial settings more difficult. This is also a challenge that has been rendered more difficult by the intensification of precarity in the aftermath of structural adjustment across much of the Global South.

To pull the above threads together, then, this book is advancing a conception of neoliberalism as a *political* project of marketisation dating roughly to the 1970s. While processes of marketisation are longstanding elements of capitalism, neoliberal interventions, broadly, are distinguished by a particular focus on market design and engineering processes of marketisation. These projects have continually run up against the limits posed by existing patterns of uneven development. These limits include both the uneven material and spatial patterns of pre-existing financial infrastructures, and wider patterns of dispossession and precarity. Thinking about neoliberalism from this angle helps us to see both why neoliberal projects are fraught, and to understand why the forms of troubleshooting pursued so often come back to efforts to 're-engineer' markets (Mirowski 2009). Markets are difficult to construct in practice – they depend on fragile articulations of material devices and on underlying relations of production, themselves enmeshed with uneven configurations of space, nature, and labour that predate the rise of neoliberalism.

Beyond 'financialisation'

Readers may have noted that, unlike many other critical accounts of fintech and financial inclusion, thus far I've avoided any mention of 'financialisation'. Financial inclusion has, in particular, often drawn attention from authors who see the project as a key extension of wider processes of the 'financialisation of daily life' (e.g. Aitken 2013; Roy 2010; Mader 2018). The latter refers to ways in which financial techniques, and associated rationalities, shape an increasingly wide range of everyday economic practices – a process usefully described by Martin (2002:3) as an 'invitation to live by finance'. It has been common for previous critical analyses of fintech applications in consumer finance to follow this broad line of argument (e.g. Gabor and Brooks 2017; Aitken 2017).

The perspective outlined in the previous two subsections, however, militates against too-easily eliding processes of neoliberalisation and 'financialisation', or of attributing experiments in poverty finance to wider processes of 'financialisation'. Neoliberalism and financialisation are often seen as conjoined developments (e.g. Fine 2013; Fine and Saad-Filho 2017). David Harvey, for one, broadly suggests that the growing dominance of financial over productive capital from the early 1970s was 'used to attack the power of working class movements either directly, by exercising disciplinary oversight on production, or indirectly by facilitating greater geographical mobility for all forms of capital' (2004:77–8). Duménil and Lévy (2004:1–2) make a similar claim that 'neoliberalism is the expression of a desire of a class of capitalist owners and the institutions in which their power is concentrated, which we collectively call "finance", to restore ... the class' revenues and power, which had diminished since the Great Depression and WWII'. The resilience of the neoliberal project in the face of failure is unquestionably sustained in no small part by the backing of powerful fractions of capital and its increasingly deep embeddedness in supranational political institutions – as per Gill's longstanding arguments about the rise of 'new constitutionalism' in global politics (e.g. Gill 1992; 1995; 1998, cf. McBride 2016).

At the same time, as I've intimated above, and as I show in more detail in Chapters 4 to 7 below, much of neoliberal governance in practice consists precisely in trying to coax capital into doing things it's not particularly interested in doing. The continued resort to building markets is perhaps better understood as reflective of severe and abiding constraints on state action, particularly in peripheral countries, imposed by the disciplinary force of financial structures (see Alami 2018; Copley and Moraitis 2021). Critically, though, the 'fiscal crisis of the postcolonial state' is deep-rooted. Trying to foster development by fostering and mobilising 'markets' is a course of action dictated, in part, by the semi-permanent condition of austerity imposed on states at the margins of the global political economy, either shut out of global capital markets or able to access them only on punitive terms. These restrictions have no doubt been amplified since the 1970s by successive episodes of structural adjustment, 'stabilisation' programmes, and conditional debt relief. However, as I show in the following chapter, they are in no small part inherited from the extraverted structures of colonial political economies.

This is an important distinction. It suggests that the history of poverty finance is perhaps less about governance directly by, or in the interests of, finance capital and more about trying to navigate embedded constraints baked into the infrastructures of global finance. Neoliberal governance is often about trying to lay the groundwork for a 'spatial fix' which may never happen (cf. Bigger and Webber 2021). In later chapters, I develop the concept of development as 'anticipatory spatial fix' to describe this mode of practice.

Studies of poverty finance as an iteration of 'financialisation' have provided valuable critiques. They have pointed to significant pathologies implicit in the ways in which new methods of credit scoring seek to make marginal livelihoods legible to financial markets – intrusive and disciplinary modes of quantification of the everyday behaviour of potential borrowers, hyper-individualising narratives framing the poor as risk-taking, entrepreneurial financial subjects (as noted in perceptive critiques from Gabor and Brooks 2017; Aitken 2017). However, in practice, starting from the perspective of 'financialisation' gives us less purchase on understanding how both financial inclusion in general and fintech applications in particular have made far more truncated and uneven progress than is assumed in the optimistic narratives discussed at the beginning of this chapter. New devices are being developed, promoted, and diffused as explicit responses to palpable and longstanding *limits* to financial accumulation, and (arguably) are likely to fail to transcend these limits. Situating these experiments in narratives of 'financialisation' – implying the ever-more pervasive spread of financial logics and subjectivities – can thus lead us to overlook or lose sight of important dynamics.

THE PLAN OF THE BOOK

In what follows, I trace out a history of poverty finance in three parts. Part I of the book outlines how the patterns of uneven development and the core paradoxes identified above are embedded in colonial histories, and how these limits were understood and addressed in the early articulation of neoliberal development governance. Chapter 1 traces the colonial histories of poverty finance. It shows how uneven access to credit was a crucial device for organising labour in many colonial economic systems. The financial sectors that emerged in colonial contexts were generally clustered around urban centres, closely linked to metropolitan merchant capital, and often made their profits primarily by providing remittance services rather than credit. Colonial banks very rarely developed the infrastructures – the routines, social relations, or physical structures – necessary to lend to the majority populations in colonised territories. The chapter considers early experiments with poverty finance, particularly from around 1930 to 1960, as efforts to address key contradictions in this system.

In Chapter 2, I show how, starting in the late 1960s and early 1970s, officials at the World Bank and elsewhere began to focus attention on access to credit, particularly for agriculture and housing, as a key factor in poverty reduction. Poverty finance, in short, was a key area where early neoliberal development interventions were articulated. Critically, though, experiments with poverty finance at the Bank and elsewhere were often based on a misdiagnosis of the underlying limits on the extension of these markets, emphasising restrictions on interest rates and poor collection practices rather than embedded colonial legacies. The chapter develops this argument empirically by tracing the evolution of World Bank and USAID approaches to housing and agrarian credit in the 1970s and 1980s.

Chapter 3 examines the role of structural adjustment in driving renewed experiments with microcredit and microinsurance in the 1990s, in response to the failures of structural adjustment. This chapter traces a notable turn towards 'local' or 'community'-based projects shaped, on the one hand, by efforts to mitigate the most destructive impacts of structural adjustment, and, on the other, by the ongoing constraints of austerity. Despite the focus across many of these projects on developing 'local' or 'community' institutions, they increasingly turned, by the end of the decade, towards efforts to promote commercialisation in order to access external resources.

In Part II, I turn to more explicit efforts to commercialise and marketise microcredit and microinsurance in the 2000s. In Chapter 4, I trace early efforts to promote the development of markets for microcredit. Concerns accumulated about the breadth of impact and scale-ability of community-oriented programmes, with microcredit promoters increasingly concerned that such programmes couldn't be scaled-up in the absence of external resources. In the continued presence of constraints on public resources, it was often assumed that such investments would need to come from global capital. Increasingly, efforts to promote commercialisation turned on the first iterations of development as anticipatory spatial fix – the construction of alternative financial infrastructures in hopes of channelling funds from metropolitan financial markets to microcredit lending.

Chapter 5 examines the crisis of commercial microcredit and the turn to financial inclusion. 'Microcredit' went rather dramatically out of fashion around 2010, as growing evidence of weak impacts was suddenly coupled with a series of microfinance crises – most notably the suicides of dozens of over-indebted farmers in Andhra Pradesh, India. Around the same time, the G20 in particular worked to articulate and popularise a wider agenda of 'financial inclusion', embracing not just microcredit, but also savings, payment systems, and insurance, and justified less in terms of narratives of bootstrapping entrepreneurs and more in terms of providing the poor with financial tools for 'risk management'. This was followed by an array of national 'financial inclusion' strategies across much of the Global South.

Part III of the book returns to the contemporary experiments in 'financial innovation' discussed in the opening pages, showing how these have often functioned as responses to the slower-than-expected progress of financial inclusion. Chapter 6 traces one key component of the 'financial inclusion' agenda – a redoubled insistence that microcredit needed to be accompanied by a wider suite of financial services, including savings, payment systems, and especially insurance. Insurance markets for the poorest have proven perhaps especially difficult to construct in practice. Precisely for this reason, efforts at promoting microinsurance are worth looking at closely. This chapter thus traces a series of unsuccessful efforts at developing commercial markets for microinsurance – simplified, low-cost insurance products targeting the poorest, typically with short coverage periods and strictly limited payouts.

Chapter 7, finally, traces the rise of fintech in global development. The chapter shows that new fintech applications in practice often replicate the limits of existing financial systems highlighted in earlier chapters. The chapter draws on analyses of the emergence, diffusion, and limits of mobile money, psychometric credit scoring, and Big Data lending applications in order to make this argument.

PART I

Poverty finance and the antinomies of colonialism

1
A colonial problem

This chapter argues that the origins of the uneven development of financial markets across the Global South are intrinsically linked to the durable social, ecological, and political regimes underpinning colonial and neocolonial extractivism. This analysis picks up from two important points highlighted in the discussion of neoliberalism and the construction of markets in the introduction. First, efforts to construct 'markets' as such are embedded in deeply uneven patterns of production and accumulation. Transactions between nominal equals in financial markets obscure from view, yet fundamentally rely upon, 'everything that happens in between' the issuance of debt and its repayment (to use Marx's terms, cited above). Second, financial markets are material and spatial. Financial transactions happen in, or between, particular places and through infrastructures bundling together routinised social practices and material objects. Contemporary efforts to redeploy financial capital into overlooked social and spatial spheres, including through new forms of poverty finance, are shaped and constrained not only by what goes on in those places, but also by the spatial and material configuration of existing infrastructures.

The argument here is that colonial legacies matter a good deal on both fronts. Extractive forms of accumulation have left many people in the postcolonial world with limited assets and incomes. Financial infrastructures are also unevenly developed in ways profoundly linked to the social and spatial dynamics of colonial capitalism. There have been, at several points from the 1950s onwards, significant forays by financial capital into peripheral territories – but, as subsequent chapters will show, these have primarily taken place in spaces with the most densely-built financial infrastructures already in place. What's critical here is that colonial political economies, as I'll show further below, depended in various ways on *uneven* access to formal credit. Colonial subjects *were* frequently in debt, and that indebtedness was a crucial organising element in colonial political economies, but small farmers and workers were very rarely indebted to formal financial institutions directly. Debts were often a means employed by merchants and by capitalist farms and mines to discipline cheap labour and to appropriate commodities cheaply.

These arrangements often became increasingly untenable over time, both politically and economically. They undermined the bases for social reproduction and inhibited investments that might have, for instance, raised agricultural productivity. It's in these contradictions, as I show in the latter parts of this chapter, that we can locate the origins of poverty finance as a site of development intervention. These interventions were often fraught and tentative. Overturning existing relations of credit and indebtedness would have entailed more radical reforms to colonial capitalisms than administrators were willing to envision. This tension strongly conditioned the subsequent development of financial infrastructures in colonial and postcolonial territories.

This chapter develops these arguments in three sections. The first section provides a broad overview of patterns of uneven development and the role of finance in colonial capitalism. The second section traces the uneven development of colonial financial systems, showing how different kinds of economic activity were associated with the development of different kinds of financial infrastructures. The third section traces early forms of poverty finance in the 1930s to efforts to respond to the contradictions implicit in these systems, and examines how these were carried over into the postcolonial period. This chapter is, undoubtedly, an exercise in generalisation. It is well beyond the scope of this book to provide a comprehensive overview of colonial financial systems. The aim here is to map out some general tendencies which, I'll argue, have strongly shaped the rollout of neoliberal poverty finance interventions.

COLONIALISM AND UNEVEN DEVELOPMENT

Finance capital has long been recognised as a major driver and beneficiary of imperialism. There is a long tradition of scholarship drawing links between imperialism and the operations of metropolitan financial capital (e.g. Hilferding 1981). From the late nineteenth century, over-accumulated capital in Europe, perhaps especially among a growing class of rentier investors in South West England (see Cain 1985:11–14), increasingly sought opportunities for investment abroad. Several influential recent contributions to the literature similarly explain contemporary forms of imperialism as being driven primarily by the resurgent power of finance capital faced with declining rates of profit from productive enterprise in core countries and seeking new outlets for over-accumulated capital (e.g. Harvey 2003; 2004; Foster 2015; Bond 2004). Recent studies have equally highlighted how colonial structures remain embedded in the kinds of financial links that persist between colonised territories and metropoles (e.g. Alami 2018; Koddenbrock 2020; Tilley 2020; de Goede 2021).

Two key commonalities across most colonial economic systems are worth underlining. First, these economic systems were extractive in character, imposing significant constraints on both productive investments and government fiscal capacity in colonised territories. This extractive character of colonial development has long been emphasised by dependency and world systems approaches (see Kvangraven 2021; Rodney 2018). In general, it's unquestionably true that colonialism enriched the colonisers – or, more precisely, some fractions of capital in metropolitan centers – at the expense of the people and territories that were colonised. Vast fortunes were extracted from colonised territories. Utsa Patnaik (2017:311) has recently estimated, for instance, that net transfers from India to Britain between 1765 and 1938 amounted to £9.18 trillion in present-day money. Finance capital was a key beneficiary of all this – the London money market was a major source of finance for governments, and for mining and infrastructure projects, globally throughout the latter half of the nineteenth century. Notably, it was not until the first decade of the twentieth century that these investments went primarily to British colonial territories (Davis and Huttenback 1985). Equally, though, the colonial 'appropriation' of cheap or unpaid labour, energy, and raw materials from colonised territories was critical to the development of industrial capitalism in the global north (see Moore 2015), often in ways not directly measurable. The centrality of slave-grown cotton and sugar, alongside the profits from the slave trade, to the first industrial revolution is one example (highlighted vividly by Williams [1994] and Inikori [2002], among others). But such patterns persisted well into the twentieth century as well. Rosa Luxemburg (2003), for instance, observed in the early twentieth century that industrial accumulation in Europe remained dependent on the ready supply of raw materials, notably rubber, obtained through colonial plunder and forced labour.

In the broadest sense, centuries of extractive development are an important part of the explanation for the patterns of dispossession, poverty, and irregular work to which neoliberal approaches to poverty finance have responded. It is precisely to the patterns of underdevelopment, insecure incomes, and ecological vulnerability left in the wake of extractive development (see Ye *et al.* 2020) that poverty finance seeks to respond. Yet, at the same time, these responses are fundamentally limited by the uneven development of financial infrastructures.

To make sense of the latter point, we need to look at how the financial sectors that emerged in colonial contexts were shaped by the extractive character of colonial financial systems more generally (Koddenbrock *et al.* 2020; Rodney 2018:138). We could justifiably speak of colonial financial systems as a particular model of banking operation. Colonial banks were clustered around urban centres and mostly made their profits by providing remittance services and lending for large-scale public works and to a few colonial enterprises. They did not usually provide productive credit for the wider colonial economy. These banks, crucially, were headquartered, raised capital, and primarily held assets in metropolitan financial centres, while operating branches across a number of colonial territories. The Finance Secretary for British Malaya would comment, towards the end of the period of formal British rule in 1953, that 'there is ... no gainsaying the fact that it is very difficult to marshal local banking credit to play its full part in the development of Malaya. This is due to the fact that such credit as exists is operated by "exchange banks" and not the type of bank interested in long-term investment in productive activity'.[2] An official in the Colonial Office in London responded that indeed, 'the whole system is primarily designed to meet the needs of the large commercial firms, and there are wide sectors of the economy not well served by this kind of institution'.[3] Koddenbrock *et al.* (2020) rightly, I think, highlight this extraverted character of colonial finance in arguing that the seeming 'divorce' between financial activity and the wider political economy of productive activity is in fact a durable feature of (post)colonial financial systems rather than an effect of 'financialisation' *per se.* Importantly, this was true of banks in formal colonies as well as overseas banks participating in more 'informal' forms of empire – as with, for instance, the dominant role of British banks in Latin America and the Caribbean in the nineteenth and early twentieth centuries (see Joslin 1962). Hudson (2017) likewise traces the rise of quite similar forms of banking practices by US banks in Caribbean territories, not necessarily under direct US rule.

The key facet of colonial banking is that colonial financial institutions generally raised funds and held the majority of their assets in metropolitan centres rather than in colonies, specialising primarily in remitting funds and in occasional lending to the colonial government and a few heavily capitalised local firms. As a result, these banks very rarely developed the infrastructures – the routines, social relations, or physical structures – necessary to lend to the majority populations in colonised territories.

The uneven development of colonial financial systems

If the generally extraverted character of colonial financial systems is a key common trait, the differentiation of colonial territory is also an important dynamic deserving further discussion. Colonial capitalisms also worked through the production of differentiated spaces within and between colonised territories. As Capps (2018) in particular has recently noted of sub-Saharan Africa, the political differentiation of urban and rural spaces, with accompanying property regimes, was intimately linked to the development of capital accumulation. While this took place in variable ways depending on the particular regimes of accumulation in place, the regulatory and physical differentiation of space – including the transformation of property regimes and the construction of transport infrastructures linking export products to coasts – were vital to colonial capitalism. Uneven access to finance was an integral element of these wider patterns of differentiation, while at the same time this produced significant patterns of uneven development of financial infrastructures themselves, both between and within colonial territories.

We could point to three ideal-typical colonial economic systems – 'économies de traite', mining and plantation colonies, and labour reserves (cf. Amin 1976; Bernstein 2010). The distinctions between these three types of colonial systems led to significant differences in the development of financial systems within territories, which often map onto important differences in the development of contemporary financial systems. I outline each of these categories further in what follows.

I should be clear here about three points. First, this tripartite scheme is a way of capturing diversity within a single system. There were, as described above, important overarching similarities between colonial financial systems across the board. Or, better put, they were fundamentally part of the same system. Second, these patterns were not fixed and often did change over time. Finally, developments in different kinds of territories were interconnected. For example, the active underdevelopment of labour reserves contributed directly to the forms of exploitation and accumulation taking place in mining and plantation economies. We should also be cautious of methodological nationalism here. Colonial political economies did not translate automatically or easily into 'national' ones even in the process of decolonisation (see Cooper 2014). Equally, individual colonial territories often contained more than one of these systems. This was certainly true, for instance, in the highly diverse mega-colony that was India. This dynamic is also visible on a smaller scale. Northern Ghana, for instance, served as a labour reserve for the cocoa farms in the southern parts of the country, and South Africa's system of 'native reserves' operated as labour reserves for the mines (see Scully and Britwum 2019). In spite of these caveats, it is still useful to think of three kinds of colonial economies, with subtle but important implications for the depth and density of financial infrastructures that developed in their wake.

Merchant economies

In parts of India and most of West Africa, we can point to the development of what Samir Amin (1974) usefully described as 'économies de traites' – roughly but imperfectly translatable as 'trading' or 'merchant' economies. These were colonies distinguished by the predominance of merchant capital and the commodification of the means of subsistence, even as 'free labour' and private property rights were visible only on a very restricted scale. Bernstein (1977; 1979), for one, argued that peasantries in Africa and across the Global South were thoroughly incorporated into 'generalized commodity relations' even in the absence of widespread private property in land and wage labour, in part through the dependence of peasant populations for means of reproduction on merchant capital (cf. Watts 2013; Banaji 2016). These were systems that depended heavily on relations of indebtedness and the *absence* of formal property rights and 'free' proletarian labour to produce cheap raw materials. In short, capital was directly involved in profitable marketing and processing activities, while shifting the costs and risks of agricultural production onto a range of local populations, mobilised in part by relations of indebtedness (see also Watts 2013; Swindell and Jeng 2006; Bernards 2019c).

Take, for instance, Amin's primary example in French West Africa. By the 1920s, West African economies were dominated by three trading companies: two French (the Compagnie Française de l'Afrique Occidentale (CFAO) and Société Commerciale de l'Ouest Africain), and one British (the United Africa Company) (see Austen 1987:130). All three operated what has usefully been described as a 'rudimentary "trading economy", wherein manufactured goods of mediocre quality destined for immediate consumption ... were offered, at greatly inflated prices, against agricultural products collected during the trading season' (Coquéry-Vidrovitch 1975:597; cf. Coquéry-Vidrovitch 1977). As Beckman (1976:47) aptly observes of these arrangements in Ghana, 'the system depended ultimately on the farmer's demand for credits, which in turn was closely linked to the seasonal nature of production'. This system of advances, often for survival items, from brokers during the off-season secured against upcoming harvests enabled merchant firms to gain control over crops on the cheap, and to transfer the costs and hazards of production onto farmers. This was a system that prohibited much investment in production, but also minimised costs and risks for merchant firms. They often recognised as much – by 1900, the CFAO was lobbying in Paris *against* the formation of concessional property in French West Africa (CFAO 1900).

It's important to underline that although indebtedness was a key fulcrum in these systems, merchant capital depended on the *restriction* of bank credit. The uneven availability of credit for farmers was in fact integral to the operation of merchant regimes – it was crucial to merchant capital that the provision of credit to farmers took place *outside* the formal banking system, by brokers lending against future crop production. This was a vital means of mobilising the production of cash crops for metropolitan markets in the absence of fully-established private property rights and 'free' labour. Merchant firms themselves were well aware of this – often actively resisting efforts to develop other sources of credit for colonised farmers and businesses. The East India Company lobbied against the formation of British-owned banks in India in the eighteenth and nineteenth centuries (see Government of India 1931:14). Uche (1999) shows particularly clearly that merchants in West Africa increasingly saw the *restriction* of bank credit to African farmers as a crucial element of maintaining their control over cheap crops. Indeed, merchant firms often actively resisted efforts to reform agricultural finance, explicitly recognising the vital role of credit in ensuring control over cheap crops.

Plantation and mining economies

In contrast to merchant economies characterised by the absence of direct investment, some colonies were dominated by large-scale, capitalised, generally European-owned enterprises, primarily concentrated on the extraction of raw materials. Financial systems in these territories were generally more extensive. They specialised in lending to expatriate businesses and settlers, in much the same way as in merchant economies – indeed it was mostly the same banks involved. But in plantation and mining territories there were, simply put, more of these 'creditworthy' enterprises. There were some notable differences between financial systems in mining and plantation economies. Mining territories, for one thing, tended to have larger populations of relatively affluent (usually white) 'skilled' workers and managers, and often consumer financial systems that were set up to serve them. Bank branch networks were developed largely following the spatial parameters of colonial capital.

Indeed, the initial development of colonial banking models, which took place in no small part in the Caribbean, was intimately linked to the perpetuation of plantation economies after the abolition of slavery in the British Empire. The Abolition of Slavery Bill in the British Parliament included truly staggering amounts of compensation to slaveholders for the loss of their property. The British government made payments to slaveholders equivalent to 40 percent of the country's GDP at the time; the debt it took out to do so was famously so large that it was only paid off in 2015. This massive influx of cash was a significant spur to the development of colonial banking in the Caribbean, as banks were founded and set up branches seeking to help manage the staggering sums of cash suddenly swirling around the region. The Abolition Bill was certainly not the only reason why colonial banks cropped up in the Caribbean in the 1830s, but it did provide a significant impetus to push forward with plans to develop colonial banks. 'It was under these conditions', writes an official history of Barclays DCO from the 1930s, 'that a group of merchants and private bankers in London conceived the plan of a Bank with a head office in London and branches in the West Indies and British Guiana' (Barclays DCO 1937:25–6). The Colonial Bank (eventually Barclays [DCO] after a series of mergers in the 1920s) and other colonial banks set up in this context were important pioneers of the model of extractive colonial banks highlighted above.

Uneven access to credit was, again, vital to the organisation of mining and plantation economies. On the one hand, in general, access to finance capital was a source of power for landed capital. In Argentina, for instance, Cain and Hopkins (2016:275) note that ready access to British finance facilitated the formation of wealthy landowning families – 'the ability to borrow on a massive scale and to make repayment through exports of primary products became the basis of the power and prosperity of the 400 or so wealthy landed families who formed the Argentine elite, and also of their allies in banking and commerce'. On the other hand, as discussed in the next section, the corollary of this was that the restriction of credit to some segments of colonised populations was a crucial means of extending large landholders' or mine operators' control over labour.

Labour reserves

Restrictive access to credit helped to reinforce colonial control over productive resources in some cases. Labour reserves were typically, sometimes actively, excluded from access to the formal financial system. But the underdevelopment of these regions was critical for the supply of migrant labour to capitalised farms or mines, and uneven access to credit helped to reinforce these relations.

One illustrative example is Kenya. Efforts to expand settler agriculture after World War I increasingly confronted both a need for cheap labour and intense competition for control over labour, both among settlers and between settler and 'reserve' economies (Berman and Lonsdale 1981:62). What's critical is that restrictions on access to credit proved vital to enabling this extraction of labour. Productive credit was, at the time, dependent on security in land. Legal land titles were, for the most part, reserved for European settlers until well into the 1950s (see Shipton 1992). In this context, as long as formal land titling was restricted to 'European' areas, both in cities and in the countryside, access to productive credit was generally *de facto* restricted to settler capital. The restriction of productive credit contributed to the underdevelopment of reserve areas, and landholder control over tenant 'squatters' was strengthened by landowner control over credit for inputs and machinery. In this sense, the intersection of credit infrastructures with racialised structures of property ownership was crucial to maintaining settler control over labour. It was not simply control over access to productive land, but also control over access to credit that enabled settler control over squatter labour in particular. We can point to similar dynamics in the system of what James and Rajak (2014) usefully call the 'credit apartheid' prevalent in South Africa through much of the twentieth century. Credit in South Africa was, in short 'given on favourable terms to white farmers and withdrawn from black ones' (2014:461), contributing to the active underdevelopment of 'reserve' agriculture and the formation of a cheap labour force for mines and settler farms.

Colonial differentiation and financial infrastructures

Three key points in the above discussion are worth underlining. First, one critical result of these patterns of uneven development is that banking systems developed in considerably more depth in territories with large-scale plantations and mines, and especially those with large numbers of European settlers. Table 1.1 demonstrates this point with a comparison within sub-Saharan Africa. Southern Rhodesia and Kenya not only had considerably more bank branches relative to their population than did trading economies in Ghana and Nigeria; they also had banks that invested a considerably larger proportion of their assets locally.

Table 1.1 Bank branches, deposits, and assets in British African territories, 1951

	Branches, 1951	Total deposits, 1951 (£'000s)	Estimated deposits per branch, 1951 (£'000s)	Local assets, 1951 (£'000s)	Local assets as percent of total deposits, 1951
Ghana	25	12 744	509.76	3 348	26.1
Kenya	31	39 176	1263.74	17 972	45.9
Nigeria	28	18 656	666.28	1 406	7.5
Tanzania	25	17 986	719.44	6 365	35.4
Uganda	18	14 604	811.33	5 839	39.9
Southern Rhodesia	47	44 499	946.78	28 615	64.3

Source: adapted from Newlyn and Rowan (1954:76–7).

Second, colonial financial systems generally relied on the restriction of formal credit to certain segments of colonised populations as a means of mobilising and controlling labour. This was true in different ways in different kinds of colonial economies, but there were very few exceptions to the overall rule. The financial systems that developed in this context were both fundamentally extractive and articulated through unevenly developed infrastructures.

Finally, these were fundamentally contradictory systems. They embedded long-run patterns of underdevelopment and vulnerable live-lihoods for most colonised subjects. Yet in many instances, states were also heavily dependent on revenues directly generated by the activities of these same populations. Albers *et al.* (2020), for instance, show that African colonial states overall relied on direct taxes – primarily head taxes – for close to 40 percent of their revenues for most of the period between 1914 and 1955, as well as on taxes on trade for roughly another 25 percent. More generally, colonial states, in Lonsdale and Berman's useful words, 'laboured under a palimpsest of accumulation and control' (1979:491) – they were partially bound to foster forms of dominant colonial accumulation, yet always needed to retain at least some degree of legitimacy among colonised subjects (see Capps 2018).

In short, colonial states came to rely very heavily on the economic activities of colonised subjects even as these were restrained and undercut by systems designed to supply cheap labour and cheap raw materials to colonial capital. Moreover, even where there were large pop-ulations of settlers, colonial states needed to retain some semblance of legitimacy among colonised populations. In many instances, this meant that colonial states were structurally bound to promote the expansion of export agriculture and other economic activities in the hands of col-onised subjects. These were, in important senses, deeply embedded, structural limits to extractivist systems that could not be transcended without radical economic and political reforms. The former were not forthcoming, and the latter happened only in part. But what's crucial here is that those partial, halting, and often truncated reforms to colonial financial systems adopted after about 1930 have played a key role in shaping enduring patterns of uneven development. These, in turn, matter a great deal in explaining the troubled progress of the neoliberal reforms discussed in subsequent chapters.

REFORMING COLONIAL FINANCIAL SYSTEMS, C. 1930–1960

Starting in the late 1920s and early 1930s, we can point to a series of efforts to reconsider the role of banking and finance in colonial terri-tories, often linked to wider reconsiderations of empire and the bases of colonial rule taking place against the backdrop of depression of war (see Cooper 2011; Woodhouse 2012). Debates about poverty finance, especially around agricultural credit, were part and parcel of the simultaneous birth of global development and the slow dismantling of formal colonial authority, a process that started in the 1930s and accelerated after World War II. There had been some efforts at reforming poverty finance in colonised territories as far back as the turn of the century – cooperatives legislation was introduced in India in 1904, and *Sociétés Indigènes de Prévoyance* (SIPs) were established in some French territories in the late nineteenth century. But from the late 1920s, and especially after 1930, these reforms were redoubled in these territories and accelerated elsewhere. The post-1930 intensification of efforts at expanding access to finance drew, in important respects, on these earlier developments. Two points about these post-1930 initiatives are worth outlining.

Spendthrift peasants?

First, a key theme throughout efforts to reform colonial financial systems in the first half of the twentieth century was an emphasis on the promotion of 'thrift' and prudent risk management by colonial populations. There are frequent references throughout colonial-era documents to the lack of understanding of principles of thrift and financial responsibility among colonial administrators.

M. L. Darling's *The Punjab Peasant in Prosperity and Debt*, originally published in 1925, was a particularly prominent example of this kind of analysis. Darling was an official with the Cooperatives Department of the Colonial Office. His book was influential well beyond India, his analysis of indebtedness finding direct echoes in discussions of West Africa, among other areas (see Kamenov 2019). Darling linked agrarian indebtedness to the rise of commercialisation. The 'Punjab peasant is not quite what he was ten or twenty years ago', Darling argued; 'now that he has tasted the comforts of a higher standard of living, his wants are multiplying' (1928:xiv). In this context, 'in spite of, or rather because of the growing prosperity, debt is increasing' (1928:xv). The problem in the Punjab, in Darling's view, was that these mounting debts were primarily 'unproductive', both in the sense that a considerable proportion of indebtedness was a product of the usurious rates charged by moneylenders, and in that borrowing was primarily for 'unproductive' purposes. He wrote: 'One of the disadvantages of unproductive debt is that it tends to increase automatically. Productive debt by fertilising the soil creates its own means of repayment, but unproductive debt is apt to be repaid with difficulty' (1928:18). For Darling the solution was, straightforwardly enough, the further development of cooperatives – 'a person who joins a co-operative credit society can in ten to twenty years clear off the whole of his debt, and in addition accumulate enough capital to supply the modest requirements of his somewhat primitive system of farming' (1928:18). While Darling's specific articulation of this thesis was influential, the basic idea had deep roots in the cooperatives administration in India. The 1915 *Report of the Commission on Cooperation in India*, for instance, opened by noting that the genesis of the cooperative movement in India was a response to the moral degradation of the peasantry in the face of rapid economic growth:

> It was found that in many parts of India … that in spite of the rapid growth of commerce and improvements in communications, the economic condition of the peasants had not been progressing as it ought to have done, that indebtedness instead of decreasing had tended to increase, that usury was still rampant, that agricultural methods had not been improved. (McClagan *et al.* 1915:10)

Farmers in this setting 'either hoarded their savings or owing to thriftlessness showed themselves unable to withstand bad seasons and to meet organised trade on equal terms' (McClagan *et al.* 1915:10).

This basic assessment – that indebtedness and poor productivity were conjoined problems, resulting from the confrontation between the lack of 'thrift' on the part of racialised colonial subjects and the exploitative activities of moneylenders – travelled quite widely around the British Empire (see Kamenov 2019). A report commissioned in 1936 by the Gold Coast government from economist C. Y. Shephard on the 'Economics of Peasant Agriculture' in the territory provides a good example. Shephard's report, citing Darling directly, deals in considerable detail with persistent problems of indebtedness – which were particularly a concern insofar as they might hamper the effectiveness of cooperatives, introduced in 1931 with legislation mostly copied directly from India, in reforming marketing (Shephard 1936:38). The extent of indebtedness was again primarily attributed to a lack of 'thrift' on the part of farmers (Shephard 1936:39). Shephard's conclusions were echoed in the report of a Commission of Enquiry on the Marketing of West African Cocoa, published two years later. Indebtedness was seen as a problem in terms of agricultural productivity because farmers whose crops were pledged to a broker were seen to have little incentive to make any investments in their farm, or indeed to pay careful attention to crops: 'Even where the farmer himself occupies his farm the incentive to careful cultivation and harvesting is frequently removed by his having pledged the usufruct as security for a loan' (Nowell *et al* 1938:22). The report clearly attributed the prevalence of indebtedness to the ostensible lack of capacity of Africans to properly manage the uneven temporal distribution of farm incomes: 'The Gold Coast African ... prefers to spend lavishly, even foolishly, when he has money; and to borrow when he has none' (Nowell *et al.* 1938:23).

French administrations likewise dramatically expanded SIPs in the 1930s (see Bernards 2019c). These were flexible institutions operated by local administrators, but they generally performed two functions – providing loans in seed and cash to farmers (predominant in cash-crop regions) and maintaining granaries (see Mann and Guyer 1999). They were nominally meant to be self-financing, with advances repaid (with interest) out of harvests. SIPs were consistently justified in terms of the lack of foresight of indigenous populations in dealing with irregular rainfall. This dated to their earliest iterations in Algeria, where SIPs were introduced as a means of protecting 'those who by their lack of foresight are not able to long survive' periods of poor rainfall (Lecoq 1903:1). The peasant's supposedly spendthrift nature and the moneylender's depravity were intimately linked in the colonial imagination.

Cooperative credit schemes were ultimately tentative and partial responses to the embedded crises of over-indebtedness they confronted – and they were resisted at every step by merchant capital. The report on cocoa marketing in Ghana explicitly recognised that efforts to reform marketing would require the replacement of existing financial arrangements, and thus would 'tend to restrict the availability of credit to small farmers, and to limit the possibilities of cheap credit' (Nowell *et al.* 1938:169) without the provision of alternatives through thrift. In Senegal, the expansion of SIPs was contested by the trading houses, who continued to favour 'indebtedness arrangements as a way to bind individual cultivators to their firms and to make the conduct of trade relatively predictable' (Tignor 1987:106). In practice, though, SIPs complicated this system by introducing a new source of seed credit, while still fundamentally seeking to keep colonised populations bound to groundnut production through relations of indebtedness (see Boone 1992:46). This was particularly the case given the extent to which the expansion of SIPs was oriented towards providing credit in seed. Merchants continued to be the primary source of credit for basic survival items during off-seasons (see Bernards 2019c). Likewise, cooperatives captured 1–2 percent of cocoa exports from Ghana (Shephard 1936:26; Phillips 1989:90). Twenty years after the first cooperatives were launched in Ghana, the colonial government commissioned a report on indebtedness among cocoa farmers, which would again note that the 'chronic indebtedness of the cocoa farmer' was a key problem (Gold Coast Government 1951: para 25). It also reiterated that cooperative society members still needed to resort to moneylenders 'at penal interest rates' for longer-term loans, and that many farmers remained unable to join cooperatives because their crops and assets were already mortgaged (Gold Coast Government 1951: para 47). But the commission again returned to familiar arguments about the 'improvident' character of African borrowers and the need for training in thrift, arguing that 'where a farmer is genuinely desirous of freeing himself from debt, and to this end is prepared to exercise restraint ... and practice thrift', the funds available from cooperative societies should be sufficient (Gold Coast Government 1951: para 111). Cooperatives were often adopted tentatively, and as a way of warding off farther-reaching reforms. They did little to address the underlying contradictions to which they were addressed.

Mobilising finance capital?

Despite their framing as devices for promoting thrift, credit cooperatives were often implicitly designed to mobilise private financial capital, directly or indirectly, to lend to agriculture. In Kenya, one official would make this particularly explicit in commenting on a proposed scheme for the expansion of cooperatives for African borrowers:

These societies are not likely, in the near future, to attract many deposits either from members or non-members. They will therefore have to depend on other sources for their working capital either government or commercial banks. No government has sufficient funds to finance many peasant cultivators and in the end finance will have to come through the commercial banks.[4]

The problems commercial banks saw with lending to colonised subjects generally included heavily racialised ideas about prudence and credit-worthiness, as noted above, but equally rather more prosaic concerns about transaction costs and collateral. One survey of Nigerian banking operations towards the end of the colonial period noted that 'Many Africans wish to operate accounts ... on which the average balance is small and the number of transactions high', and that 'such accounts could only be profitable under (rare) conditions where returns on assets were sufficiently high to outweigh the cost of making many small transactions' (Rowan 1952:166). These were pragmatic issues, of course, that intersected with colonial racial hierarchies in complex ways. In the first instance, colonial economic systems produced large numbers of dispossessed people with precarious incomes, who needed to make 'many small transactions'. Equally, it was because financial infrastructures were built up to facilitate extractive modes of development that they were spatially and socially distant from colonised populations – a point which Walter Rodney makes very well in reference to sub-Saharan Africa (2018:138). But in any case, alongside paternalistic efforts at developing 'thrift', colonial authorities also sought to develop ways of mobilising finance capital for agriculture in colonised territories, in essence by constituting colonised populations in ways that 'fit' existing financial infrastructures.

One possibility was to pool risks. Cooperative structures were often designed to do this. Sometimes this entailed more or less direct inter-mediation by the state. For instance, the rapid expansion of SIPs in French West Africa in the 1930s was very much a process driven and organised by the colonial state, but one into which it worked to enrol financial capital (see Bernards 2019c). The *Caisse Centrale de Crédit Agricole Mutuel* (CCCAM), an agricultural bank modelled on the French *Crédit Agricole*, was established in Senegal by decree in 1931. The CCCAM borrowed funds from the central government and private lenders in order to lend on to SIPs or to larger cultivators. In one of the rare instances where a commercial bank was directly involved, Barclay's DCO set up a proto-microcredit village-lending scheme for agriculturalists in Mandatory Palestine at the behest of British authorities. This scheme likewise mobilised group structures to minimise the cost to the bank of making many small transactions and provided some security against default through collective liability (Barclays DCO 1937:100–1).

Other approaches sought simply to make members into more attractive prospects for commercial lenders by assembling borrowers into groups without involving capital directly. In India, the cooperatives legislation passed in 1904 provided for unlimited liability for rural cooperatives – that is, members would be jointly responsible for outstanding loans made to the society in the event that a cooperative was insolvent. The explicit aim here was to enable cooperatives to channel credit to members in the absence of acceptable collateral (see Kamenov 2020:105). Yet, as Kamenov (2020) notes, there was a critical tension here – very much the tension between inclusion and stratification highlighted in the introduction. On the one hand, the goal of the cooperatives from the start was to enable 'inclusive' access to credit, particularly for peasant farmers who might otherwise only have access to finance through moneylenders. On the other, unlimited joint liability was meant to encourage cooperatives to operate along more businesslike lines. This quite often ran counter to the first objective, particularly insofar as it discouraged cooperatives in practice from admitting or lending to members who didn't have access to security. The point is that cooperatives and the like were, in many instances, very much vehicles by which states sought to mobilise finance capital. They sought to do this by assembling collectives of borrowers, which might borrow in larger amounts and provide security in the absence of collateral.

The other dimension of mobilising finance capital was a series of, often quite tentative, efforts to reform land tenure in particular with an eye to facilitating wider access to credit. This was a longstanding concern of officials in a variety of colonial settings. In Senegal at the turn of the century, for instance, one French official justified continued efforts to extend the scope of private property by arguing that secure property titles would 'above all, allow the owner to make use of the largest possible credit' (Boudillon 1911:26).

Kenya – where reforms began much later, with officials starting to discuss credit for 'African' farmers only in the early 1950s – is a particularly good example. In Kenya, as noted above, African agriculture was often explicitly and directly underdeveloped. A cooperatives ordinance had been passed in Kenya in 1931, but in the late 1940s there were still only a handful of registered societies, almost entirely made up of white farmers, and few if any credit societies (see CPK 1950:85). The colonial government likewise established a Land and Agricultural Bank (LAB) to provide long-term agricultural credit from 1931. The LAB nonetheless required security in land, much the same as commercial banks, which meant that it generally lent money only to European farmers. It did not begin to lend to African farmers until 1945, and even then, only narrowly (see Shipton 1992:365). In Shipton's words, until the 1950s, 'the British colonial government's policy in Kenya was to try to protect African smallholders in the "reserves" from moneylenders by forbidding land mortgages' (1992:365). This 'protective' impulse, of course, dove-tailed quite closely with the interests of settler farms in maintaining a steady supply of tenant and casual labour.

Policies to expand access to credit for Africans were given a significant impetus by colonial officials grappling with the Mau Mau insurgency in the 1950s. The colonial government appointed Roger Swynnerton, Assistant Director of Agriculture in Kenya, to develop a scheme for agri-cultural development in late 1953. Swynnerton's report – commonly referred to as the 'Swynnerton Plan' – marked a significant shift towards encouraging the development of African agriculture.[5] The plan was intended to create a small 'middle class' of property-owning African farmers employing wage labour and, crucially, able to access productive credit. Second, rather than changing the way that either the banks or the state-backed agricultural lending agencies operated, the main thrust of the Swynnerton reforms was to change the way that African farmers held land, in order to make this more compatible with existing financial infra-structures. Swynnerton's report (CPK 1954:54–5) makes much of this explicit, suggesting that it was impossible to mobilise sufficient resources from public sources alone. Some lending from public sources was nec-essary, but 'were each farmer with a registered title to his land to borrow up to [£300] against the security of his title, ultimately borrowing would greatly exceed the resources of Kenya'. The solution mainly consisted in encouraging the much wider adoption of formal land titling. Ultimately, the explicit purpose of land titling was to encourage much greater access to commercial credit for African borrowers: 'If Africans are to develop their lands to their full potential they will require much greater access to finance and if they achieve titles to their land in economic units, much greater facilities should be made available to them for borrowing against the security of their land'.

These were, much like the promotion of thrift elsewhere, efforts to allay and offset wider calls for reform. In one particularly clear example, the colonial government in Ghana responded to repeated demands in the 1950s for a 'national bank' for Ghana by setting up the state-owned Bank of the Gold Coast (BGC) in 1952 (see Bernards 2021b). Where national-ists had variously pushed for a central bank and a dedicated agricultural and industrial development bank for the territory, the BGC was explicitly designed to operate along commercial lines. The Managing Director of the new bank made abundantly clear, in a press release announcing its formation, that the BGC would operate on commercial lines and would continue not to be able to lend to the 'African trader' as long as his [sic] small capital made him 'a bad banking risk *in isolation*'.[6] The bank was, however, open to developing new forms of group lending to collectively responsible groups of African farmers and businesses.[7] Collective responsibility for loans, in short, was widely embraced as a means of making colonised populations more suitable for existing colonial financial infrastructures.

Ultimately, these were all limited responses that failed to address the underlying social and ecological contradictions to which they sought to respond. Early efforts to mobilise capital for seed credit in Senegal ultimately 'saddled the Senegalese Provident Societies with a large debt' from the first years of the 1930s (Tignor 1987:103), which was amplified because the price of seeds nearly tripled in the time between the planning and implementation of the expanded SIPs scheme (costing 29 million francs rather than the 10 million originally budgeted). The SIPs were forced to take out a 50-year loan to enable repayment (Tignor 1987:103). As a result of the persistence of merchant credit described above, moreover, SIPs systematically struggled to collect repayments. Arrears accumulated steadily throughout the 1930s and 1940s – in 1937–38, Senegalese SIPs reported arrears of 12,220 metric tons of groundnuts; by 1946–47, the figure was 57,278 (Tignor 1987:112).[8]

POSTCOLONIAL ECHOES

I have presented above a very brief sketch of the configuration of colonial financial systems, and of what we can properly label the first experiments with poverty finance. In the final section of this chapter, I want to briefly highlight how much these interventions laid the groundwork for postcolonial poverty finance. Agricultural credit, in particular, was a key focus of reforms taking place alongside decolonisation. 'It is no exaggeration', noted a report from a US State Department-sponsored conference on agricultural credit in 1952, 'to say that since World War II one of the major social movements has been a demand for the reform of many of the basic agricultural institutions throughout the world', especially 'in those countries which have heretofore been dominated by subsistence agriculture' (Blaisdell *et al.* 1953:3).

There were, in a number of instances, dramatic expansions of commercial banking systems in the decade before decolonisation. There was, for instance, a significant expansion of branch networks across sub-Saharan Africa, particularly in British territories, in the 1950s (Engberg 1965). What's notable, though, is how much the density of bank branches in 1950 seems to have shaped the density of branches at the end of the decade (see Table 1.2). Kenya was a major focus of this expansion, along with Ghana, Nigeria, and then-Rhodesia (see Engberg and Hance 1969:196). Historians have often attributed this expansion in part to efforts by banks in Kenya and elsewhere in sub-Saharan Africa to navigate the political and economic pressures created by decolonisation, as well as to capitalise on business opportunities seemingly opened up by the 'developmental' colonialism (see Cooper 1996) of the postwar period (see Bostock 1991; Engberg 1965; Engberg and Hance 1969; Morris 2016; Velasco 2020). While this is broadly true, we can usefully situate this development, and understand its limits, with reference to the patterns of uneven development and contestation described above. If the expansion of branch banking in the 1950s was in some senses a spatial fix (for British finance capital in particular, which was tentatively seeking out new spaces for accumulation in colonised territories), it was also one that was strongly shaped by the configuration of existing financial infrastructures.

Earlier concerns about informal moneylenders and indebtedness were amplified in the postcolonial period as well. A major study of interest rates 'outside organized money markets' by an IMF staffer in the 1950s was a significant landmark here (Tun Wai 1957). The moralistic conclusions about peasant indebtedness highlighted above are prominent. On its first page, along with noting that interest rates charged by moneylenders were, as a rule, significantly higher than those charged either by commercial banks or cooperatives in the 'official sector', the report suggests that 'a significant portion of the demand for loanable funds in rural areas is for financing consumption at levels much higher than are warranted by the low income of the peasant' (1957:80). Equally, the report emphasises the primarily rural character both of exclusions from the formal banking system and of 'unorganized' lending: 'Unorganized money markets are located mainly in rural areas therefore the demand for and supply of loanable funds originate from the agricultural

Table 1.2 Bank branches, and estimated bank branches per 1 million people, 1950–57

	Bank branches, 1950	Bank branches, 1957	Population, 1960, millions	Est. branches per 1m people, 1950	Est. branches per 1m people, 1957
Côte d'Ivoire	8	11	3.50	2.28	3.14
Gabon	7	9	0.50	13.97	17.97
Ghana	21	82	6.64	3.16	12.36
Kenya	29	97	8.12	3.57	11.95
Senegal	8	13	3.21	2.49	4.05
Tanzania	29	55	10.05	2.88	5.47
Zimbabwe	38	130	3.78	10.06	34.42
Benin	4	5	2.43	1.64	2.06
Cameroon	8	20	5.18	1.55	3.86
Chad	3	8	3.00	1.00	2.67
D. R. Congo	53	66	15.25	3.48	4.33
Liberia	7	8	1.12	6.26	7.15
Malawi	7	8	3.66	1.91	2.19
Mali	3	6	5.26	0.57	1.14
Togo	3	2	1.58	1.90	1.27
Zambia	23	45	3.07	7.49	14.65
Congo	9	13	1.02	8.84	12.77
Ethiopia	14	32	22.15	0.63	1.44
Guinea	5	12	3.49	1.43	3.43
Niger	1	1	3.39	0.30	0.30
Nigeria	22	142	45.14	0.49	3.15
Sierra Leone	3	14	2.32	1.29	6.04

Data sources: Author calculations based on data from Engberg and Hance (1969) and World Bank Population Data, available https://databank.worldbank.org/home.

sector' (1957:83). The diagnosis for the reliance on informal lending in agricultural finance was, straightforwardly, that 'the existing financial institutions tend to restrict their lending activities mainly to urban areas and do not generally wish to engage in the more risky field of lending to the agricultural sector' (1957:88). Collateral requirements were again highlighted as a reason for borrowing from 'unofficial' sources (1957:88).

Finally, the state-backed systems for poverty finance, particularly in agriculture, were carried forward after the end of formal colonialism. In many instances, they were expanded. Large-scale cooperative systems were adopted in India and across much of sub-Saharan Africa.

State-backed agricultural banks were also dramatically expanded after the end of colonial rule, often with the explicit backing of the World Bank. The following chapter focuses on these institutions, and the role that efforts to reform them and to juggle with their attendant contradictions played in the rise of neoliberalism in global development.

CONCLUSION

In the wider context of this book, this chapter has developed two key points. First, in order to understand the truncated progress of poverty finance, we need to understand the patterns of uneven development shaped by histories of colonial capitalism. Colonial modes of development systematically produced dispossession, ecological vulnerabilities, and insecure livelihoods across much of the colonised world. Moreover, the financial systems generated in these contexts mirrored important patterns of uneven development between colonies and metropoles and within and among colonial territories. Colonial financial systems were fundamentally extraverted; they were dominated by a few banks run from and fundamentally oriented towards the metropole. These extraverted financial systems gave rise to the uneven development of financial infrastructures both within and between colonised territories. Second, these patterns of development generated important contradictions and limits, to which early poverty finance initiatives were ultimately a response. It is, fundamentally, to these inherited contradictions – to credit systems that failed to mobilise or even militated against credit for local economic or social development, and which set the stage for intensified uneven development after formal decolonisation – that most poverty finance interventions in the period since have been addressed. It makes sense, then, that the negotiation and articulation of poverty finance sits very much at the root of neoliberal approaches to development and indeed played a key role in their early articulation. The next chapter turns to this process, looking at developments in agricultural and housing credit from the 1960s and 1970s onward.

2
Poverty finance and nascent neoliberalism

We saw in the last chapter how colonial political economies often rested on the uneven availability of credit and how, in many instances, this generated important contradictions that colonial authorities negotiated only with considerable difficulty, especially after 1930. We also saw, in the final few pages of the chapter, how the financial systems that emerged during these years of reformist colonialism laid important parts of the groundwork for postcolonial efforts at mobilising credit, for agriculture in particular.

The main argument outlined in this chapter is that poverty finance was a key focus of neoliberal development interventions from the start, but that early neoliberal articulations of poverty finance foundered on their inability to address the patterns of uneven development inherited from the colonial era. Early academic articulations of neoliberal approaches to development emphasised promoting the efficient allocation of credit through the removal of 'market distortions' caused by state interventions. The incorporation of these ideas into policy, however, was halting, murky, and error-prone. It was one thing to say that the market should allocate credit, but quite another to actually build markets to do so. Housing and agricultural credit programmes at the World Bank and USAID were particularly important in this respect. Colonial and postcolonial interventions had generally assumed that poverty finance needed to be provided on cooperative or state-backed terms. We can see a line of thought emerging in the 1960s and 1970s that poverty finance needed to be provided, instead, by remaking financial systems along market lines. The successive failures of various efforts to organise agricultural and housing credit on a market basis in the 1970s and 1980s played a critical, but often under-acknowledged, role in paving the way for the more widely discussed microfinance 'innovations' that followed in the 1990s and 2000s.

This chapter examines the evolution of these interventions, showing how officials at the World Bank and USAID grappled with the underlying contradictions highlighted in the previous chapter, and how efforts to do so were increasingly articulated in terms of marketisation. In the first section below, I show how the liberalisation of interest rates was central to neoliberal diagnoses of development failures. In the second and third sections, I examine efforts to put these visions of marketisation into practice, in reforms of agricultural and housing credit respectively.

CREDIT, INTEREST RATES, AND COLONIALISM IN
THE RISE OF NEOLIBERAL DEVELOPMENT THEORY

Notably, the implicit or explicit rejection of colonial legacies as an explanation for postcolonial underdevelopment was a key tenet of what has been called the neoliberal 'counter-revolution' in global development (Toye 1993; Bair 2009). Insofar as neoliberal economists saw colonial legacies as being relevant, they emphasised the rise of state interference in the economy in the final years of colonialism. P. T. Bauer, for instance, while arguing that colonialism had likely led to greater economic development than would have taken place in its absence, insisted that if colonial rule had had any deleterious effects, these were 'the introduction of state monopolies over agricultural exports' in the late years of colonial rule, which had given 'governments close and direct control over the livelihoods of the producers' and had 'served as a powerful source of patronage and finance for the rulers' (1971:154). More generally, 'distortions' in agricultural markets, ostensibly induced by state monopsony and an emphasis on developing heavy industry, were a key focus of the neoliberal counter-revolution. This was not an intellectual revolution from 'outside' major development agencies. Indeed, World Bank economists themselves conducted a good deal of research on such 'price distortions' and their detrimental impacts on agriculture (e.g. Lutz and Scandizzo 1980).

Arguments about the role of finance were central here, maybe most notably in the articulation of the 'financial repression' thesis. This was outlined in a pair of widely cited books published in the mid-1970s by Edward Shaw (1973) and Ronald Mckinnon (1973) – these remain, incidentally, influential among IMF staff in particular (e.g. Jafarov *et al.* 2019). Both Shaw and McKinnon were primarily focused on the role of financial institutions, and particularly 'financial deepening' in economic development. Both insisted that developmentalist efforts to control the distribution and pricing of credit had introduced important distortions that actually impeded the access of small farmers to formal credit. McKinnon is especially interesting insofar as he did recognise some of the problematic inheritances of colonial finance:

> In the colonial period, organized banking served mainly expatriates who were engaged in developing exports of raw materials ... Funds would be channeled to banks – controlled largely in, say, London – which would then reinvest funds with borrowers whose collateral and reputations were known to overseas bankers. (1973:69–70)

After independence, though, McKinnon argued that interventionist governments had introduced 'neo-colonial' banking systems 'where favored private and official borrowers still absorb the limited finance available at low rates of interest, which are often far below the opportunity cost of scarce capital' (1973:70). The 'neo-colonial' aspect of this system, for McKinnon, consisted mainly of close links between the state and a small financial sector. Small farmers, the argument ran, remained 'repressed' because banks were unlikely to lend to them as long as they were unable to charge rates high enough to compensate for the risks of agricultural lending and the cost of reaching places remote from their predominantly urban branch infrastructures.[9] McKinnon argued, 'Usury ceilings on the interest rates charged on bank loans have emasculated the ability and willingness of commercial banks to serve small-scale borrowers of all classes' (1973:73). There was 'no economical substitute' for expanding the role of the commercial banking system in rural areas, but this couldn't be done without the removal of restrictions on interest rates, particularly because detailed information on borrowers and collateral were lacking and risks were high (1973:77). Similar views emphasising the distortionary harms of credit subsidies were shared (and published) by some economists within the World Bank and with close links to USAID as well (e.g. von Pischke 1978; von Pischke and Adams 1980). (Though, as we'll see shortly, the Bank's actual policy on credit subsidies was quite a bit fuzzier than this.)

For the moment, the important point is that the marketisation of agricultural credit and other areas of poverty finance was understood primarily as a question of removing regulatory restrictions which had inhibited the efficient allocation of credit to poor farmers. These early neoliberal perspectives all understand markets as a kind of natural state that exists in the absence of distortions induced by government interventions. The emphasis on deregulating (in this case, often taken as synonymous with raising) interest rates is particularly telling in this respect. Higher rates would allow, in theory, the efficient allocation of credit for productive purposes. The colonial infrastructures of existing financial systems, discussed in the previous chapter, were largely overlooked. Markets could be conjured simply by clearing the way for them to operate. In a few instances, neoliberal thinkers explicitly sought to rehabilitate colonial rule, or to minimise its negative impacts (Bauer 1976). But even where neoliberal economists were generally critical of colonial financial systems – McKinnon (1973) being a good example – theirs was a line of thought that wasn't really capable of recognising the materiality of colonial legacies. Indeed, they often directly dismissed the relevance of colonial legacies alongside wider structural power relations as inhibiting development. McKinnon argued explicitly that 'As long as potential access to international trade remains remarkably free, as it has in the postwar period, successful development rests largely on policy choices made by national authorities in the developing countries' (1973:2). We can describe much of the trajectory of actual efforts at expanding agricultural and housing credit in terms of a confrontation between this market fantasy and the actually existing patterns of postcolonial capital accumulation they found on the ground.

AGRARIAN POVERTY AND DIRECTED CREDIT

If agricultural credit and the 'financial repression' of small farmers were core elements of emerging neoliberal diagnoses of poverty in the 1970s, the actual implementation of neoliberal financial initiatives entailed a number of complexities. The Bank's report (World Bank 1980) *Accelerated Development in Sub-Saharan Africa* (often referred to as the Berg Report after its main author), identified improving the productivity of smallholder agriculture as a key point of emphasis for economic reform in sub-Saharan Africa. The report notes that smallholder farms produced the bulk of agrarian output from the region, but at comparatively low yields per acre; that, as poverty was overwhelmingly rural, raising smallholder productivity was an effective way of reducing poverty; and that raising productivity among smallholders would be more cost-effective than other available means of increasing output (World Bank 1980:50–

51). But what's critical is that the Berg Report was not a major departure from the Bank's work on agriculture and agricultural credit through the previous decade. Indeed, the arguments about smallholder agriculture in the Berg Report were heavily influenced by research carried out by Paul Collier and Deepak Lal under the auspices of the Bank several years earlier in Kenya (Collier and Lal 1980). By the late 1960s and early 1970s, more than half of agricultural lending from the Bank was for credit programmes, with a growing emphasis on targeted programmes for smallholders (World Bank 1974:2). USAID ran a similar programme of lending, with over half of its direct assistance to agriculture in Latin America going to agricultural credit programming by the end of the 1960s (see Adams 1971). In the latter case, agricultural credit was clearly part of a wider strategy of anti-communist imperialism in the region.

Credit was increasingly identified, in terms that would not have been entirely alien to colonial officials in the 1930s, as a 'key element in the modernization of agriculture' (World Bank 1974:1).[10] As one summary from the early 1970s put it, the prevalent thinking at the Bank and at USAID was that 'Credit shortage is one of the major bottlenecks causing low land and labor productivity in traditional agriculture ... the future transformation of less-developed agriculture will also require major credit infusions' (Adams 1971:163). The World Bank's landmark 1975 *Assault on World Poverty* report explicitly framed the introduction of effective access to credit as a key means of promoting technological upgrading, while noting that 'credit facilities are also an integral part of the commercialization of the rural economy' (1975a:105). The shortcomings identified in existing credit markets were things that would largely have been familiar to colonial officials in the 1930s. Most credit went to large farms, and the credit that was available for smaller farmers was primarily from informal sources. Even formal credit was only available for short-term loans – at best purchases of inputs, or more likely for basic survival needs – and not available in amounts or over terms that would allow investments in machinery or irrigation (World Bank 1975a:105).

What was distinct from previous efforts to resolve these challenges, though, was that even in the mid-1970s the Bank proposed addressing these challenges primarily by efforts to engineer more effective markets, or to marketise existing state-backed financial institutions. In two areas in particular – in the marketisation of the pricing of credit (i.e. interest rates) and the commercialisation of credit provision itself – we can point to a series of troubled efforts to engineer more effective markets.[11]

Fixing interest rates

The 'common sense' at the start of the 1970s had very much been that subsidised interest rates and the mobilisation of external resources through concessional lending and grants were vital to the expansion of agricultural credit (see Adams 1971). This consensus did not last very long after the Bank (and USAID) started to mobilise these programmes on a much larger scale – largely, however (as I'll show below), for reasons that had more to do with the embedded fiscal constraints facing developing country governments than with any ideological crusade by the Bank, however. The appropriate response to rural credit shortages, the Bank came to argue in the first *World Development Report* a few years later, was 'not to subsidize interest rates, but to increase the availability of medium-term credits, avoiding institutional forms that are highly bureaucratic and inflexible' (World Bank 1978:42). Concerns about the efficacy of interest rates as price signals in the context of government involvement had seeped into Bank policy quickly: 'Capital/credit markets in developing countries are imperfect in varying degrees and as a consequence interest rates may not allocate resources among competing uses as effectively as they should' (World Bank 1974:5). Particularly relevant here was the role played by public or subsidised lenders in driving down interest rates, worrying about subsidised credit distorting markets or promoting corruption and political patronage (1974:7–8). The long-run goal for the Bank was 'positive interest rates reflecting costs of lending; an intermediate objective might be to cover at least the opportunity cost of capital' (1974:9).

But achieving this was difficult in practice, and often took place only haltingly. It's worth bearing in mind that the distribution of credit was never entirely about poverty reduction. It was deeply political. In USAID interventions in particular, agricultural credit served a dual purpose as an anti-communist measure for the US in Latin America. As Bateman notes, the distribution of small loans was part of a wider strategy aimed at bolstering US 'soft power' in Latin America: 'The hope was that the reduction in poverty would be just enough to contain the rising pressure for much more radical change, though not enough to encourage any upset to the prevailing structure of power and wealth' (2018:19). Subsidised rural credit schemes were means of mitigating rural disquiet in times of crisis, and more generally of propping up fraught modes of small-scale agricultural production under pressure from degrading ecological conditions and world market pressures for many governments in developing countries.

More importantly, while neoliberal economists within and outside the Bank pushed for the deregulation of interest rates, it was a series of operational failures that actually cemented Bank support for liberalised interest rates in practice. Loan agreements for agricultural credit projects included conditions regarding the lending rates charged to ultimate borrowers. In early projects, these were typically fixed at a specific rate for the duration of the project. Earlier World Bank agricultural credit projects had run into a recurrent problem where interest rates fixed in project documents turned out to be negative in real terms because of high inflation in project countries (World Bank 1976a). It was a growing concern for Bank officials that a number of projects seriously strained the finances of the project participants: agricultural development banks which were generally meant to be self-financing. In Gujarat, India, for instance, a project evaluation concluded that because the rate of inflation exceeded the rate of interest on project loans, the project had enabled borrowers – mostly large farmers with access to commercial credit elsewhere – to gain access to very cheap credit, while heavily decapitalising the project partner. The latter had 'thus subsidized them, at the expense of its own balance sheet' (World Bank 1976b:9). A major review of agricultural credit projects completed in 1976 likewise concluded that across most of the projects examined, 'the structure of interest rates imposed by the program and by the financial system in which it operates not only subsidizes the farmer but threatens the viability of the channel and forces it to act in a manner contradictory to the purposes of the project' (World Bank 1976a:70). The review, notably, was explicit in emphasising not so much the effect of subsidies on borrowers or incentives, but more narrowly 'the effect the interest rate and cost structure has on the participating institutions' (1976a:70).

Projects in the latter part of the 1970s initially sought to resolve this issue either by setting a floor below which rates paid by farmers could not sink, but permitting rises, or by making a much greater effort to predict inflation rates over the term of the project and setting rates accordingly. In practice, these policies did not often have the desired impact. In the latter case, simply raising fixed rates involved making predictions, which often turned out wrong in unstable macroeconomic conditions. Interest rates on a project in Ecuador in 1977, for instance, had been set at 11 percent per annum for 'small farmers', and 14 percent for other end-borrowers, levels explicitly justified because they were seen as 'likely to be positive over the long term if, as expected, the anti-inflationary policies adopted since 1975 continue to be successful' (World Bank 1977:12). In practice, project funds were used up because the legal documents around the loans had made no provisions for adjusting interest rates once faced with higher-than-expected inflation (World Bank 1988:v).

The more common response was the former, namely setting minimum interest rates. Here the Bank set a floor below which rates were not allowed to fall, but which permitted raises. For instance, in a project in Pakistan launched in 1979, the Bank raised concerns during negotiations that interest rates were both too close to the rate of inflation and set at a level that gave the Agricultural Development Bank of Pakistan (ADBP) an insufficient spread over its own cost of funds to build up reserves. Minimum rates set at prevailing rates (then 11 percent annually) were a compromise agreed by the Bank when the Pakistani government refused to consider higher rates (World Bank 1979a:14). Indeed, it's a sign that the Bank's priorities here ultimately had more to do with the balance sheets of partner banks that the compromise Bank officials ultimately agreed was for the government to cut the rate it charged the ADBP, allowing the ADBP a profitable spread. The trouble the Bank encountered with these approaches was that while project documents permitted interest rate hikes (unlike projects that simply raised fixed rates), they also didn't contain any provisions compelling interest rate rises. In practice, governments were often reluctant to raise rates on loans to farmers.

In this context, the increasing turn to various 'market'-based pricing mechanisms in the latter part of the 1980s was in no small part a reaction to the failures of projections aimed at achieving positive real rates, or minimum rates adopted in the absence of clear procedures for raising rates. In the Philippines, to take a typical example, in previous projects 'interest spreads available to retail banks on [project] funds proved insufficient to cover default costs' (World Bank 1985:12). In response, a new project launched in 1985 was set up to 'introduce market-oriented rates on its loans to participating banks without any regulation of spreads to be retained by the latter' (World Bank 1985:12). But these strategies were also fraught. By the late 1980s, the preoccupation of the Bank with interest rates itself started to come in for criticism in project evaluations. In Zimbabwe, the evaluation of a 1982 project for small farmers – which had included provisions that indexed interest rates directly to prime commercial rates, but which also allowed the government to guarantee losses made by the Agricultural Finance Corporation – noted that 'The principle of not subsidizing farmers' interest rates so as to provide them with the right cost signals, as well as to provide the credit institution with sufficient independent revenue, seems inconsistent with then demolishing the earnestness of the business relationship between farmer and credit institution by providing that government will pick up any bad debts and operating costs' (World Bank 1990a:vi). The Bank's conception of the marketisation of credit thus began to embrace a wider range of concerns, reaching beyond the pricing of credit itself into the commercialisation of the financial sector as a whole and the introduction of more competition in rural lending.

Commercialising agricultural banks

Another explicit objective of many of these programmes from the mid-1970s onwards was the reform of agricultural credit institutions along more explicitly commercial lines. Given that state-backed agricultural banks were often established to provide forms of credit that commercial banks were generally not interested in providing, there was always some degree of tension here. This was a long-unfolding concern, and the intensification of efforts to commercialise agricultural bank operations after about 1980 was a reflection of long-running trends as much as a sudden conversion to neoliberalism. Here again operational concerns, particularly around the growing pressure put on partner institutions by arrears and overdues across a number of projects, were important drivers.

Institutional reforms to state-backed lenders to increase their operational autonomy and reform operations along explicitly commercial lines were thus increasingly a major component of most projects adopted after about 1980. Sometimes this took the form of support for developing the mundane infrastructures of banking activity. Some projects included funds for (among other things) staff training, computer systems, accounting software, vehicles, and upgrades to headquarters or branch buildings. More often, projects introduced conditionalities related to loan recoveries and amendments to loan appraisal procedures in an effort to improve recovery rates. The reforms to interest rates above, aimed at ensuring credit to small farmers was made on profitable terms, were also closely related. By the 1980s these direct lending projects were often understood, sometimes explicitly so, as stepping stones towards the development of project structures that would involve commercial banks, or the independent development of private financial markets. For instance, a 1983 project in Thailand, based around direct on-lending by the state-owned Bank for Agriculture and Agricultural Cooperatives, was explicitly described as an 'interim step' towards the development of a rediscount facility at the Central Bank which would support wider commercial lending for agriculture (World Bank 1983a:12).

Yet the Bank nonetheless remained ambivalent about precisely how far agricultural credit – especially longer-term credit for mechanisation or land development, rather than seasonal loans for inputs – could be delivered on purely market terms. Efforts to expand projects to include commercial banks had mixed impacts and often failed. The Bank's tentative initiative to involve commercial banks directly in the revived Pakistani project in 1979, for instance, was abandoned because commercial banks had little interest (1983b:19). There were equally growing concerns that support for state-backed lenders, even if geared to promote the commercialisation of those institutions, might inhibit the development of competitive private credit markets. In Morocco, an audit in 1992 suggested: 'there is little indication that the World Bank Group is actively encouraging greater participation by financial institutions other than [Caisse Nationale de Credit Agricôle (CNCA)] in rural finance' (World Bank 1992a:24). Partly for this reason, by the early 1980s, as structural adjustment lending took off, agricultural credit projects were increasingly also seen as a means of influencing broader financial policy reform.

Agricultural credit projects continued to be negotiated alongside structural adjustment loans and were often framed as a means of supporting or driving wider sectoral reforms. The usefulness of these projects as a means of compelling policy adjustments was, however, limited in practice. The Bank increasingly viewed narrow sectoral projects, particularly those focused on a single institution, as less efficient instruments for prompting policy reforms. Project evaluations conducted by the late 1980s and early 1990s virtually all concluded that directed credit programmes were not effective instruments for compelling policy reforms. The evaluation of a 1989 project in Honduras would note that 'a sector-specific credit project, like this one for agricultural credit, is a weak instrument for addressing problems of financial intermediation in a subsector when the overall banking system is unsound' (World Bank 1995a:v). Much the same was concluded of the much larger series of projects in India – the evaluation of a fourth loan to the national Agriculture Rediscount and Development Corporation (ARDC) would note that 'The main lessons under ARDC IV (and indeed previous ARDC projects) ha[ve] been that [the ARDC] alone cannot bring about sustained or permanent improvements in policy and institutional environment for agriculture credit through its powers to sanction refinance facility' (World Bank 1989a:vi). The point here is that while agricultural credit projects had increasingly come to be seen as a means of reforming financial systems, the truncated progress of actual reforms was interpreted as a sign that targeted programmes were ineffective in this aim.

One of the very final agricultural credit projects run by the Bank is telling with respect to both this shift in emphasis towards wider reforms and the seeming unsuitability of agricultural credit projects for that purpose. After making six previous loans directly to the ADBP, the Bank shifted its approach to agricultural credit in Pakistan in a final project in 1990. The 1990 loan was made to the Pakistani government, rather than to the ADBP as in previous loans, and open for on-lending to farmers both by the ADBP and commercial (and at the time, nationalised) banks. It was explicitly intended to promote greater competition and the development of a self-sustaining market, and designed in conjunction with wider structural adjustment programming in Pakistan: 'Through further financial sector liberalization and progress in increasing competition among banks, the project would support the consolidation of the gains already made in strengthening agricultural credit' (World Bank 1990b:3). The project appraisal was unequivocal: 'Only a market driven agricultural credit system can meet the expanding needs of the agriculture sector and increase its productivity' (World Bank 1990c:19). In practice, the project went, in the Bank's estimation, quite poorly. Both the Pakistani government and the ADBP failed to adopt agreed reforms phasing out subsidies to interest rates, and to meet targets for deposit mobilisation. Loan disbursements from the World Bank were suspended in 1993, and eventually cancelled altogether in 1994. The Bank concluded from the experience that '[a] sector specific credit project is a weak instrument for addressing problems of financial viability and financial intermediation in a sub-sector when the overall banking system is unsound' (World Bank 1997:v), and that 'Unless agricultural/rural credit interest rates are identical to the market-based interest rates, participation of the commercial banks in any rural credit operation will never become meaningful' (World Bank 1997:v).

It wasn't really until the early 1990s, then, that the Bank decisively rejected targeted agricultural credit projects. By the early 1990s, the Bank had concluded that there was, in fact, something of a tension between the commercialisation of financial systems and widespread access to credit. The basic paradox identified in the introduction to this book – that poorer borrowers' low and unpredictable incomes are both the reason they are held to need credit *and* the main reason why they constitute poor credit risks – is evident here. An evaluation of the agricultural credit project in the Philippines noted above was uncommonly explicit about this, noting that the project experience had underlined that commercial banks

> are profit maximizers and risk averters ... that they prefer to remain on short exposure, especially in periods of inflation and economic uncertainty, that they will seek secure loans, that they never like to make small loans to small farmers, that they are slow to open rural branches, and that they cannot be expected to respond enthusiastically to the development objectives of Government and the Bank. (World Bank 1992b:x)

Commercial banks, in short, were unlikely to be enthusiastic participants in agricultural credit programmes, particularly if these targeted small farmers. This conclusion drove the Bank's increasing turn towards microcredit, as a means of delivering wider access to credit for impoverished smallholder farmers, by the early 1990s (see Chapter 3).

MARKETISING SHELTER FINANCE

Similar narratives began to emerge in relation to housing. As Rolnik (2013), Soederberg (2017) and Van Waeyenberge (2018), among others, have recently noted, housing policy was one of the earliest areas where neoliberal development frameworks were articulated in practice. Given that we've spent far more time on agricultural credit up to this point, it is worth providing some brief background on housing policy in global development here. Through the 1950s and 1960s, public house-building programmes were widespread through the Global South. In the latter years of the colonial period, housing would far more likely have been spoken of in social policy contexts (see e.g. Bernards 2018b:71–2). Housing finance was more or less an afterthought in this period, even if establishing urban housing systems based on nuclear family owner-occupiers was a key element of postwar colonial 'stabilisation' policies seeking to establish a stable urban proletariat (see Cooper 1996; Bernards 2018b).

From the early 1970s, we can trace the rise of a kind of celebratory discourse around informal housing, and a concomitant turn towards slum upgrading programmes, which was embraced enthusiastically by the Bank. John F. C. Turner, and his 1972 book *Freedom to Build* (Turner 1972), was hugely influential over Bank policy. Turner articulated an approach to housing development which was deeply skeptical of state involvement in housing, particularly for the poorest (which, to be fair, did in fact far too often consist of bulldozing informal settlements at the time he was writing). Turner instead celebrated the self-organising capacity of slum-dwellers and called for targeted 'self-help' programmes aimed at providing access to basic services and secure tenancy. The Bank's own employees and consultants cite Turner's influence directly. One retrospective written in 1999 notes that the Bank's dominant modes of housing intervention in the decade were 'primarily influenced by [Turner's] theoretical writing' (Werlin 1999:1523). From the mid-1970s, the Bank's discussions of housing policy reflect an explicit embrace of informal housing as legitimate dwellings, while regularising their residents' access to land tenure and key services – the latter category including credit, alongside basic utilities and social services: 'The acceptance of squatter settlements as legitimate forms of shelter, and the provision to these settlements of secure land tenure, credit, water, sewerage, electricity, schools, clinics, and other services would greatly benefit their inhabitants and stimulate private construction' (Grimes 1976:26).

Yet, clearly only some elements of Turner's arguments actually carried through. As Van Waeyenberge (2018:293) shows, site and service policies remained dominant throughout the 1970s. To an extent, this was because the Bank's emphasis on 'self-help' was always much less about empowerment and much more about 'self-financing'. The Bank's first housing project was a site and service scheme in Senegal (see Van Waeyenberge 2018:293). The project itself is indicative. The appraisal report makes note of the government's turn to a more widespread sites and services approach based on 'a growing awareness of the impossibility of providing more than a small proportion of families' with homes on a public or state-owned enterprise basis (World Bank 1973:6). The project was explicitly meant to be organised around 'self-help' principles, while subsidies for public housing were meant to be phased out:

> with the assistance of community organizers and practical technicians, occupants would participate in making and carrying out decisions to advance their own welfare. They would build their own housing and community structures, such as mosques and social centers, and establish cooperative institutions such as savings and credit mechanisms, building materials production co-ops, and child-care centers. (1973:9)

Critically, this was justified as a means of 'freeing' public resources to be spent elsewhere. We can see an early articulation here of ideas about development through 'self-help', which would be enthusiastically embraced (again) in other areas of policy by the Bank in the 1990s through the promotion of microcredit – to which I will return in the next chapter. The embrace of 'self-help' narratives around housing at the Bank was always oriented at least in part around the conditions of permanent austerity inherited from the colonial state, which I've highlighted previously. A 1983 review, for instance, of housing interventions at the Bank frames the turn to slum upgrading in precisely these terms: 'During the early 1970s it became clear that it was beyond the financial resources of all but a handful of developing countries to solve a problem of this magnitude' (Bamberger 1983:95; cf. Werlin 1999:1524). Such invocations also echo colonial arguments about thrift outlined in Chapter 1 in important respects. Indeed, there's a fairly direct through-line here: USAID supported efforts to promote homeownership through 'thrift' in the 1950s and 1960s in a number of favoured countries in Latin America and East and Southeast Asia (e.g. Harold 1966). Thus, the turn to 'self-help' in the 1970s drew on a language of local empowerment through responsibilisation, and an assumption of austerity as a background condition, that both had longer lineages. The point I want to pick up here, though, is the growing role that access to credit took on in these programmes.

The Bank was considerably less ambivalent in its embrace of financial liberalisation for housing purposes than it was with respect to agriculture, even from the mid-1970s. Echoing neoliberal economists' discussions of agricultural credit (e.g. McKinnon 1973; Shaw 1973), restrictions on access to credit for housing were largely blamed on government interference. Expanding access to mortgage finance was understood primarily in terms of liberalisation, particularly the 'freeing of interest rate restrictions, measures to encourage competition between banks, [and] the promotion of life insurance companies and pension funds' (World Bank 1975:30). Likewise, a study commissioned by the Bank on financing housing in developing countries argued that 'Points of view that interpret usury as an evil have often led to the pegging of commercial bank interest rates at artificially low levels ... With excessive demand thus created by controlled interest rates, banks prefer lending to the least risky borrowers' (Grimes 1976:57). As compared to the rather more ambivalent discussions of interest rates for small farmers at around the same time, even in high level policy documents, the unambiguous embrace of 'financial repression' arguments here is notable.

The increasing shift towards financial reform as a housing policy strengthened the role of USAID. The predominant housing finance framework remained the Housing Investment Guaranty Fund (HIGF) throughout the period in question. The HIGF was launched, with $10 million, by the US Congress in 1961; by the mid-1970s, it guaranteed more than $1 billion in loans. The HIGF was designed, in essence, to mobilise American commercial lenders for housing projects in favoured countries in the Global South. The HIGF worked with national governments and local lenders to design projects, often with a strong 'institutional development' component, aiming to

assist in the accumulation of local capital for long-term mortgage finance operations, the promotion of effective cost recovery systems, the reduction of subsidies, the elimination of unrealistic standards for Basic services and the stimulation of the private sector to expand economic development opportunities in urban centers. (USAID 1983:3.2)

In a parallel to the directed credit programmes for agriculture described above, the commercialisation of various financial institutions – many of which were cooperative or public institutions – was a key objective of the programme. The HIGF subsequently guaranteed 'the return of one hundred percent of the outstanding balance of the loan plus accrued interest' to the commercial lender backing the project (USAID 1983:5.3). Initially, the HIGF primarily supported lending to middle-class borrowers in developing countries, but was increasingly pushed to lend to low-income borrowers in the 1970s. This shift was formalised by legislative changes in 1975 which required at least 90 percent of new guarantees issued under HIGF to be used for low-income borrowers (see USAID 1983:3.1; USGAO 1978:1).

There are two things worth underlining about the actual distribution of funds under the HIGF. First, the programme was never designed to serve the poorest. This remained the case even after the 'new direction' focus on lower-income borrowers. Indeed, this point was made explicit in a number of evaluations: '[USAID] does not believe that countries with very low per capita incomes are suitable recipients for [HIGF] project loans, since these loans are made on commercial rather than concessional terms' (USGAO 1978:3). Likewise, 'The commercial-rate financing provided under the ... program is not, for the most part, appropriate to meet ... the shelter needs of the very poorest income levels (below the 15th income percentile)' (USGAO 1978:5). Second, the loans were, emphatically and explicitly, used to advance US political objectives, even more than was the case with small loans for farmers. Fully two thirds of loans disbursed between 1974 and 1978, for instance, went to four countries – Korea, Chile, Israel, and Portugal (USGAO 1978:3) – the geopolitical significance of which I probably don't need to elaborate at length. Programming in Israel and Portugal, in particular, went somewhat against the stated objectives of the programme in lending to the poorest, but was explicitly mandated by Congress for what were euphemistically described as 'specific foreign policy reasons' (USGAO 1995:4).

However, the way the HIGF worked changed over time, in ways that were mirrored at the Bank. In another parallel to agricultural credit debates, there was a gradual shift both at the World Bank and at USAID through the 1980s away from individual projects and towards efforts to press for sector-wide reforms. USAID commissioned efforts to develop more systematic frameworks for evaluating housing policies and reforms to mobilise finance, primarily by removing restrictions on interest rates (see Struyk et al. 1985; Struyk and Turner 1987). World Bank officials were developing similar analyses in tandem, again emphasising the need to remove restrictions on interest rates: 'Arbitrarily low interest rates are a threat to the viability of housing finance institutions. This threat explains the great reluctance that market-oriented institutions have either to developing or to taking over low-income programs sponsored by the government in many countries' (Renaud 1984:58; cf. Renaud 1985). The Bank's housing provision, as Van Waeyenberge (2018) shows, shifted decisively towards efforts to mobilise housing finance through the 1980s, with a relative de-emphasis of site and service and slum upgrading programmes.

This push for more systematic reforms involved some rethinking of the HIGF. The HIGF was in theory meant to deliver small 'demonstration' projects, which would ostensibly show the value of self-help approaches to delivering housing. This was probably always a questionable premise. Increasingly, the HIGF was seen as a potential mechanism for reforming housing policies more generally. Interest rate subsidies were, again, a key focus – highlighted, for instance, in Government Accountability Office reviews of the programme:

> The general practice in many developing countries of subsidizing shelter costs has ... threatened the financial viability of these institutions. Interest-rate subsidies result in financial losses, which have forced the institutions to turn back to their central governments for new funds. (USGAO 1984:12)

The economic crisis in the early 1980s, though, ostensibly provided an opportunity to press for reforms: '[Housing guaranty] loans are dollar-denominated and thus attractive to governments trying to deal with foreign exchange shortages. The Office has used the promise of new ... loans to get governments to take steps toward needed reforms' (USGAO 1984:14). As with agricultural credit, then, USAID increasingly embraced a view of HIGF projects less as a means of providing housing, and more as a means of driving wider financial sector reforms.

The Bank's landmark 1993 publication *Housing: Enabling Markets to Work* encapsulated much of this broader shift (World Bank 1993a). The report is widely cited as a key moment in the neoliberalisation and financialisation of housing policy (see Rolnik 2013; Soederberg 2017; van Waeyenberge 2018). The report didn't so much signal any major changes as formalise the wider shifts that had been ongoing both at the Bank and at USAID throughout the preceding decade. It made explicit the shift from housing as an area of social policy to an 'economic' problem: 'The key problem is one of managing an important economic sector with crucial links to overall economic performance, and not simply one of managing a component of the social welfare system' (World Bank 1993a:10). The kind of austerity logic highlighted throughout this book was a key component of this argument: 'Governments too often perceive housing solely as a welfare issue, requiring the transfer of physical or financial resources to households unable to house themselves adequately. Available resources, however, are rarely adequate' (World Bank 1993a:11). The state, in short, could not provide housing except for a small number of people. Enabling the titular markets to 'work' would direct private sector resources towards the provision of housing. Available credit, along with competitive, profit-oriented housing finance, were presented as key conditions for effective markets in housing (World Bank 1993a:16). If this emphasis on market provision and the removal of subsidies didn't exactly look much different from the conclusions nearly 20 years prior (e.g. World Bank 1975b), the specific approach to achieving those ends had changed a lot. This was articulated explicitly as a shift away from targeted interventions aimed at building physical infrastructures or providing credit towards the wider reform of housing and financial sector policies (World Bank 1993a:1).

The HIGF came in for a similar rethinking two years later. A 1995 assessment found that the programme was in significant financial difficulty because a number of borrowers had defaulted, triggering guarantees well beyond the reserves budgeted for the purpose. Equally, the programme had generally failed to mobilise credit for low-income housing, both in that it had done little to mobilise private credit, and that 'in nearly every country visited for this review, GAO observed program-financed shelter projects that were outside the reach of the poorer families that the program is supposed to target' (USGAO 1995:3). Or, in what was a recurrent problem, credit directed to housing under the HIGF did not stimulate the development of private markets for housing finance, particularly for the poorest. The debt crisis and changes to financial rules in the US had also meant that credit was, even more than previously, being disbursed to middle-income countries under the programme. The GAO recommended dismantling the HIGF.

CONCLUSION

This chapter has identified a series of lines of thinking that, even prior to the debt crisis, linked poverty and irregular livelihoods to the exclusion of smallholder farmers and informal workers from mainstream financial markets. We can see, in the trajectories traced above, how neoliberal approaches to development were premised on an explicit denial of the importance of colonial legacies. We can also get a sense of how difficult it was in practice to articulate new markets, or to coax existing institutions into operating in the 'market-like' way that development authorities wanted, in the context of inherited patterns of uneven development. The idea that markets constituted a kind of default setting on human behaviour, which needed to be shielded from interference to operate properly, was in practice increasingly confronted with a financial sector that was not designed to lend to farmers, especially the poorest smallholders or landless farmers, or for housing in informal settlements.

Three points are worth underlining here. First, these trajectories, albeit to different degrees, should make us reconsider the history of structural adjustment. Looking at housing and agricultural finance in this light helps us to see that poverty finance was integral to the rise of neoliberalism in global development governance. Neoliberal approaches to development were being worked out, albeit with some difficulty, in relation to housing and agricultural finance before Reagan or Thatcher came into office, before the Third World debt crisis and structural adjustment took hold, and even before Pinochet's coup in Chile. The latter should appear much less as a 'Big Bang' kind of moment in global neoliberalism, then, and much more as a continuation by other means of a wider and more longstanding project of the commodification, commercialisation, and marketisation of housing and agriculture. Directed agricultural credit programmes at the World Bank and the HIGF (a directed credit programme in all but name) continued alongside the first structural adjustment loans. Second, and relatedly, we can see from this history that there's no clean break between neoliberalism and the approaches that preceded it. 'Self-help' approaches to housing owe a good deal to the colonial-era veneration of 'thrift' and were adopted by the Bank and others in no small part because they promised to work in the context of inherited conditions of entrenched austerity. Finally, there are very clear echoes of the dynamics traced here in the rise of microfinance. It is to microfinance that I turn in the next chapter.

3
Structural adjustment, backlash, and the turn to the local: Explaining the rise of microfinance

This chapter examines the rise and adoption of microfinance in the 1990s. The rise of microfinance has been widely discussed globally and in different contexts, with a number of authors emphasising the role of the World Bank and USAID, as well as a number of key NGOs and microfinance evangelists, in promoting the rise of microfinance globally and in different contexts (see Bateman 2017; 2020; Dalgic 2007; Aagard 2011; Mader 2015). Here I argue that the vogue for microfinance in the 1990s was a reflection of efforts to grapple with the failures of early rounds of neoliberal reforms within the confines on the wider patterns of uneven development mapped in this book. Microfinance sought to make an end run around the limits imposed by the colonial financial infrastructures and constraints on state action described in Chapter 1. This is made even clearer when we widen our lens slightly to look at other contemporary areas of poverty finance alongside microcredit. In this chapter, I situate the rise of microcredit as a policy fad alongside the rather less closely studied, but simultaneously emerging, micro*insurance* (see Bernards 2018a). The latter provides a useful contrast with microfinance. Microinsurance emerged out of different but parallel debates about the reformulation and expansion of social protection amidst the devastation of structural adjustment. It was, at least in its initial articulations, explicitly counterposed to the 'market'-based solutions proffered by the World Bank, the IMF, and their allies. Yet, by the early 2000s, microinsurance and microcredit were being promoted in strikingly similar terms to the approaches they had initially opposed, and by the same actors.

Microcredit has often been discussed as a kind of twin project of mitigating backlash against the brutality of structural adjustment while clearing new ground for further neoliberalisation (e.g. Weber 2002; 2004; Bateman 2017). Microfinance, in Bateman's words, 'gained its initial support and then became a dominant feature of international development policy in the longer term largely because it could be ... deployed to legitimize, maintain, and extend the global neoliberal project' (2018:17). This dynamic, in which microfinance simultaneously helped to rescue neoliberalism from itself and to extend its reach into ever-wider spheres of social life (reflective of a wider tendency of neoliberalism to 'fail and flail forwards', in Peck's [2010] evocative phrase), is certainly a key element of the story here. Yet we also need to understand how poverty finance initiatives in the 1990s sought to respond to the social crises of structural adjustment by working around the limits of the colonial structures described above – both the logics of permanent austerity and the limits of existing financial infrastructures. Microfinance was an effort to mitigate the contradictions of neoliberalisation while working around deep-rooted patterns of uneven development. As we'll see in subsequent chapters, microfinance wound up by largely reinforcing both.

This chapter develops these arguments by examining how microcredit emerged out of two initially divergent streams of activity: the promotion of social protection for informal workers in the Global South and global neoliberal development governance. This convergence laid the groundwork for the renewed emphasis on commercialisation and marketisation seen in the 2000s (explored in the next chapter). I make this argument in three steps. First, I briefly recap the long-run backdrop to these developments, highlighting the intensification of precarity across much of the Global South in the context of structural adjustment. Second, I show how microinsurance as a policy scheme emerged out of efforts at the International Labour Organization (ILO) to expand access to social security to non-standard workers in the Global South – such as precariously employed or casualised wage workers, 'informal' sector workers, and small-scale farmers. Finally, I return to the rise of microcredit, showing how USAID, the World Bank, and others picked up and started to aggressively promote microfinance in the 1990s.

NEOLIBERALISM, AUSTERITY, AND PRECARITY

Before getting into the details of the poverty finance interventions traced in this chapter, it's worthwhile briefly mapping out the global context in which they took place. These dynamics constitute the problems to which poverty finance interventions sought to respond and the key limits they had to confront. This will, of necessity, be a very brief discussion. None-theless, three background developments are important to understand.

First, the Third World debt crisis, alongside global financial deregula-tion (see Helleiner 1994), restructured global financial flows in ways that exacerbated the persistent restrictions on resources available to develop-ing country governments. Access to credit for many developing country governments is increasingly determined by global market conditions over which they have little control. This is exacerbated by political imperatives to privatise key industries and assets and to restrict public spending, especially for social purposes, perhaps especially by the endur-ing political commitment of key regulatory agencies, notably the IMF, to implementing austerity measures in the name of 'fiscal consolidation' (see Kentikelenis et al. 2016). Together these dynamics have created the conditions for recurrent debt crises and deepened quasi-permanent con-ditions of austerity (see Alami 2018; Bassett 2018; Bonizzi et al. 2020). As I've noted in previous chapters, these dynamics are ultimately deeply rooted in the modes of insertion of colonial and postcolonial economies into hierarchical global financial systems. They have been intensified and exacerbated by developments in recent decades.

Second, global production has been radically restructured in ways that have extended the reach of corporate power, both directly and indirectly, across a number of sectors. Manufacturing and agricultural industries in particular have increasingly come to be dominated by complex supply chains. The lowest-margin, highest-risk, and most competitive aspects of production processes have been externalised to locations primarily in the Global South. Studies across a number of sectors point to a tendency for firms beholden to equity markets to prioritise share buybacks and dividends, driving supply chain reorganisations and, at times, under-investment in productive capacity (Milberg 2008). Other authors have highlighted links between the organisation of global supply chains and hyper-exploitation through various forms of unfree labour (Phillips 2013; McGrath 2013). Selwyn (2019) argues that, given these imbalances and tendencies towards the hyper-exploitation of workers at the periph-ery of global supply chains, they are better understood as 'global poverty chains'. Agricultural production has likewise been marked by a dramatic concentration of corporate control over inputs and marketing by a few large firms on one hand, and by increasingly volatile prices on the other – the risks of which are borne predominantly by peripheral small farmers or by states (see Clapp and Isakson 2018; Staritz et al. 2018).

Finally, the upshot of the confluence of semi-permanent austerity and growing corporate power has been deepening precarity and exposure to climate breakdown for working classes globally, but especially in the Global South (see Bernards and Soederberg 2020). Cuts to social services, currency devaluations, privatisations and restructurings of public enterprises, and the retrenchment of public employees under the auspices of structural adjustment created social dislocations that have yet to be resolved in many places. Elaborate chains of subcontracting in global production networks have worked to squeeze peripheral workers into ever-cheaper and faster modes of work (see Phillips 2016; Selwyn 2019). Rural producers in the Global South, meanwhile, are increasingly displaced from land and livelihoods by land grabbing and volatile prices, and the effects of the above processes have amplified longer-term dynamics of exposure to variable climates (see Li 2009; Bernards 2019c; Natarajan *et al.* 2019).

This context is worth bearing in mind for two reasons. First, it helps to underline the background against which all of the below experiments with poverty finance have taken place. It has been continually necessary to articulate new means of mitigating the worst consequences of neoliberalisation. One of the lesser remarked facts about the history of neoliberalism in global development is that it has been a spur for a considerable development of alternative forms of protective institutions. Despite (or perhaps because of) the acceleration of austerity, privatisation, and dispossession, the past thirty years have in fact witnessed an *expansion* of flagship social protection programmes in the Global South, albeit often through a variety of different forms of non-contributory social transfers rather than conventional contributory social security. Harris and Scully (2015), invoking Polanyi, call this a 'hidden counter-movement'. There are decided limits to these programmes. There's little question that they are pitched in neoliberal terms, aimed as they are at maintaining peoples' capacity to consume, and often come with conditionalities aimed at producing productive labourers (Cammack 2004). But this 'hidden counter-movement' points to a key dynamic that does help us understand the forms that poverty finance interventions took in the 1990s. Second, these developments have deepened and entrenched the constraints within which development policies must be articulated. The long-run conditions of austerity are a clear echo of the colonial era. But they have arguably been exacerbated by the political constraints imposed by the 'constitutionalization' of austerity (per McBride 2016). Moreover, these developments have accelerated patterns of uneven development and increased the precarity of urban and rural working classes across the Global South.

Structural adjustment was, emphatically, a disaster. It was a disaster that required complementary efforts to offset its worst effects. Yet these efforts have been strongly constrained by the broader structural constraints induced by the long-term colonial legacies introduced in Chapter 1, and strengthened by the constitutionalisation of austerity. In this way, in Peck's words, neoliberalisation can be understood as a dialectical process in which 'the forever-incomplete triple commodification of land, labor, and money sets the stage for, indeed inescapably provokes, various forms of "protective" socioinstitutional counteraction, which become entangled as contradictory externalities of the exchange process' (2013b:1560). Poverty finance initiatives have formed an important part of these responses. It's particularly useful, before we turn to the more widely-discussed story of microcredit, to look first at a perhaps less well-known example: the articulation of 'community'-level insurance mutuals as a means of delivering social security or access to healthcare for non-standard workers across the Global South.

THE ORIGINS OF MICROINSURANCE

In the late 1970s and the 1980s, the ILO led a significant push to expand social security coverage to non-standard workers in developing countries. The development of social security schemes for rural populations was a point of emphasis, although this was perceived as a particularly complicated problem. A report for the ILO's 1977 African Regional Conference, for instance, notes that 'The obstacles are enormous and relate especially to the living conditions of the populations concerned, which aggravate current constraints – supporting public services, for instance, are fewer and worse in rural areas than in town – and cause new difficulties, such as the scale and type of contingencies to be covered, and to the poverty of the agricultural sector' (ILO 1977a:40). Apart from general concerns about fairness, this was also seen, much like many of the programmes discussed in the previous chapter, as a means of slowing down rates of urbanisation and the supposed depopulation of the countryside. But, notably, this argument was articulated in expressly non-market terms: 'raising the rural population's standard of living – an absolute necessity – could better be done by using increased income for community purposes, rather than by increasing cash incomes with the probable result of inflating useless and dangerous kinds of consumption' (1977a:41). In fact, this framing expressly prioritises collective modes of poverty reduction over the raising of individual incomes. So how did we get from here to the emphasis on marketisation of microinsurance policies in the early 2000s?

Efforts at expanding social protection faced a bind. Contributory social security programmes modelled on pensions, unemployment, and social security programming developed for salaried, formal workers in the Global North were problematic for workers with insecure employment and low and unpredictable incomes. Where workers could only afford to make small contributions and lacked steady, predictable incomes, contributions were simply not an effective financing mechanism. But non-contributory programmes required the mobilisation of external resources – through taxation or otherwise – in ways that would have stretched the constraints posed on postcolonial economies by their peripheral insertion into global financial structures. Already in the ILO report, there was some emphasis on fiscal constraints as limits on the expansion of new programmes. Where workers' contributions were already high and incomes precarious, 'the most serious constraint lies in the great difficulty of finding other sources of finance ... The situation varies greatly according to countries. In each of them political, economic and social considerations fix limits, and because of these priorities have to be established' (ILO 1977a:32). These constraints were already apparent in the 1970s – and, as noted in the previous chapters, they dated to the colonial period – but they would only grow more pronounced as the structural adjustment era wore on.

These dilemmas are reflected very clearly in ILO reports on social security for non-standard workers prepared for a number of countries during this time. These reports outline a number of alternatives for the financing of social security schemes for irregular workers. An ILO mission to Iran noted that 'government subsidies remain the only practical source' of financing for the extension of social security in rural areas (ILO 1977b:9). In Malaysia, ILO officials advocated a compulsory insurance scheme for farmers and fishermen subsidised with a 'solidarity levy' on an existing provident fund for urban workers (ILO 1980:50–51). Officials even proposed a non-contributory scheme for the long-term unemployed in Gabon (ILO 1982). In the context of the wide adoption of austerity measures at the time, however, public-financed programmes were often considered untenable in practice. A 1989 report to the Cameroonian government on social security for agricultural workers noted this explicitly. The report suggests that the 'general economic situation' wouldn't permit any public subsidies, so 'the balance between what is desirable and what is possible in the social sector has to be met through the collective participation of beneficiaries' (ILO 1989:130).

The ILO's advisors were thus faced with a dilemma: effective contributory schemes would be near-impossible for workers with small and unpredictable incomes, and public subsidies were difficult to provide in the context of fiscal crisis and structural adjustment. Officials in the Social Security Department of the ILO therefore increasingly began to advocate for the expansion of small-scale schemes organised at the community level and funded out of local contributions. A pair of officials published an article advocating the use of 'traditional' institutions and village associations in Francophone Africa, including rotating savings and credit societies (referred to as 'tontines' in much of Francophone West Africa), harvest insurance, informal associations, and mutual benefit schemes, as a means of providing social protection to 'self-employed' workers (Mouton and Gruat 1989:52). The ILO ran a project along similar lines in Rwanda, Mali, and Togo between 1982 and 1988, which had sought to organise small-scale craftsmen into self-governing associations as a means of facilitating access to credit, organising training, and providing a greater political voice (Maldonado 1989). There are, of course, clear parallels here with the embrace of self-help and the positive view of 'informality' outlined in the housing interventions in the previous chapter. Yet at the ILO, there was initially much more stress on the 'community', and on collective self-help, than on individuals and discrete households. Autonomous organisations of informal workers and smallhold farmers were increasingly emphasised as alternative means of poverty reduction and social protection for precarious and irregular livelihoods not generally covered by conventional social security.

A number of research projects and policy missions in the 1990s explored similar options. These were given additional impetus by the expanded emphasis at the ILO and elsewhere on the role of the 'informal' economy in the 1990s (see Bernards 2018b). The Social Security department ran a pilot project applying a similar approach in four countries – Tanzania, Benin, India, and El Salvador (Van Ginneken 1996). Separate social insurance schemes were, in practice, the major emphasis. The interventions in Benin and Tanzania started by scouting out appropriate informal workers' organisations in target cities to run social insurance programmes. In Benin, the pilot project proposed involved using several informal workers' organisations to collect contributions, while drawing on a public-private microfinance institution, the Fédération des Caisses d'Épargne et de Credit Agricole Mutuel (FECECAM) to manage money. The basic model proposed was to have officials of informal sector organisations collect contributions and deposit them at an account with the local branch of FECECAM. Agreements would be established with local clinics to permit card-carrying members to draw on the funds to pay for medical care (Gauthé 1997:24). The Beninois project was never implemented in full, but the basic model was carried forward. In Tanzania, the project proposed extending the model of the Dar es Salaam intervention to Arusha and Mbeya (Kiwara and Heijnis 1997). It identified 'viable' groups of informal workers in the two cities, based on criteria including having upwards of four hundred members, a common bank account, stable leadership, and the nearby availability of healthcare providers (1997:75–6). The Tanzanian government also organised a similar pilot scheme in the rural Inguna region on the basis of the Dar es Salaam experiment – although in this case, member contributions were augmented by matching funds from the World Bank (Kiwara 1999:138–140).

This work on healthcare mutuals laid much of the groundwork for the subsequent development of microinsurance – indeed, this and other work done by the ILO on healthcare mutuals (e.g. Atim 1998) is cited directly in many of the regulatory documents discussed in Chapter 6. The first usage of the term 'microinsurance' was, in essence, an effort to develop a consistent concept for this loose series of experiments. Officials in the Social Protection department of the ILO initially advanced the concept of 'microinsurance' to refer to autonomous community-directed organisations linked into larger structures to facilitate the pooling of risk, to describe these emerging alternative forms of social protection (Dror and Jacquier 1999). As an explicit alternative to both 'state'- and 'market'-led alternatives that had largely failed, they proposed 'microinsurance' as a set of 'autonomous enterprises' operated at the community level, with 'networks to link multiple small area- and occupation-based units into larger structures that can enhance both the insurance function (through a wider pooling of risk) and the support structures needed for improved governance (through training, data banks, research facilities, etc.)' (1999:77). 'Microinsurance' was initially articulated as a 'community'-based response to the limits of market-led models of development, in a context of permanent austerity. Critically, this articulation of microinsurance as a form of community provision is explicitly defined in opposition to the (presumed permanent) incapacity of the state to provide effective social protection to the poorest:

> In many LMICs [low- and middle-income countries] where the State has never provided more than rudimentary services, such as in sub-Saharan Africa, exclusion is linked to the inability of the market and of society to incorporate certain subgroups that cumulate a different profile of impeding characteristics, such as low income, malnutrition, low health status (and hence low insurance status within for-profit insurance schemes), rural habitat, low education levels and ethnic/tribal origin. (Dror and Jacquier 1999:72)

In short, we can trace this turn to the community as a means of providing social protection through microinsurance to efforts to mitigate the worst impacts of structural adjustment, within the confines of the semi-permanent austerity increasingly imposed on peripheral states in the global financial system.

Yet, there was a growing recognition by the late 1990s that it would be impossible to develop these kinds of systems at scale without the mobilisation of external resources. 'Microinsurance' in the guise articulated by Dror and Jacquier's article (1999) ran into essentially the same problem that state-backed initiatives for social protection had a decade earlier. Contributory systems didn't work for the poorest, but given conditions of public austerity across much of the Global South, the state wasn't a viable source of external resources. The emphasis was increasingly placed on the mobilisation of global capital markets. The promotion of 'microinsurance' was subsequently taken up by a number of other actors beyond the ILO, particularly through the establishment of a working group on insurance at the Consultative Group to Assist the Poor (CGAP). The group of participants in the microinsurance working group contrasted somewhat with CGAP's microcredit activities – the ILO, in particular, remained an important participant in the microinsurance group (see Bernards 2016; 2018a). Growing emphasis was nonetheless placed on developing markets rather than mobilising community solidarities. In a strong parallel to claims about microcredit, there was a growing consensus that 'The future success of microinsurance depends on achieving prudent, profitable and continuous growth and development' (Botero *et*

al. 2006:583). I'll defer a discussion of what this push for commercialisation and marketisation entailed in practice to Chapter 6 (suffice to say,
it met with limited success). For the moment, the point is that the turn
to poverty finance here needs to be understood as an effort to respond
to the worst consequences of structural adjustment, while at the same
time to navigate the limits posed both by neoliberal reforms themselves
and by deeper constraints imposed by patterns of uneven development
engendered by colonialism.

MICROCREDIT GOES GLOBAL

I dwelled in the previous section on a story that will likely be less familiar
to many readers than the much more widely discussed origins of microcredit. This contrast is useful in understanding the rise of microcredit
itself. The adoption and promotion of microcredit at the World Bank
and USAID was driven by many of the same institutional and structural
forces as the ILO's push towards microinsurance. Microcredit was also,
in no small part, a reaction to the failures of directed credit schemes in
agriculture and housing traced in Chapter 2.

It's worth noting, to begin, that Grameen Bank (which was, along with
its founder Muhammad Yunus, the microfinance poster-child in the
1990s and 2000s, often credited with pioneering microfinance in 1970s
Bangladesh and eventually awarded the Nobel Peace Prize in 2006) was
in many ways a direct outgrowth of the kinds of programmes examined
in the previous chapter and in the discussion of microinsurance above.
As Roy notes, Grameen Bank, along with similar organisations like the
Bangladesh Rural Advancement Committee (BRAC – to which we will
return in the next chapter) and the Association for Social Advancement
(ASA), emerged out of a cluster of postcolonial civil society organisations in Bangladesh, oriented around the 'delivery of a wide range of
services, including microfinance, to the poor' (2010:100). Such organisations explicitly rejected the emphasis placed by USAID and the World
Bank on building markets, specifically emphasising the need to go
beyond market provision to meet the needs of the 'ultra-poor'. Grameen
Bank thus represented part of a considerable apparatus of development
organisations stretching well beyond the state, but also closely entangled
with it in important ways. Grameen Bank was initially a village-level
pilot project led by Yunus in 1976. The project was rapidly scaled up in
the late 1970s, in collaboration with branches of the Bangladesh Krishi

Bank (BKB, a government-owned commercial bank), Bangladesh Bank (with matching support from the International Fund for Agricultural Development), a number of other nationalised commercial banks, and a guarantee fund financed by the Ford Foundation (although never actually tapped). It was finally incorporated as a separate financial institution in its own right in 1983, with 40 percent of its capital owned directly by the Bangladeshi government, 40 percent by members and 10 percent each by BKB and Sonali Bank (another nationalised commercial bank) (Hoque and Ahmed 1989:19; von Pischke 1991:239). Grameen, BRAC, ASA, and the like thus represented, albeit on a much more extensive scale than in most other countries, part of the same terrain of interlinked state and voluntary organisations and community services onto which the ILO pinned many of their hopes for social protection provision for the poorest in Africa's informal sectors around the same time. Heroic narratives about Yunus aside, then, Grameen Bank was very much a product of a particular set of postcolonial institutional circumstances – which Roy (2010) goes as far as to describe as the 'Bangladesh Consensus'.

Of immediate interest, though, is less the specific origins of Grameen Bank itself and more how the 'Grameen model' was taken up and circulated in global development circles in the 1990s. USAID started to embrace microlending into the 1980s, primarily in its programmes in Latin America. As noted in the previous chapter, various small-scale credit schemes, particularly those backing anti-communist governments, had been rolled out in housing and agriculture in the 1970s (see Bateman 2017). Support for 'microenterprise' and 'informal' economies was, in many ways, an outgrowth of some of the rethinking of the programmes examined in the previous chapter, particularly the growing concern about state-backed agricultural credit. In a retrospective discussion, one former USAID official attributes this to the rethinking of directed agricultural credit (prompted by, among others, Adams 1971; von Pischke 1978; Adams and von Pischke 1980) alongside the growing emphasis on the 'informal' and the embrace of private sector initiatives after Ronald Reagan's election in 1980 (Rhyne 2014). Rhyne narrates the turn to microcredit as a more or less direct substitute for targeted credit: 'If public development banks were sidelined, who would lend to the poor?' (Rhyne 2014). This view, however, understates some of the threads linking programming in the 1970s with later developments.

One notable continuity, for instance, was the use of guaranty funds to promote microcredit abroad. USAID set up a microcredit guaranty fund, along the same lines as the HIGF, with Boston-based NGO Accion in 1986. The basic problem was framed in much the same way as well. The USAID/Accion project, for instance, described the 'shortage' of small enterprise credit from the formal financial system in terms that will be familiar (and which, implicitly and indirectly, point to key continuities with colonial financial systems):

> street vendors, household manufacturers, etc. almost never have access to commercial credit channels. Bankers have a hard time dealing with them: they are seldom able to provide collateral, and the size of the loans they require is too small to compensate a bank for its administrative costs in processing a loan. (USAID 1986:3)

The project was premised on the idea that previous microlending programmes' reliance on grant funding rather than commercial credit had led to a lack of attention to the credit-worthiness of borrowers and an unwillingness to charge high enough rates to secure the financial self-sufficiency of the programmes. The programme, echoing the Bank's activities on agricultural credit around the same time, included a number of conditionalities for local partner organisations, including charging positive real interest rates to end-borrowers (USAID 1986:9).

The World Bank was somewhat slower in embracing microcredit, but it began to do so in the late 1980s. Here the example of Grameen was hugely influential. The Bank included a quite positive discussion of Grameen Bank in its 1989 *World Development Report*. This was, of course, reflective of an earlier embrace of Grameen as a key model for rural finance in particular, hinted at in later agricultural credit projects. It also reflected a very explicit preference for private initiative over state-backed projects: 'While the government struggled to create a viable rural banking system in Bangladesh, a small private initiative was started in 1976 to help the landless without normal bank collateral to obtain credit' (World Bank 1989b:117). It's hard not to read this embrace of Grameen in the light of the recurrent concerns about many of these issues through the Bank's agricultural credit programming in the 1970s, particularly around repayment performance. The repayment performance of Grameen Bank, with loan recovery rates nominally at 97–99 percent, was strongly emphasised (World Bank 1989b:117). Future Chief Economist of the Bank Joseph

Stiglitz (1990) argued a year later, in more formal terms, that Grameen's 'peer monitoring' system allowed it to do two crucial things. First, it worked around the absence of credit-information infrastructures, that had left rural finance predominantly under the control of moneylenders. It also managed to create incentives for monitoring repayment performance, which were supposedly lacking among government lending programmes. The Grameen Bank, for Stiglitz, was 'able to exploit the local knowledge of the members of the group. It has devised an incentive structure whereby others within the village do the monitoring for it' (1990:353). While this came at the cost of exposing borrowers to heightened risks – ones which, admittedly, 'could be much better absorbed by the bank' (1990:353) – this should be offset by interest rates adjusting to better monitoring and hence lower default risks (1990:362).

Some of the Bank's internal critics of directed credit were also explicit in their embrace of Grameen as an alternative to the former. For instance, von Pischke rhapsodised the virtues of Grameen:

> It appears to have operated on a financially sound basis for almost ten years. It has linked savings, credit and social progress in a sound and creative matter through a radically innovative instrument, while targeting those far beyond the frontier of formal finance: primarily women in rural households that are virtually landless. (1991:232–3)

Von Pischke did sound a few notes of caution. He highlighted, notably, that certain claims of Grameen – about, for example, 98 percent repayment rates – were to some extent an artefact of the fact that such rates were calculated by comparing loans more than a year in arrears against the total value of the outstanding portfolio. In short, repayment rates were calculating by measuring a fairly restrictive portion of loans heavily in arrears against an (at the time) rapidly expanding denominator (von Pischke 1991:234). Nonetheless, the implicit contrast here between the 'payment discipline' and commercial interest rates achieved by Grameen and poor collection rates and subsidies prevalent in directed credit programmes is core to this argument. Official documents similarly contrasted the successes of Grameen with the failures of directed credit. The Bank's official handbook on poverty reduction strategies, published in 1993, likewise stressed that while subsidised credit schemes had failed, and had 'weakened the financial sector' in the process, more recent programmes had shifted to mutual guarantee arrangements whereby social pressures are brought to bear on borrowers, thereby increasing repayment rates and reducing lender risks. They charge market-determined interest rates, establish deposit facilities, and target poor clients rather than nonpoor sectors. (World Bank 1993b:46)

The point here is that the embrace of Grameen in the late 1980s and early 1990s needs to be understood, not just in terms of the deepening thrust of a cohesive neoliberalising or financialising project, but also as a response to a particular diagnosis of earlier failures to create commercial financial markets.

As I've noted above, these are failures that must be understood at least in part in terms of the awkward confrontation between marketising projects and the uneven financial infrastructures developed under colonialism. The Bank's 'failing and flailing' (*per* Peck 2010) into an embrace of microcredit reflected a partial recognition of these issues. This is true in the sense of a deepening recognition that markets would not simply emerge on their own through deregulation, without the construction of particular informational infrastructures (for instance, Stiglitz's emphasis on 'peer monitoring'), and because Grameen seemed to promise a model that would resolve the problems of low repayment and subsidised interest rates that had frustrated Bank officials in their efforts to develop agricultural credit systems over the previous decades. Grameen spoke effectively both to the turn to the 'local' in response to the failures of structural adjustment and to the more prosaic concerns around interest rates and collection performance that had dogged directed credit projects over the previous decades.

Microcredit became an increasingly central part of both USAID and the Bank's work – as well, increasingly, of the wider international development community's – into the 1990s. The US and other major donors drove a widespread embrace of microcredit across the UN system alongside associated narratives about women's empowerment, self-reliance, and entrepreneurship in global development. As one critic would note in 2002, 'The idea that microcredit – as the road to self-reliance – is an effective intervention for the "empowerment of women" in particular, and poverty reduction more generally, has come to occupy the status of a hegemonic discourse' (Weber 2002:539–40).

A landmark event here was the Global Microcredit Summit in 1997, held in Washington and attended by roughly 2,500 delegates from various UN agencies (including the World Bank), as well as NGOs, governments, and corporations. The Summit launched a campaign to 'reach 100 million of the world's poorest families, especially the women of those families, with credit for self-employment and financial services by the year 2005' (quoted in Kidder 1997:432). The Microcredit Summit and the '100 million' pledge were subsequently endorsed by the UN General Assembly and received widespread media coverage. The elevation of microcredit to the status of miracle cure for poverty and gender inequality, and the articulation of associated tropes of poverty reduction through 'women's empowerment' and 'self-reliance' (expertly critiqued by Rankin [2001], among others) are decidedly important here. These narratives were often ambiguous about just how 'market'-oriented the delivery of microcredit should be. As Roy (2010) in particular notes, the 'Bangladesh consensus' reflected in the Grameen Bank and others emphasised the interlinked delivery of a variety of services including microcredit, targeting the 'ultra-poor' who might not be viable to serve commercially. This sat awkwardly with some of the more explicitly commercialising views of microfinance articulated in, for instance, the Accion/USAID project discussed above – and increasingly at the World Bank.

This emphasis on commercialisation was particularly reflected in the institutionalisation of CGAP within the World Bank. This reflected, among other things, the consolidation of growing concerns at the Bank about the need to put microfinance institutions on a more explicitly commercial footing in order to enable their expansion. CGAP was launched in 1995, following a donor working group meeting in Paris that proposed setting up a permanent consultative group to govern microfinance programming (CGAP 1998a). Initially, CGAP included bilateral development agencies from Canada, the Netherlands, and the US, as well as the African Development Bank, the Asian Development Bank, IFAD, the UN Capital Development Fund, the UNDP, and the World Bank. In its early years, CGAP's activities were heavily focused on work with microfinance institutions (MFIs). In planning, it was envisioned that CGAP would be 'a major financing facility for MFIs' (Bresnyan 2004:13), with the Bank's own original capital contribution of US$30 million to be matched by US$70 million from other participating donors, either in cash or by allowing existing microfinance portfolios to be managed by CGAP. In the end, these contributions mostly went unrealised and CGAP provided a relatively minor proportion of grant funding to MFIs (Bresnyan 2004:14). CGAP was pushed into a primarily technical assistance and knowledge dissemination role as a result. In this capacity, though, it played a major role in laying the groundwork for the commercialisation of both microcredit and microinsurance, as discussed in the following chapters.

For the moment, it's relevant to lay out some of the reasons behind the push, primarily at the World Bank and CGAP, towards marketising and commercialising microcredit. By the mid-1990s, the Bank, in particular, was already circulating some more skeptical assessments of microcredit. Indeed, some of the earliest studies highlighting the 'consumption-smoothing' function of microcredit – which we'll discuss further in Chapter 5 – were published by the Bank around this time (cf. Weber 2002). The bulk of the Bank's concerns on microcredit, though, had more to do with the continued dominance of NGOs, reliant on donor funds, in the microcredit sector. This had been a concern in places for some time – the Accion credit guaranty project with USAID mentioned above, for instance. The push toward a more explicitly market-oriented approach to microcredit followed a similar logic to that of microinsurance. Put simply, mobilising financial capital, in place of donor funds, was necessary to expand programmes beyond their relatively limited scope. In 1995, the Bank published guidance on acceptable intermediaries for small- and micro-enterprise credit schemes that included a strong emphasis on avoiding arrears, charging positive (and profitable) real interest rates, and a clear plan or tendency towards full commercial independence: 'a solid and growing funding base with clear business plans, backed by operational capacities, that lead to mobilization of commercial funds from depositors and the financial system, and eventually to full independence from donor support' (World Bank 1995b:3). The Bank's assessments of Grameen increasingly reflected this analysis as well: 'The Grameen Bank needs to expand its activities (both membership and lending) over time in order to be more cost-effective, especially when it will have to depend more on the market than on help from donors and the government to finance its lending' (Khandker et al. 1995:83). The emphasis on reforming microcredit programmes themselves – implicit in the reference to 'cost-effectivness' in the above passage – persisted in wider efforts to marketise and commercialise microcredit, as I'll show in the next chapter. However, the emphasis of these efforts to commercialise microfinance (including microcredit and other areas like microinsurance) increasingly took the form of seeking to construct new enabling frameworks, both new financial infrastructures linking poverty finance to global circuits of financial capital, and new regulatory frameworks conducive to commercial operation.

For the moment, the point is that such concerns were very much baked into CGAP from the beginning. One early discussion of CGAP's role, for instance, begins by noting that 'Despite the growing number of [MFIs], back-of-the-envelope calculations indicate that they have penetrated less than 2 percent of the total market for microfinance services' (CGAP 1998b:1). Indeed, some of CGAP's earliest activities were very much framed in this vein of expanding the reach of microfinance by developing more formal markets and mechanisms to allow the investment of formal financial capital in microfinance. One of the network's first activities, in 1995, was a conference on developing frameworks for the regulation and supervision of microfinance. This was framed explicitly in terms of enabling the conditions for market expansion: 'MFIs probably reach fewer than 5% of potential clients. Serving this market will require funding far beyond what donors and governments can provide' (CGAP 1996:1). Critically, 'MFIs and microloan providers cannot be safely funded from commercial sources ... unless appropriate regulation and supervision regimes are developed' (CGAP 1996:1). The actual estimates of the reach of MFIs here are evidently somewhat arbitrary, and depend on an understanding of the universe of 'potential clients' that incorporates virtually all the inhabitants of the Global South. Nonetheless, the general sense that (1) the sector needed new sources of funding to operate on a wider basis, and (2) that mobilising finance capital was the only viable means of doing so, is very clearly evident in CGAP's early work. There's also a clear parallel here with the similar turn to marketisation in microinsurance described above.

CONCLUSION

The preceding discussion has examined two parallel but converging histories. First, 'microinsurance' emerged out of efforts, primarily at the ILO, to articulate new modes of social protection for informal and agricultural workers in the context of structural adjustment. Second, I traced out the more familiar story of microcredit, echoing Weber (2002), Mader (2015), Bateman (2017), and Roy (2010) among others in highlighting the ways that microcredit was simultaneously a response to the failures of structural adjustment and an extension of neoliberal modes of governance. The convergence of microinsurance and microcredit on a particular emphasis on marketisation by the late 1990s and early 2000s is indicative of the underlying dynamics that drove the turn to 'community'-level experiments and pushed them towards efforts to construct more explicitly marketised forms of operation. These experiments in market-making are taken up in more detail in the next chapter.

The high-profile evangelism of people like Yunus, to say nothing of the frequent pronouncements about 'self-reliance' from US policymakers, can perhaps give the impression that microfinance was no more than a neoliberalizing mission. But we miss out on important parts of the story if we don't account for just how much the embrace of microfinance by the global development community reflected an effort to grapple with the twin failures of structural adjustment and directed credit in the preceding decades. This is perhaps especially apparent if we look at the emergence of microinsurance. Out of fairly different institutional settings, with broadly different ideological commitments, we got not only a similar emphasis in the 1990s on voluntaristic 'community' organisations as a self-conscious alternative to ostensibly 'state'- and 'market'-oriented development models, but also a similar tendency towards commercialisation and marketisation moving into the 2000s. As I've sketched above, this convergence makes sense if we take it as a product of efforts to grapple simultaneously with the worst consequences of structural adjustment within the constraints of entrenched austerity, and with the institutional and infrastructural limits of the financial systems developed under colonialism. By the turn of the millennium, the development of global frameworks around both microcredit and microinsurance were strongly influenced by the World Bank, particularly CGAP, and increasingly turned towards developing new means of marketisation. As I'll show in the next chapter, this involved, once again, grappling with embedded colonial legacies in financial infrastructures.

PART II

Making markets for poverty finance

4
Commercialising community: Experiments with marketisation

The turn to 'community'-based schemes began to give way in the late 1990s and early 2000s to efforts to shift such programmes onto a more explicitly market-oriented footing. While there were (as yet) few widely reported examples of community development programmes based on microcredit or cooperatives doing active harm in the same way that structural adjustment had, concerns accumulated about the breadth of their impact and their scalability. If community-oriented programmes had initially been advocated as a way of redressing market failures in an austerity context, it was of increasing concern to their promoters that such programmes couldn't be scaled up in the absence of external resources. In the continued presence of constraints on public resources, it was often assumed that such investments would need to come from global capital markets. As shown at the end of the previous chapter, this particular concern with scaling up through commercialisation was institutionalised by the World Bank and major donors through CGAP. But this was increasingly allied to a recognition that removing constraints on markets was not enough. Markets, in short, had failed to materialise on their own, so the Bank and others increasingly sought to build the infrastructural substrates of markets in the hope that buyers and sellers of credit would turn up.

This chapter analyses two parallel forms of activity through which global development actors, often loosely centered on CGAP, sought to commercialise and marketise microfinance: (1) the promotion of regulatory reforms and (2) the construction of various metrics and information-sharing mechanisms in the hope of channeling capital to MFIs. The chapter takes up these developments in turn. I emphasise two points throughout. First, these activities identified obstacles to market development that were remarkably consistent with those flagged up in colonial debates decades earlier: transactions costs, a lack of collateral, and the difficulty of assessing credit risks, in particular. Second, these same concerns have profoundly shaped later efforts to 'innovate' responses to the failures of microcredit and financial inclusion. These activities are worth reviewing, in short, because they show the continuity of the limits posed by colonial financial infrastructures very clearly, and because they show the beginnings of neoliberal responses to these concerns.

There have been extensive debates about the merits and demerits of the commercialisation of microcredit (e.g. Roodman 2012; Sinclair 2012; Bateman 2010). Some previous analyses have also looked at the specific mechanisms of commercialisation examined here. Soederberg (2013; 2014) places considerable emphasis on the processes of securitisation mediating between global capital and localised MFIs as enabling a kind of 'spatial fix' in Harvey's (2006) terms – the redeployment of overaccumulated capital into new spaces. Aitken (2013) shows in fine-grained detail the particular practices of securitisation, reintermediation, and valuation through which commercial microcredit markets were assembled. This chapter builds on these analyses by placing this episode in its longer context. Debates in the early 2000s about microcredit mark some of the first real appearances of a mode of development practice that I think we can usefully call the 'anticipatory spatial fix'. This can be defined as efforts to promote development and poverty reduction by coaxing capital into collecting in particular places for particular purposes, through the construction of regulatory frameworks and infrastructures suitable for the circulation of financial capital. The interventions traced in previous chapters mainly sought to substitute state or community resources for activities capital was unable or unwilling to undertake alone, whether by mobilising community ties, by reforming individual financial institutions, or by removing supposed regulatory fetters. More recent interventions, beginning with the microcredit projects traced in this chapter, have instead often sought to lay the groundwork for profit-seeking financial capital in hopes it will turn up.

In framing the commercialisation of microcredit in this way, I build on recent analyses of the growing emphasis on multilateral donors and developing country governments 'escorting' financial capital into particular development projects (Gabor 2021; Jafri 2019; Mawdsley 2018; Tan 2021), and previous analyses of poverty finance through the lens of the 'spatial fix' (e.g. Rankin 2013; Soederberg 2013; Frimpong Boahmah and Mursid 2019). Perhaps less directly, the rise of the anticipatory spatial fix also speaks to a broader turn in development governance towards 'provisional' modes of governance, emphasising often-indirect modes of experimental tinkering with underlying institutions and infrastructures over direct and coercive interventions (Best 2014).

Situating experiments with commercialising microcredit in the longer history of poverty finance traced in this book is informative. It helps us to see how efforts to promote the commercialisation of microfinance reflect a mode of practice which is fundamentally anticipatory. It seeks to foster spatial fixes yet to come. And, critically, it seeks to foster spatial fixes which – as the following chapters make clear – might never actually appear. Bigger and Webber note a similar dynamic in describing the rise of 'green structural adjustment' in the World Bank's urban infrastructure programming, seeking to produce cities as sites of investment through policy conditionalities, describing this as a 'preparatory program for creating "surfaces" to which spatially fixing capital *might* adhere' (2021:37, emphasis added). This matters insofar as it underlines the need for caution in attributing efforts to expand financial markets to the interests of the financial sector, as is often done (whether implicitly or explicitly) in analyses drawing on the lens of 'financialisation' to understand the development of poverty finance. The experiments sketched out here and in the following chapters have, by and large, not been driven by finance capital itself. It is reflective of the enduring structural power of finance in the global political economy that states and international organisations have felt increasingly compelled to try to coax financial capital into participating in development projects. But the fact remains that the global diffusion of financial logics and the formation of new financial markets appears much more selective and uneven than is often assumed.

In this chapter I trace out these efforts to commercialise microcredit. The first section looks at efforts to mobilise capital for microcredit through regulatory reform. The second section examines three different kinds of more direct efforts to mobilise financial capital: through the development of microcredit ratings, through the formation of dedicated investment funds, and through a range of techniques for mitigating risks in microfinance investments.

REGULATING MARKETS INTO BEING

At the end of the previous chapter, we saw how CGAP and others had started to frame the normalisation of regulatory frameworks for microfinance as a necessary step towards channeling commercial financial capital (rather than donor money) into poverty finance. This emphasis was ramped up in the early 2000s. Within a few years, though, it had run into growing scepticism as regulatory changes largely failed to engender new markets on their own.

Developing new regulatory frameworks to assist the development of commercial markets for microfinance was an area of activity CGAP, in particular, was engaged in nearly from the start (CGAP 1996). This was framed primarily as a means of expanding the reach of microfinance through the mobilisation of commercial investment. In early discussions, the emphasis was clearly on mobilising local resources in developing countries, either by enabling commercial banks to get involved in offering microcredit or by enabling MFIs to draw on deposits to increase their available funds. Equally, enabling MFIs to register as banks and operate on a profit-seeking basis, and hence to take deposits, would ostensibly allow them to leverage their funds much further. In an influential formulation, Rosenberg (1994) argued that for MFIs chartered as banks, each dollar in donor or depositor funds would yield up to twelve in assets made available to borrowers – if MFIs were subject to the normal reserve ratios applied to commercial banks.

Bolivia's Banco Solidario (BancoSol) was often cited as a model (e.g. CGAP 1996:3; Cuevas 1996). In 1992, BancoSol became the first MFI to 'graduate' to registration as a commercial bank, a move which was widely credited with enabling it to expand rapidly in the first half of the 1990s. BancoSol originated in the operations of the microfinance NGO PRODEM, which was established in 1987 with backing from USAID. BancoSol was in this sense very much an outgrowth of the US-backed expansion of microcredit and microenterprise programmes in the region described in Chapter 3. PRODEM remained a prominent investor in BancoSol after the latter's establishment in 1992, along with a number of international NGOs and philanthropies (including Accion and the Rockefeller Foundation), as well as a number of Bolivian politicians and wealthy individuals. The profit orientation required as a result of BancoSol's registration as a commercial bank was credited with the bank's ability to rapidly expand its portfolio. According to one influential evaluation published by the Ohio State University's Rural Finance Programme: 'BancoSol's shareholders expect profits, and they will probably reinvest them in the quest for additional outreach, as they believe a profitable organization best serves their altruistic goals' (Gonzalez-Vega et al.

1996:4). A 'strong concern for financial viability' was the root cause, in this evaluation, of BancoSol's performance (Gonzalez-Vega et al. 1996:4). This was a diagnosis that CGAP subsequently publicised (CGAP 1997). And early results did seem to validate this point.

BancoSol's portfolio expanded dramatically – both in dollar terms, from a monthly average outstanding portfolio of US$3.25 million in 1991 to US$30.2 million by 1995 (Gonzalez-Vega et al. 1996:32), and geographically, growing from four branches in 1991 to twenty-nine by 1995. While BancoSol inspired a degree of imitation among Bolivian MFIs, the government did not outright permit any further MFIs to charter as banks. Instead, it introduced an intermediate category of 'fondo financiero privado' (private financial funds, or FFP) which were authorised to take deposits and adopt less-complex loan documentation procedures, but not to offer current accounts or engage in foreign exchange transactions (Mosley 2001; CGAP 1996). Like BancoSol, these FFPs were never entirely commercial banks, as most remained owned by local or international NGOs – indeed, PRODEM's non-profit wing would launch an FFP separate from BancoSol, but focused primarily on rural borrowers (Mosely 2001). The boom in FFPs would turn out to have its limits, and was ultimately rather short-lived. By the end of the 1990s, 'organizations onlending … concessional credit' were 'a small, rare, and endangered species' (Mosley 2001:107). Under pressure from the global financial crisis, growth had stalled, there were signs of increasing consolidation in microfinance markets and the rate of loans in distress had risen dramatically (see Mosley 2001; Navajas et al. 2003). In 1999, the overall proportion of microloans in default rose from 4.6 percent to 7.8 percent (Mosley 2001:106).

We would do well to understand this cycle of microcredit boom and bust in Bolivia with reference to the ways in which BancoSol fit into the wider history of colonial uneven development and neoliberalisation in Bolivia. Bolivia reflected many of the contradictory patterns of development traced in Chapter 1. The territory was a leading exporter of silver under Spanish rule, and by the beginning of the seventeenth century, the Bolivian silver complex centered on the city of Potosi accounted for half of all Spanish American silver exports (Brading and Cross 1972). The rise of Potosi drove the development of large landed estates to produce food for mining operations, and the brutal dispossession of indigenous communities through mobilisation as unfree labour for mining and agriculture (see Mahoney 2010:74–6). As the productivity of the Potosi mines declined in the seventeenth century, landed capital gained increasingly entrenched control over the state (Mahoney 2010:76). This was partially disrupted in the late nineteenth century by the rise of tin exports, in which a small number of families, building on the financial and transport infrastructures that had been developed in nineteenth-century efforts by agro-mining elites supported by Anglo-Chilean financial and commercial capital, gained control over a burgeoning tin industry that quickly overtook silver (Dunkerley 1984:6–8). By the first half of the twentieth century, three family firms controlled 80 percent of tin exports (Dunkerley 1984:6). All three were plugged closely into imperial financial systems – with listings and headquarters in the US or in London, and investments in tin production globally – and dominated the domestic financial system in Bolivia (Dunkerley 1984:9–11). Hesketh and Morton note that this left a durable, 'highly parcelised' configuration of national space, split between mining enclaves, an entrenched stratum of large semi-feudal landholdings, and increasingly marginalised indigenous spaces (2013:152).

The political history of Bolivia in the latter half of the twentieth century can be usefully narrated as a series of truncated efforts to mitigate the contradictions inherent in these postcolonial patterns of uneven development – through what has been described, in Gramscian terms, as recurrent episodes of 'passive revolution' (Hesketh and Morton 2013; Hesketh 2020). The 1952 revolution, enabled in no small part by the weakening position of the tin mining families against the backdrop of US efforts to secure supplies during and after World War II (see Dunkerley 1984:12), initiated a partial process of transformation. Its effects were not dissimilar to the processes of formal decolonisation underway at the same time in Asia and Africa. The state took control of the major tin mines (and importantly the banks), established some new political rights and began a truncated process of land reform, which primarily had the effect of solidifying the capitalisation of agriculture (Hesketh and Morton 2013:153–4). The nationalised banks were perpetually undercapitalised; elite-owned money capital was generally held abroad, where higher returns were possible, and banks were left both with limited resources to lend and little incentive to lend to riskier smallholder agriculture or micro-enterprises (Moseley 2001:104). The nationalised banks, in short, did little to expand the infrastructures developed during the nineteenth and early twentieth centuries. They also retained the extraverted, urban-focused character of the pre-revolutionary banking sector.

The country's economy went through a dramatic episode of boom and bust in the 1970s, with rapid growth heavily reliant on state investment financed through petrodollar debts. This was followed by a disastrous series of efforts to negotiate the repayment of debts with the IMF as these became unmanageable following the 'Volcker shocks' (in which the Federal Reserve, under chairman Paul Volcker, unilaterally and sharply raised interest rates in an effort to slow inflation in the US, thus driving up the cost of debt service for many developing countries with loans contracted in New York).

In 1985, Bolivia's new centre-right government adopted a programme of 'shock therapy', including widespread privatisation and drastic cuts to public spending, infamously advised by Jeffrey Sachs (see Sachs 1987). Two related impacts of these reforms are particularly important. First, this programme saw the liberalisation of the financial sector – including, notably, the removal of restrictions on interest rates. At the same time, the stabilisation programmes effectively wiped out the existing nationalised banks (Moseley 2001). In this context, the capacity of MFIs to work partially around the infrastructures of the existing financial system, by mobilising informal social ties, was particularly important. Second, structural adjustment had devastating impacts on agriculture and mining, undercutting agricultural prices at the same time as increasing transportation costs. Farm gate prices dropped substantially, and the price of crops dropped radically relative to the price of fuel for farmers more distant from key markets (Morales 1991). Coupled with the large-scale retrenchment of tin mining following the dismantling of the nationalised mining company, this prompted a considerable movement of people into major cities, particularly into informal settlements around the capital city, La Paz. The upshot of this was the confluence of a newly liberalised financial sector, the development of the institutional bases for microfinance through donor and state activity, and a rapid influx of precarious workers in close proximity to existing MFIs.

In this context, Bolivia's commercialised microfinance sector saw a rapid cycle of boom and bust. The potential market for MFIs had expanded rapidly, and there were few alternative sources of finance. Yet the boom was always limited. Commercial microlending was predominantly concentrated on urban, relatively less poor borrowers – a situation reflective of the broader tension between inclusion and stratification highlighted throughout this book. BancoSol, notably, lent considerably less to the poorest borrowers than other MFIs, even in Bolivia (Mosley

2001:115–16). Indeed, the widespread role of commercial MFIs in the country's banking system seems to have exacerbated the effects of the global financial crisis from 1998 to 2004 (Marconi and Mosley 2006). The commercial microfinance boom in Bolivia, in short, reflected the confluence of a particularly brutal process of neoliberalisation with a longer colonial history of uneven development. While it enabled the rapid expansion of the microfinance sector, the longer-run impacts on poverty and vulnerability were, at best, uncertain. Yet neither the micro-finance bust, nor its uneven impacts, nor the wider context in which it took place received much attention in the official discussions that took BancoSol as a model for the commercialisation of microfinance. The lesson CGAP and others took from BancoSol was largely that its formal-isation, and the attendant commercialisation of its operations, offered a promising model for the development of the microfinance sector else-where – if one that was difficult to apply where MFIs weren't already operating on an explicitly profit-oriented basis.

The problem that the Bank and CGAP *did* see here was, as one Bank official observed in 1996, that despite the strong consensus among economists and practitioners behind the benefits of formalisation-cum-commercialisation in terms of so-called 'outreach' and expansion, very few MFIs globally had actually chartered as banks. Other than BancoSol, Cuevas (1996) could locate only two other cases at some stage of formalisation, in Ecuador and in Mexico. While this slow progress might be attributed to potential trade-offs at institutional level to formalisation, these needed to be understood in relation to the wider 'enabling environment' provided by financial regulation. In particular, 'successful graduation of MFIs requires financial sector deregulation and liberalization' (Cuevas 1996:197). This was echoed in official CGAP publications: 'countries experiencing substantial financial liberalization offered a far more promising opportunity for experiments in microfinance [by commercial banks] than those under a regime of financial repression' (CGAP 1998b:2). Here already, then, we can see an emphasis on fostering an 'enabling' regulatory environment to allow the expansion of MFIs, and more generally the delivery of microcredit, on a self-sustaining basis.

We can detect a subtle shift in emphasis in the late 1990s and early 2000s in debates around the formalisation of microcredit. This was linked in part to wider institutional changes at CGAP itself, which made a strategic shift, following the renewal of its funding in 1998, away from technical assistance and funding for individual MFIs and towards knowledge production and information-sharing among donors (Bresnyan 2004:10–11). But in any case, both the development of regulatory frameworks and encouraging the commercialisation of microfinance were identified as key strategic goals from 1999 (Bresnyan 2004:13). Key early activities here included a scoping study of microfinance regulation in countries covered by the West African Central Bank (BCEAO), and work on what would eventually be a wider set of guidelines on regulating microfinance (see CGAP 1999:22). This echoed the wider strategic shifts taking place at the World Bank at the time. A review of the Bank's microfinance programming in the 1990s found that greater attention in project design and in the selection of partners needed to be given to commercial viability, and that regulatory reforms permitting MFIs to operate on a more explicitly commercial basis were likely necessary, in many instances (World Bank 1999).

This was not quite a straightforward process. By the early 2000s, the relationship between formalisation and commercialisation had started to look more ambiguous. One early concern from CGAP staff revolved around the capital structure of MFIs, which were still largely run by NGOs. Licensing alone, one discussion paper argued, could do little to address the basic fact that without shareholders with capital at risk, incentives to closely scrutinise portfolio quality and management decisions were somewhat attenuated. Indeed, some key supervisory tools, particularly capital calls, were unlikely to be effective where the sole shareholders were NGOs. This was because NGOs were unlikely either to have capital that could be called up or a financial stake in the survival of the institution in the same way that commercial banks would (CGAP 2000:3–4). This 'ownership problem' could ostensibly be solved 'only where the ownership moves into the hands of people who will lose large amounts of money if the institution goes under' (CGAP 2000:3). This argument evidently drew on some questionable ideas, increasingly prevalent at the time, about shareholder oversight and corporate governance – which were reflected in the vogue at the time for 'shareholder value' and the wider rise of managerial capitalism. There's an implication here that licensing alone needed to be complemented by farther-reaching processes of marketisation and commercialisation, including the privatisation of ownership. The 'shortage of licensable MFIs is the binding constraint to the growth of microfinance, rather than the absence of a tailor-made regulatory regime' (CGAP 2000:12). Officials also worried about whether governments could avoid political pressure to restrict interest rates on microloans if they had clearly established supervisory responsibility for MFIs – which was an unexpected effect of the above-mentioned efforts to harmonise regulations for non-bank financial institutions in West Africa (CGAP 2000:7).

These debates culminated in the publication, in 2003, of a set of consensus guidelines on regulation and supervision in microfinance (Christen *et al.* 2003). The guidelines drew a clear distinction between the impact of prudential regulations (aimed at protecting deposits and wider financial stability) and non-prudential regulations. The former were seen as potentially costly and inappropriate for many MFIs, both in the sense of requiring extensive supervisory effort on the part of regulators, and in terms of compliance costs for MFIs. Where the aim was to promote the expansion of microfinance, 'the right type of non-prudential regulation can frequently have the desired promotional effect with relatively low associated costs', while offering licences for MFIs with different prudential rules risked 'a proliferation of under-qualified depository institutions' (Christen *et al.* 2003:8). CGAP advocated a suite of limited non-prudential rules – granting permission to lend, extending consumer protection rules (such as truth in advertising rules and protections against abusive lending practices), fraud prevention, and establishing credit information services (Christen *et al.* 2003:10–13) – coupled with selective deregulation. On the latter, liberalised interest rates were (yet again) a key issue (Christen *et al.* 2003:13).

In short, by the early 2000s, there was a consensus that an 'enabling environment' for the expansion of commercial microcredit would entail both the deregulation of certain elements and the availability of inexpensive routes to formalisation. But equally, that formalisation could be premature without the commercialisation of microfinance institutions themselves. This reflected, in part, the much slower-than-expected pace of chartering observed in the 1990s. Notably, the optimistic arguments about commercialisation permitting greater leverage were mostly absent by the time these guidelines were published. As I trace further in the next section, this ambivalent consensus around regulation was increasingly accompanied by more direct efforts to mobilise global capital for investment in MFIs.

INFORMATION AND MARKET-MAKING

Perhaps not surprisingly given some of the ambivalences around efforts to commercialise microfinance through regulatory reforms, promoters of microfinance increasingly turned to more direct means of expanding commercial microcredit, especially in the latter parts of the 2000s. Some of these mechanisms have been well recounted elsewhere (particularly Aitken 2013; Soederberg 2013; 2014). I leave the question of some of the inherent contradictions – and new sources of risk and vulnerability – inherent in these projects mostly to the next chapter, where I'll trace the abandonment of microcredit as a development tool in favour of a wider emphasis on 'financial inclusion' after about 2010. Before that, however, I want to discuss two key features of the efforts to expand microcredit in the late 2000s.

The first is that efforts to build markets for microfinance often took the shape of mobilising different kinds of information about MFIs in forms legible to financial capital. This is a key point to emphasise. This problem of information and legibility is a vital problem towards which many of the fintech applications discussed in Chapter 7 are fundamentally addressed. Moreover, the push to commercialise microfinance represents the emergence of development interventions tinkering directly with the infrastructures of (micro)financial markets, in hopes of overcoming the reluctance of financial capital to invest in poverty finance. Previous reforms, traced above and in previous chapters, put a much stronger emphasis either on providing funds or on changing institutional frameworks. Starting with the push to commercialise microfinance, the World Bank and others increasingly tried to 'engineer' market infrastructures in more fine-grained ways.

Second, this is a process that was scarcely ever driven directly by finance capital. The latter participated at times, but the impetus behind the development of new market infrastructures for commercial microcredit more often came from donors and development agencies, or from consultancies seeking to sell services. The projects described below represent significant efforts to carve out ways to 'escort' capital into poverty finance, or, as noted in the introduction to this chapter, a kind of 'anticipatory spatial fix'. Indeed, it is worth underlining that these efforts to expand access to capital markets for microfinance were driven, to a considerable degree, by the efforts of microfinance promoters to work around the narrow and extraverted financial sectors that existed in most postcolonial contexts: 'Foreign capital assists MFIs that are ready for capital investment, but are unable to access it locally, because local capital markets are weak' (Reddy 2007:1). This was often not so much about finance capital 'prospecting' (to borrow Leyshon and Thrift's [2007] useful phrase) for the poor, but rather about microfinance promoters trying to create infrastructures through which finance capital might be circulated in hopes of attracting investment.

In what follows, I map out some of the different ways that microfinance promoters sought to construct new infrastructures linking global capital markets with MFIs. I examine how they did this through the construction of credit scoring systems for microcredit, and through the development of new structures of intermediation and risk-shifting for investment in microfinance. These experiments were more or less simultaneous, and broadly took place among a network of microfinance professionals centered on CGAP and a few key donors including USAID.

MAKING MFIS LEGIBLE: MICROCREDIT RATINGS

A number of microcredit rating agencies (MCRAs) emerged in the early 2000s. The first, and still largest, of these were launched between 1997 and 2000: MicroRate in 1997, MicroCredit Ratings International (now M-CRIL) in 1998, Planet Rating in 1999, and MicroFinanza Rating in 2000. All of these have a different (loose) geographical focus, with MicroRate predominantly operating in Latin America, M-CRIL mainly in India, South Asia and Southeast Asia, and MicroFinanza and Planet Rating being comparatively global. Alongside the emergence of the MCRAs, Accion, in particular, had worked to develop standardised metrics for assessing the commercial viability of MFIs in the 1980s and 1990s. Accion, particularly in the context of efforts to operate guarantee funds for MFIs, had begun efforts to adapt the 'CAMEL' methodology that had been developed by US financial supervisors in the late 1970s – taking account of measures of Capital adequacy, Asset quality, Management, Earnings, and Liquidity (see Saltzman and Salinger 1998). The Accion CAMEL method was strictly focused on financial indicators, to the explicit exclusion of indicators of social and economic impacts on borrowers (Saltzman and Salinger 1998:5). Accion's rating method was geared towards promoting private investment in MFIs: 'Any MFI interested in gaining access to capital must be able to provide accurate, consistent, and verifiable financial performance data, both to microfinance managers focused on achieving maximum results and to potential depositors, lenders, and investors interested in the microcredit industry' (Saltzman and Salinger 1998:3). This emphasis on financial indicators over measures of social impact notably reflects its origins in efforts to manage guarantee funds for microcredit.

CGAP once again played an important role, both in developing guidelines and in pushing to orient more clearly towards capital markets as a key audience for microcredit ratings. Along with major global ratings agency Standard & Poor's (S&P), Accion, the Inter-American Development Bank (IADB), and several smaller microfinance consultancies, CGAP participated in a 'Micro-Finance Rating Methodology Working Group' started in 2007. Notably, none of the main microcredit ratings agencies were involved in the Working Group, although Accion's adapted CAMEL method was discussed directly and substantially influenced the Working Group's conclusions. The justification for the group's activity emphasised the need for harmonised ratings to allow investors to compare between different MFIs as a precondition for mobilising sufficient capital: 'Mobilizing large sums of capital requires suitable instruments that allow investors to define parameters of risk and reward' (S&P 2007:7) Yet it remained a significant obstacle that different ratings agencies adopted different approaches. Moreover, they did not always strictly provide a straightforward estimate of the likelihood of repayment in the same way that conventional CRAs did: 'products of the various specialized MFI rating agencies use widely varying criteria developed to meet diverse needs and they do not readily correspond to the rating categories with which mainstream investors are familiar and often wish to integrate into their decision-making process' (S&P 2007:14).

This initial report was followed up by a pilot project on microfinance ratings in Latin America, jointly run by S&P and the IADB. The pilot aimed to bring ratings for a select group of MFIs across the region in line with S&P's global scale for corporate credit ratings. It involved some selective adjustments to S&P's normal criteria for rating financial institutions. In so doing, it incorporated more qualitative judgement about management and governance than the Accion CAMEL model. The project was once again justified in terms of encouraging institutional reforms to bring MFIs more in line with 'normal' financial institutions and fostering the investment of globally mobile capital as a result (S&P 2009:27–8). At the time, the relative lack of success on the latter front could be attributed to 'current market conditions' (S&P 2009:28), given the global financial meltdown taking place in 2008–9. The longer perspective in this book suggests otherwise, however – the relative disinterest of financial capital in participating in poverty finance is probably the historical norm. The IADB did subsequently continue to support efforts to harmonise and increase comparability between microcredit ratings, particularly in a collaborative project with the four main MCRAs run out of the IADB's Multilateral Investment Fund (FOMIN, after the Spanish) in 2011–12 (Abrams 2012). It also followed the S&P pilot with a project that financed conventional credit ratings for a range of smaller MFIs in the region (Buyske 2014).

These projects encountered some consistent limits. One key controversy throughout these debates was around the relative weight that rankings might give to straightforward financial indicators and to the social objectives of microfinance. The issue had been a controversial one among the established microcredit ratings agencies, partly in a reflection of wider controversies within the microfinance community about whether commercial or poverty-alleviating priorities should take precedence (see Roy 2010) and what exactly the 'social goals' of microfinance were. Accion, evidently, had settled on narrowly financial metrics from the 1990s, while most of the MCRAs sought to incorporate some measure of the 'double bottom line' of MFIs. An added complication here was that social objectives in themselves were vastly more difficult to conceptualise and measure in a consistent way. These were problems that the microfinance ratings agencies themselves had struggled with essentially from the start (e.g. Sinha 2006). The Methodology Working Group would conclude that 'a limited review of social mission focused primarily on how management delivers on its stated objectives should be incorporated into the rating methodology, not as a separate factor, but as a subcomponent under the wider management and strategy evaluation' (S&P 2007:18). Notably, this 'limited' review would entail no direct judgement based on the contents of MFIs social objectives, merely a more managerial assessment of whether or not they were monitored and met. The Working Group's preferred methodology thus 'does not include an assessment of the social impact or quality of the MFI's mission, but looks only at evidence that the MFI's board of directors and management have established their own social mission targets, and actively monitor how well it performs in achieving these targets' (S&P 2007:18).

Although making MFIs legible to global capital markets was always a key objective of microcredit ratings, the degree to which microcredit ratings could be made to conform to the standardised metrics used in conventional corporate credit ratings was a matter of some debate. The Accion CAMEL was evidently an effort to render MFIs comparable with conventional financial institutions, but even there, significant adaptations to some of the normal benchmarks for creditworthiness and allowances for limited data needed to be made (see Saltzman and Salinger 1998). Initial IADB efforts to work with S&P likewise aimed to assign conventional credit ratings to MFIs with an eye to ensuring greater comparability between microfinance and other categories of financial assets. These debates always overlapped at least in part with the institutional imperatives of agencies providing ratings – while CGAP and the IADB were seemingly agnostic on the question, different projects sought either to adapt conventional credit ratings to MFIs, or to foster the wider adoption of specialised microcredit ratings. The FOMIN project with the MCRAs, for instance, was explicitly intended to ensure that specialised microcredit ratings would be 'branded' more clearly and 'differentiated from a traditional credit rating' (Abrams 2012:3). Equally, the degree to which MFIs actually sought out ratings varied widely – within Latin America, for instance, Ecuador, Bolivia, and Peru made up the vast majority of microcredit ratings in large part because their governments had brought in regulations requiring MFIs to seek credit ratings (Buyske 2014:7). Elsewhere in the region, it was primarily a few larger institutions seeking to tap global capital markets that were rated, and outside of Latin America microcredit ratings were rather rarer in practice.

Microcredit ratings could also only rate MFIs, rather than borrowers themselves. In this sense, credit ratings continued to rely on MFIs themselves to provide the infrastructures of credit risk assessment 'on the ground'. The Methodology Working Group's report makes this explicit. It notes that the MFIs' own credit decision processes are often somewhat contingent and need to be evaluated on a case-by-case basis: 'Because borrowers in the informal sector do not have formal records, all microfinance lending methodologies use alternative ways to assess borrower repayment capacity, either delegating the task to the peer group (in the case of group lending), or to the loan officer (using guided reviews)' (S&P 2007:55). Critically, this meant that microcredit ratings had to involve some assessment of the effectiveness of these processes, and only therefore an indirect assessment of borrowers themselves. In this sense, the development of microcredit ratings was indicative of the wider tendency in microfinance to rely on the mobilisation of alternative financial infrastructures to assess and manage credit risk 'on the ground'.

MOBILISING INVESTMENT

Alongside efforts to make MFIs legible to metropolitan financial markets, microfinance promoters also sought to develop means of tapping global capital markets directly. There are three key developments worth discussing here: (1) a few MFIs launched initial public offerings (IPOs), (2) a few MFIs sought to securitise loans, and (3) there was a much broader development of 'microfinance investment vehicles' (MIVs), capital funds dedicated to investments in microfinance. I take each of these up in turn here.

Microfinance IPOs

Compartamos, a Mexican MFI heavily backed by a number of donors, and including the World Bank's International Finance Corporation (IFC) as a major shareholder, listed 30 percent of its shares in New York and Mexico in April of 2007. SKS, a major Indian MFI, followed suit in 2010. The Compartamos offer was thirteen times oversubscribed and sent the share price surging more than 20 percent on the first day of trading (Rosenberg 2007:1). Both IPOs drew considerable attention and raised controversy at the time.

Compartamos was very much a product of the microfinance interventions traced over the last two chapters. It was founded in 1990 as an NGO, and supported at various stages by CGAP and a range of development agencies. In 2000, Compartamos was incorporated as a non-bank financial company, owned by the nominally not-for-profit NGO. The move was heavily backed with technical assistance and funding by a USAID grant administered by Accion. At the time of incorporation, Compartamos operated solely in Oaxaca and Chiapas. It had a portfolio composed of 70 percent of loans to women traders, and maintained an explicit policy against lending for agriculture (Chemonics International 2000:68). The company continued to raise money in loans and grants from a number of donor agencies while also starting to list bonds, guaranteed by the IFC on the Mexican stock exchange in 2002 and 2004 (Dugan 2005:1). CGAP published a celebratory brief in 2005, trumpeting the fact that Compartamos was independent of donor money: 'No longer reliant on donor funding, Compartamos is now a highly profitable (with 18 percent adjusted return on assets), pro-poor microfinance bank that is fully integrated into the financial sector' (Dugan 2005:1). Compartamos obtained a full banking licence in Mexico in 2006. It's also worth noting that even prior to the IPO, there was a degree of controversy over the eye-watering interest rates charged on Compartamos loans (over 100 percent per annum in most cases; see Rosenberg 2007:3; Dugan 2005:4).

SKS had a similar history. It was established as an NGO in 1997, receiving grant and loan funding from the Small Industries Development ment Bank of India (SIDBI) and incorporated as a non-bank financial corporation in 2005. SKS received additional equity capital at the time of incorporation from SIDBI and a number of philanthropic investors. In the years after, the firm was able to mobilise a good deal of private equity capital and expanded rapidly: SKS's portfolio under management grew from just over US$20 million in 2006 to $960 million in 2010, and its number of borrowers from 173,000 to 5.8 million in the same period (Sinha 2011:6). SKS raised US$350 million with an IPO in August of 2010, once again massively oversubscribed (Bajaj 2010).

The IPOs kicked off a considerable debate. The very high interest rates charged by Compartamos, in particular, were an area of contention. As noted above, this was a subject of some debate even prior to the IPO, but became even more contentious afterwards. Accion argued that unusually high profits were necessarily a part of the expansion of Compartamos: '[t]he returns received have become retained earnings and allowed the institution to nearly double its reach over the last three years, something it could not have done any other way' (quoted in Rosenberg 2007:11). Nonetheless, even sympathetic critics questioned whether clients' interests were really being served by financing shareholder returns through usurious interest rates. Rosenberg, for one, noted that 'it is hard to avoid serious questions about whether Compartamos' interest rate policy and funding decisions gave appropriate weight to its clients' interests when they conflicted with the financial and other interests of the shareholders' (Rosenberg 2007:12).

Along with controversy about high interest rates, critics suggested that the push for rapid growth, in particular as Indian MFIs led by SKS took on private equity capital and sought to build up portfolios, had led to a weakening of lending controls and a predatory rush to push expensive loans on clients reliant on precarious incomes (Sinha 2011). The rapid

growth of loan portfolios also masked the accumulation of bad loans, as
the director of M-CRIL argued:

> The MFI perspective, in this situation, was that as long as overall loan
> recovery did not fall below 1–2% of overall portfolio they could carry
> on growing. Both the big rating agencies (without a specialized knowl-
> edge of microfinance) and, by extension, the commercial banks (as
> lenders/providers of funds to the MFIs) also bought into this line of
> thinking. They all forgot the first lesson of microfinance performance:
> large recent disbursements mask portfolio quality ratios because the
> denominator of the ratio (total portfolio) grows faster than the numer-
> ator (quantum of bad loans). (Sinha 2011:9–10)

Readers will recall that this issue – rapid expansion of loan books artificially inflating recovery rates – had been raised in discussions of
Grameen at the World Bank in the 1990s. Equally, in India in particular,
the microfinance boom was in fact centered on a few provinces where
MFI operations were already relatively well-established – above all, in
Andhra Pradesh. Sinha noted an important dynamic at work in this
situation:

> The cost of developing new operations in [marginal] areas relative to
> offering multiple loans in developed areas is high and the rewards of
> being the first mover are limited; in such a highly charged atmosphere
> as soon as an MFI opened a new area, others rushed in to capitalize on
> the investment of the first mover. Thus, large numbers of the poorest
> families in India were (and continue to be) excluded even as others,
> better off due to their locational advantage, were increasingly falling
> into a debt-trap due to the culture of easy money. (2010:10)

While attributing the rise of over-indebtedness to a 'culture of easy
money' is questionable given the complex workings of agrarian change
and ecological distress into which microloans were circulated in Andhra
Pradesh (see Taylor 2011; 2013; Young 2010; Maclean 2013), the general
pattern of geographically-concentrated credit booms and busts Sinha
traces is quite typical of the development of microcredit in particular
and commercial forms of poverty finance in general. It is, moreover, one
intimately linked to the already-uneven development of financial infra-

structures. The results, as I'll discuss further in the next chapter, have been catastrophic.

For the moment, though, it's worth emphasising that for all the controversy and human misery they generated, Compartamos and SKS were exceptions to the rule insofar as they were able to mobilise private capital directly. Only a handful of other MFIs listed shares publicly – Equity Bank in Kenya, Bank Rykat in Indonesia, and BRAC in Bangladesh. Equally, it's worth noting that it's not a coincidence that the massive IPOs for Compartamos and SKS took place in countries that had been the site of international poverty finance interventions for decades. For instance, as we saw in Chapter 1, India had been host to a massive cooperatives programme under colonial rule in the early twentieth century. Mexico and India were also key focal points of the World Bank agricultural lending schemes discussed in Chapter 2. Ten successive projects were launched in Mexico between 1965 and 1987, supported by Bank loans totalling more than US$1.8 billion in nominal terms. India, likewise, hosted fifteen regional and national projects backed by just under US$1.6 billion in loans. Collectively, these two countries accounted for about 40 percent of the Bank's total lending for agricultural credit.[12] These programmes, in both cases, track the general shift (traced in Chapter 2) from financial and operational support for directly state-led agricultural finance to the development of a wider rediscount scheme meant to bring on board commercial banks and linked to policy conditionalities around structural adjustment. It's not a coincidence, in short, that the largest microfinance IPOs happened in places where substantial infrastructures for poverty finance had been built up over decades and where channels for investing metropolitan capital were already well-worn.

MIVs

The bulk of private investment in MFIs elsewhere came through MIVs. MIVs are investment funds dedicated to investments in microfinance. They proliferated rapidly in the 2000s, but a handful of important funds largely dominated the market – Blue Orchard, Oikocredit, Omidyar, and ProFund in particular. These large, relatively diversified MIVs are accompanied by several hundred smaller funds which generally specialise in a regional or thematic niche (for example, investing in MFIs specialising in the poorest borrowers). There are significant differences between these firms in terms of how they are set up, but in general MIVs are intended to channel funds from metropolitan investors to MFIs in developing countries. Differences between MIVs notwithstanding, the basic model is fairly straightforward. Investors buy shares in a specific fund offered by an MIV, and the MIV takes those funds and invests in MFIs, either by buying equity or (more likely) by lending funds to MFIs.

MIVs play a key role by essentially mediating between capital markets and MFIs themselves. Rather like microcredit ratings, MIVs represent an effort to mobilise capital for microfinance through the production of specialised knowledge. As Aitken notes, 'In order to fully constitute micro-credit as an investable asset, there need to be formalized and regularized routes opened through which it can be accessed by global capital' (Aitken 2013:483). Investors in MIVs are essentially delegating decisions about where profitable returns can be made by investing in different MFIs. In the period in question, the MIV sector did expand rapidly. Between 2005 and 2012, the estimated global portfolio held by MIVs grew from just over US$1 billion to just over US$8 billion (Micro-Rate 2013:4).

Yet the impact of MIVs was distinctly uneven. At least in principle, MIVs were heavily marketed to 'ethical' investors concerned with their social impact, and the market for 'socially responsible' investments was identified as a key potential source of further investment in MIVs (CGAP 2007). In practice, it's questionable how much additional capital they really managed to mobilize – international financial institutions (IFIs), including the IFC as well as regional development banks, have consistently been the largest investors in MIV funds. MIV investments are, moreover, heavily skewed towards a few large MFIs; in 2007, 10 MFIs accounted for 26 percent of total MIV investments (S&P 2007:15). More generally, they were heavily weighted towards a few countries primarily in Latin America (Peru, Ecuador, Mexico, and Bolivia) and post-Soviet Eastern Europe and Central Asia (Azerbaijan, Georgia, and Serbia), along with Cambodia and India (MicroRate 2013:7). They also lent predominantly to MFIs, rather than equity investments. A survey carried out by MicroRate found that 82 percent of assets held by MIVs in 2007 were debts (MicroRate 2008:13). This ratio held fairly consistently over time – in fact, the same exercise in 2012 returned the exact same figure, with 82 percent of MIV assets being debts (MicroRate 2013:10). In short, while MIVs certainly reached a wider range of MFIs than were able to raise funds through IPOs, they nonetheless remained concentrated on a handful of places that already had comparatively easier access to funds.

Securitising microloans

Finally, there were some experiments – by both MFIs and MIVs – with the securitisation of microloans and the development of more complex structured finance products out of microcredit. 'Securitisation' refers to the pooling of income from a bundle of different payment streams (such as loan payments and utility payments), out of which rights to a portion of the income are sold to investors. 'Structured finance' refers to securitisation coupled with the 'tranching' of rights to payment into different risk levels. In the simplest terms, this means a division between 'senior' securities, who have the right to be paid first so face the least risk, but earn lower rates of return, and 'junior' ones who are paid last but earn higher rates of return. As a number of authors have noted, efforts to expand the securitisation of microfinance represented the application to microfinance of financial techniques that had become pervasive in mainstream financial markets in the 1980s and 1990s (Soederberg 2013; 2014; Gruffydd-Jones 2012).

Securitisation and structured finance were seen as a means of mitigating information problems and managing investor risks in ways that might enable greater commercial investment in MFIs. One contemporary author described the appeal as follows:

> instead of the MFI itself borrowing in the capital market to finance its lending to the microborrower, it can simply transfer the actual assets (the microloans) from the balance sheet to the investor. This is securitization and it could potentially be a viable way for microborrowers to get access to capital. One reason for this is that the creditworthiness of the MFI is of subordinate interest and it is now the (historically impressive) credit health of the pool of microloans that is important for the capital market. *By bringing the actual borrower closer to the global capital market*, there might also be efficiency gains to make. (Byström 2008:2114, emphasis added)

The appeal here to 'bringing the borrower closer' to capital markets is a familiar one from longer-term debates about securitisation in global finance.

There are good reasons to be skeptical about such claims. Appeals to the 'disintermediated' character of financial systems marked by the spread of securitisation and structured finance were particularly common in the 1990s and 2000s. French and Leyshon (2004) rightly argue that talking in terms of 'disintermediation' can serve to black-box the complex practices, processes and infrastructures that enable firms to bypass 'traditional' forms of intermediation and access financial markets directly.[13] The development of widespread securitisation, and especially of complex structured finance, depended on the development of increasingly sophisticated computer models of historic risks (see Lockwood 2015; Campbell-Verduyn *et al.* 2019) and a greatly expanded role for credit rating agencies (CRAs) as arbiters of credit risk 'at a distance' (see Sinclair 1994). Structured finance, in short, did not so much remove intermediaries as pose new chains of intermediation through complex calculative infrastructures linking lenders/investors and borrowers. Equally, while processes of disintermediation were frequently understood as the roots of a process of financialisation which divorced speculative profits ever-further from 'real' economies (e.g. Lapavitsas 2013), in practice, as Leyshon and Thrift (2007:98) note, financial accumulation remained 'dependent on the constant searching out, or the construction of, new asset streams, usually through a process of aggregation, which then – and only then – allows speculation to take place'. This dependence on assembling new asset streams has lent restructured financial markets a kind of expansionary character: 'The financial system ... must continuously prospect for new asset streams that can be turned into collateral, a process which itself provides examples of novel strategies of capitalization, as agents turn to all kinds of activity for sustenance and replenishment' (Leyshon and Thrift 2007:98; cf. Bryan and Rafferty 2006).

Yet the securitisation of microfinance often looked like the obverse of this. It was in practice a series of efforts by a few commercial MFIs, but also by the complex of development actors involved in their promotion, at constructing the calculative infrastructures necessary to build securitisations or structured finance products *in hopes of* attracting finance capital. The securitisation of microfinance, in short, epitomises the anticipatory spatial fix as development practice.

Securitising microfinance was typically framed as a way of ramping up access to lending capital and driving expansion, but it always invoked fundamental difficulties and tensions around the commercialisation of microfinance. The IFC pulled out of a planned securitisation deal with Grameen in 1998 in the context of growing concerns about the latter's reliance on subsidies and questions about whether its accounting system inflated its actual repayment rates (Mader 2015:60). These questions had been kicking around since the early 1990s (e.g. von Pischke 1991), as noted in the previous chapter.

The first actually completed microfinance securitisations took place in India, led by ICICI Bank in 2003 and 2004. Notably, these deals entailed buying loan portfolios from a pair of relatively small non-commercial MFIs, Bhartiya Samruddhi Finance Limited and Share Microfin limited, respectively (Basu 2005:15). In lieu of collateral assets backing the original loans (such as cars or houses), ICICI held cash collateral in the form of a 'first loss guarantee' fund largely financed by the Grameen Bank's US foundation (Meehan 2004:13). These were justified as a means of enabling wider access to funds for MFIs. For instance, one member from the structured finance division of India's ICICI Bank, a participant in the first MFI securitisations in India, wrote a year later:

> From an originator's perspective, the main advantages of securitization include the ability to raise finance at a relatively low cost, partial or total removal of assets from its balance sheet, diversification of funding sources, access to the capital markets for unrated entities and access to liquidity. Thus it serves as an effective balance sheet management tool for originators, through which … risks could be hedged and an enhanced return on capital and equity could be managed through the continuous churning of portfolio. (Basu 2005:4)

Securitisation was held out for MFIs, even non-commercial ones, as a means to 'provide a steady supply of money to … MFIs/NGOs and enable them to build up their portfolios to a sizeable scale' (Basu 2005:12). And the Share deal did allow the MFI to access funds at notably cheaper rates than commercial bank loans. Its cost of funds under the securitisation was 8.75 percent, rather than the 12–13 percent it apparently normally paid on loans (Meehan 2004:13).

Several dramatically bigger securitisation issues followed in the next couple of years. Blue Orchard, later in 2004, launched a US$40 million collateralised debt obligation (CDO) to fund a set of nine MFIs (Meehan 2004:15–16). The CDO was split into four tranches, a senior tranche backed by a US$30 million guarantee provided by the US Overseas Private Investment Corporation (OPIC, which was at the time the US government's development finance arm) and three junior tranches. The CDO financed a group of MFIs, predominantly in Latin America.

A follow-up issue was launched in 2005, referencing a slightly larger group of MFIs, and with slightly less participation from OPIC (Byström 2008:2123). In 2006, Blue Orchard again followed up these earlier issues with a public CDO referencing twenty-two MFIs and raising US$106 million. Critically, the Blue Orchard CDOs were not collateralisations of microloans directly, but rather of loans to MFIs. And, indeed, to a geographically uneven handful of MFIs.

BRAC followed suit in 2006 with the first actual securitisation of microloan payments, raising USD 180 million in a securitisation issue traded in local currency in Bangladesh. At least part of the aim for BRAC in securitising its receivables was to diversify its sources of funds, and hence to evade political pressure to reduce interest rates that had tended to come with financing from official sources in Bangladesh (Rahman and Mohammed 2007:3). Like most of the other microfinance securitisations, BRAC's issue was underwritten by a guarantee from development banks – in this case, German KfW Group and Dutch Financierings-Maatschappij voor Ontwikkelingslanden (FMO). One of the distinct challenges with securitising microloans themselves, as opposed to loans to MFIs, was the distinct lack of formalised credit infrastructures at BRAC. The consultants who helped structure the securitisation made note of challenges posed by the lack of historical data in analysable form; BRAC had only just finished computerising its records in 2005, lacked demographic data, and had fundamental time-lags in reporting loan data to the head office in Dhaka. In the latter case, 'the infrastructure simply does not exist for more frequent transfers of information to head office' (Rahman and Mohammed 2007:8). While adjustments were made to work around these issues in the BRAC case, they are an indication of the importance of complex structures of reintermediation in enabling supposedly 'direct' mobilisation of finance capital for microloans. The need to assemble new and complex calculative infrastructures – drawing in data that MFIs simply weren't collecting and systems they didn't have – in order to enable securitisations is an important hint at why they weren't more widespread. Only a few MFIs globally had the resources to do so, and they were, again, concentrated in a handful of places which had long been focal points for poverty finance interventions.

Previous critical analyses (Aitken 2013; Soederberg 2013; 2014; Mader 2015) have rightly pointed to the costs and risks associated with these moves for borrowers. One of the reasons why MFIs were able to retain low default rates, apart from the statistical illusion sometimes created by rapid portfolio growth, was that historically they had been flexible with borrowers. Where the rights to repayment had already been sold off to distant investors, though, much of that flexibility stood to disappear. Equally, the 'churning' of loans through securitisation issues exacerbated the already-uneven development of microfinance markets. It helped to amplify the existing tendencies towards localised crises of over-indebtedness (those highlighted in the discussion of SKS and IPOs above), rather than to widen access to microfinance in geographical terms. Nonetheless, the need to assemble complex new infrastructures for gauging default risk, often at a much more individualised level than in the past, in practice meant that securitisation and CDOs were relatively rare. The Blue Orchard CDOs and BRAC securitisation were by some distance the largest and most prominent. They weren't widely emulated, and it's doubtful they could have been. SKS followed suit with a securitisation of US$42.6 million worth of microloan receivables brokered by ICICI in 2009 (Mader 2015:168), but as has been made clear in the discussion of their IPO above, SKS was already one of the largest and most commercially oriented MFIs. Even the promoters of microfinance commercialisation often conceded that only a handful of MFIs would viably interest commercial financial markets. Like other experiments with commercialisation, then, maybe the most important effect of microfinance securitisations was in fact to amplify existing tendencies towards uneven development. As French and Leyshon (2004:270) note, this was also characteristic of wider processes of reintermediation, predominantly in the Global North. It piled new sources of credit into already-saturated markets in places like Andhra Pradesh, exacerbating growing crises of over-indebtedness, but skipped over large numbers of potential borrowers and places in between. We can thus see an incipient tendency for the anticipatory spatial fix as a mode of development to exacerbate existing patterns of uneven development. In this respect, it is not unlike the other poverty finance interventions examined in this book.

CONCLUSION

As noted above, I'll delay most of the discussion of the grimly violent consequences of the rollout of commercial microfinance until the next chapter. Here I want to bring out two points. The first is that, while periodic crises of over-indebtedness and their bleak human costs have –

rightly – drawn much of the critical attention directed at microfinance, the fundamentally *uneven* nature of the development of microcredit markets is important too. MFIs, for the most part, have remained small and reliant on subsidies and public financing. Despite the rapid growth of MIVs in the preceding years, in 2010, 70 percent of cross-border funding for MFIs still came from governments and multilateral financial institutions (CGAP 2011:1). In 2018, two World Bank economists published a large-scale review of profitability in microfinance, drawing on a data set from precisely the peak years of commercial microfinance from 2005 to 2009 (Cull *et al.* 2018). MFIs remained reliant on subsidies throughout this period. Indeed, because larger loans came with larger subsidies, commercial institutions serving larger borrowers were disproportionately subsidised more per borrower than were smaller NGO-based non-profit MFIs. Commercial institutions also made proportionately much larger loans, primarily to 'less-poor' borrowers (Cull *et al.* 2018:226). All were only modestly profitable without subsidy.

The 'financialisation' of microcredit, as such, was a decidedly partial achievement, even on its own terms. We will see a similar dynamic at play in Chapter 6 in the discussion of microinsurance – where commercial markets have remained vastly smaller and more reliant on public resources than their promoters' hopes and expectations would suggest, and concentrated on a few, more profitable but less developmentally beneficial areas of practice. The key tension between inclusion and stratification highlighted in the introduction is plainly visible here, in the tendency for commercial MFIs to lend primarily to 'less-poor' borrowers.

These dynamics are worth keeping in mind when we think about the place of 'financialisation' in poverty finance. Commercial microfinance was always first and foremost a political project. The embrace of microfinance in the first instance, as Chapter 3 argued, was an effort to simultaneously respond to the failures of structural adjustment and efforts to reform postcolonial financial systems through directed credit, while working around the infrastructural constraints inherited from extraverted colonial financial systems. The push to commercialise microcredit reflected a need to respond to the relatively slow development of microcredit in the 1990s, within the constraints of the quasi-permanent austerity conditions increasingly baked into the global financial system for peripheral economies, by building new financial infrastructures to ease the circulation of capital. It's not a coincidence that attempts to build new systems of credit rating, intermediation, and risk management were ramped up as the promotion of greater leveraging and investment through formalisation proved increasingly complicated. While the effort to coax capital markets into financing microcredit certainly does suggest a degree of structural power for global finance, it also calls into question the ostensibly 'inescapable' spread of financial logics and subjectivities (to use Hall's [2012] evocative terms) highlighted in many discussions of financialisation.

A second key point, to which I'll return in Chapters 6 and 7, is that the peculiarly neoliberal understanding of markets and market-design, discussed in the introduction, does a lot to explain the nature of the interventions traced in this chapter. We can detect, in the fraught experiments with constructing new metrics and infrastructures for translating dispersed microfinance activities into forms legible to global capital, a shift from the reform of regulatory frameworks and the commercialisation of particular state and community institutions towards efforts to engineer systems to mobilise some approximation of information used by financial institutions to assess risks. The interventions traced in Chapters 6 and 7 seek to mobilise new technologies to deliver ever-more fine-grained information at the level of individual borrowers or insurance clients. They nonetheless continue, in the same vein of the interventions discussed above, in the effort to develop market infrastructures into which spatially-fixing capital *might* be steered.

5
From microcredit
to financial inclusion

In the last two chapters, I've described how the emergence of microcredit as a development fad, and the initial articulation of microinsurance, had their origins in responses to the failures of structural adjustment in the 1990s and 2000s. I've also highlighted efforts in the 2000s to put micro-credit and other forms of poverty finance on a more explicitly commercial footing. Microfinance – insofar as it was seen as a means of 'empower-ing' the poor in developing countries, particularly marginalised women (see Rankin 2001), by giving them access to credit that in theory would allow them to participate in entrepreneurial activities – exemplified a wider movement towards more dispersed forms of development practice aimed at producing markets (see Cammack 2004). Microfinance was also an effort to mobilise localised social solidarities in new ways, in order to work around the deficiencies of conventional financial infrastructures. These infrastructures were still very much rooted in urban physical bank branches and property collateral, which was very unevenly available. But in the context of quasi-permanent conditions of austerity, mobilising commercial capital and leveraging depositors' funds were increasingly seen as necessary adjuncts to the expansion of microcredit. As traced in the previous chapter, efforts to build new infrastructures suitable to the commercialisation of microfinance generally wound up exacerbating patterns of uneven development, themselves deeply rooted in colonial histories. In retrospect, the period from 2000 to 2010 was probably the peak of commercial microfinance, certainly as a centrepiece of the global development agenda. By the late 2000s, the accumulation of doubts about the benefits of microfinance, compounded by a catastrophic crisis of over-indebtedness in Andhra Pradesh and the meltdown of the global financial system, had forced a reconsideration of the place of microfi-nance in global development. Microfinance was increasingly subsumed into a wider agenda of 'financial inclusion'.

This chapter traces the collapse of commercial microcredit and its gradual replacement with 'financial inclusion' initiatives. As with the previous two chapters, this is ground that is by now well-trodden by previous critical analyses (e.g. Taylor 2012; Soederberg 2013; 2014; Mader 2018). The main purpose of this chapter is to reconsider these developments in light of the longer trajectory traced out in this book. Two points are significant. First, we can usefully understand the shift to financial inclusion as part of the wider pattern of failure and adaptation in neoliberal development (Peck 2010; Best 2016; 2020). In common with most of the other examples discussed in this book, the push for 'financial inclusion' represented a shift towards efforts to engineer markets for poverty finance by different means – increasingly emphasising wider 'enabling environments', particularly broader regulatory reforms and the adoption of new technologies rather than targeted microcredit schemes. It has also, perhaps predictably, failed in important respects – even on its own terms. We would usefully understand the various turns to fintech solutions, which I will trace in the final two chapters of this book, as so many efforts to respond to these failures by doubling down on the neoliberal politics implicit in financial inclusion.

At the same time, it's crucial to underline that 'financial inclusion' is addressed to fundamentally the same patterns of uneven development as previous poverty finance interventions. Marketising solutions to poverty are applied against a backdrop of persistent contradictions, which they have continually failed to navigate. Present-day financial inclusion interventions should be understood, then, as part of a long series of fraught efforts to respond, through financial reforms, to deeply embedded social and ecological contradictions rooted in colonial capitalisms. We have seen above that poverty finance has, historically, been an important mechanism by which states and international organisations have sought to navigate capitalist restructuring in the face of intensifying social and ecological contradictions. Financial inclusion represents a new configuration of this very longstanding pattern.

MICROCREDIT: WHAT WENT WRONG?

The broader problems with microfinance are well documented (see Rankin 2001; Maclean 2013; Bateman 2010; Taylor 2012; Mader 2015; Bateman *et al.* 2019). Put simply, microfinance transfers responsibility for poverty alleviation onto impoverished workers, often women. It promises 'empowerment' and access to entrepreneurial livelihoods, but – particularly after the push to commercialisation in the 2000s –

more often resembles a grimly exploitative mechanism for extraction (see Soederberg 2014). Rather than freeing marginalised people from poverty, it has amplified exposure to changing ecological conditions (Taylor 2011; 2013; Natarajan *et al.* 2019) and to new sources of dispossession (Green 2019). More generally, microcredit has multiplied the dangers inherent in precarious livelihoods (Bond 2013; Soederberg 2014). Whatever the intentions of its promoters, commercial microcredit, in particular, did more harm than good. Here, I want to focus less on these failures themselves – which are, at this point, hard to dispute – than on why microcredit has increasingly been *recognised* as a failure by key institutions of neoliberal development governance.

In this respect, it's worth noting two problems that even advocates of microfinance started to recognise in the midst of the push to commercialise microcredit described in the previous chapter. First, as has become apparent at a number of points in the previous chapters, the development of commercial microfinance was profoundly uneven. Commercial MFIs rarely lent money to the poorest. Even microfinance advocates ultimately had to concede that 'most institutions serving the poorest borrowers attract profit rates too small to attract profit-maximizing investors' and pointed to a 'profit-outreach tradeoff' (Cull *et al.* 2009:13). Cull *et al.'s* diagnosis of this problem will be familiar if you've read this far: transaction costs. In their words, 'Even if information asymmetries were not a major problem, the high transactions costs mean that reaching the very poor with small-scale services remains a tough business and often entails charging high fees or depending on steady subsidies' (Cull *et al.* 2009:2). Or, to put it slightly differently, commercial microcredit replicated or exacerbated the patterns of uneven credit development described throughout this book, particularly the tension between inclusion and stratification.

Second, where and when microloans *were* made, an increasing number of studies called into question the sweeping claims about poverty reduction made by microfinance advocates (see Bateman 2010; Taylor 2012). Evidence accumulated that showed very limited impacts on poverty reduction. Some authors sought to redeem microcredit by arguing that what it did was not, in fact, to reduce poverty, but to help the poorest navigate precarious livelihoods. These arguments had been circulating since at least the mid-1990s, as noted in Chapter 3, but they gained considerable traction in the 2000s. Some authors did frame these 'consumption smoothing' effects as virtues. Roodman's is one of the most prominent statements to this effect: '[microcredit's] strength lies *not in lifting people out of poverty* ... It lies, rather, in leveraging modest subsidies to build financial institutions and industries that *give millions of poor families more control over their finances*' (2012:6, emphasis added). These claims for the 'consumption smoothing' benefits of microcredit are, incidentally, directly echoed in the framing of financial inclusion as a tool for financial management rather than poverty reduction, as discussed in the next section. But they did, nonetheless, clearly represent a walking back of the grand claims about bootstrap entrepreneurialism and empowerment promulgated by Yunus and others in the 1990s.

Particularly challenging for many microfinance advocates was a pair of high-profile randomised control trials (RCTs), whose results were initially circulated in 2009, showing that microfinance had little impact of any sort. By the late 2000s, the 'randomistas' had quite successfully established themselves as influential actors in global development politics, and RCTs were widely adopted as the 'gold standard' for the evaluation of development interventions. The reasons for the rise of RCTs in many ways mirrored those underlying the broader push to community-based development and to markets. Fiscal constraints in developing countries, particularly in the aftermath of structural adjustment, along with constant restrictions on aid budgets in the Global North, pushed both a 'projectisation' of development aid and a growing reliance on frequently-cash-strapped NGOs to administer projects. This created fertile ground for a methodological orientation which promised cost-effectiveness (by 'rigorously' identifying 'what works') and conceived of 'development' action as so many dispersed, small-scale, testable interventions (see Bédécarratts *et al.* 2019; Donovan 2018; Kvangraven 2020, Leão and Eyal 2020).

A pair of 2009 studies was particularly important in calling the benefits of microcredit into question. The first, from Dean Karlan and Jonathan Zinman (2011), was eventually published in the high-profile journal *Science*, but was also widely covered when first released as a working paper in 2009. Karlan and Zinman worked with a Manila-based MFI, randomising loans allocations to a sample of credit applicants. Applicants who were unambiguously 'creditworthy' or 'uncreditworthy' according to the MFI's credit scoring system were loaned (or not loaned) money according to their scores, but loan decisions for 'marginally creditworthy' applicants were made randomly. Perhaps not surprisingly to readers recalling the discussion of credit scoring for microlenders in the previous chapter, the latter category in this case made up 74 percent of the total pool of borrowers (Karlan and Zinman 2011:1279). The authors then followed up with borrowers 1–2 years after the fact. Their results showed that there were negligible differences in terms of business development (measured by the share of each group operating businesses and their number of employees). In fact, borrowers were slightly less likely to be operating businesses. The study also measured no differences in terms of subjective wellbeing (other than marginally higher levels of stress among male borrowers). The second, from a team including eventual Economics 'Nobel' Laureates Abhijit Banerjee and Esther Duflo (eventually published as Bannerjee et al. 2015), centered on an MFI in Hyderabad. It employed a somewhat different study design, and traced results over a longer time period. The study worked with a local MFI, Spandana, randomly selecting 52 of 104 neighbourhoods in Hyderabad in which to open up a Spandana branch. It found, in the first instance, that vastly fewer households took out microloans than expected (26.7 percent of surveyed households, as against 80 percent expected by Spandana) (Banerjee et al. 2015:24). The few unambiguously positive impacts of microloans were concentrated almost entirely amongst existing businesses, and indeed increases in profits were concentrated among businesses that were already in the top 5 percent of businesses by earnings.

The preliminary results of both the Karlan and Zinman and Bannerjee et al. studies were picked up and reported in the media (e.g. Bennett 2009; Harford 2009), alongside wider concerns about 'microcredit bubbles' (Gokhale 2009). Roodman's narration of this calling-into-question of the benefits of microfinance is typical: 'Until a couple of years ago, the microfinance industry got on pretty well with stories and opportunistic use of academic studies … But the last two years have dealt the industry a series of blows [including the RCTs above] that have left insiders and outsiders increasingly muddled' (Roodman 2012:4). I will leave for readers to judge what it says about whose voices are listened to in global development that two non-reviewed working papers from prominent economists showing indifferent results were given far wider credence within the development community than a couple of decades' worth of often-qualitative work showing real harms (e.g. Rankin 2001) – much less the concerns of the affected communities themselves. The point here is to highlight the political significance of the RCT evidence showing limited benefits of microloans, in the context of the growing influence of

the randomistas in the settings in which microcredit-promoting interventions were developed and negotiated.

Microfinance (in) crises

These concerns about the limited impacts of microfinance were compounded by two crises. The first was the wider collapse of the global
financial system, starting with the sub-prime mortgage crisis in the US
in 2007–8. The second was a series of devastating crises in microfinance,
most notably in Andhra Pradesh in late 2010. I take up each of these in
turn in this subsection. First, it is hardly coincidence that the turn to
arguments about 'inclusion' in global finance came in the aftermath of the
global financial crisis of 2007–8. Indeed, the project of 'financial inclusion' is usefully understood as part of a wider patchwork of post-crisis
regulatory reforms that have incorporated new technical, ethical, and
political concerns without fundamentally altering the market-oriented
foundations of financial governance. The crisis was seen by many at the
time as a potential turning point towards a more socialised global financial system, but post-crisis reforms generally wound up by reasserting
the neoliberal bases of global finance (see Helleiner 2014). 'Financial
inclusion' and the G20 principles were key elements of this shift (Soederberg 2013).

Given the focus of this book, the second series of events – specific
microfinance crises – merits more direct attention. There were certainly failures of individual microlenders throughout the whole period
covered in the previous chapters, and instances – such as the example of
BancoSol and the FFPs in Bolivia – where MFI operations exacerbated
the effects of wider financial turbulence. In terms of its depth and devastation, though, as well as the extent of its wider reverberations, the 2010
collapse of the microfinance sector in Andhra Pradesh province in India
was unmatched.

Andhra Pradesh, as noted in Chapter 4, was the site of a remarka-
ble boom in commercial microfinance operations in the 2000s, it was in
the epicentre of India's microcredit industry nationally (see Mader 2015,
Chapter 5). But in October of 2010, the sector went bust with remarka-
ble speed and gruesome violence. A spate of suicides by over-indebted
farmers facing aggressive pressures to repay led to new restrictions on
loan collection practices (see Mader 2015:177). The provincial government passed an emergency ordinance requiring MFIs to publicise

interest rates and to register the names of their recovery agents in each district, forbidding the collection of loans or the issuing of new ones until this was completed. The ordinance also banned the collection of collateral and the issuance of multiple loans to the same self-help group. While these measures effectively shut down the microfinance sector only very briefly, borrowers stopped paying *en masse*. The microfinance sector in India shrank dramatically in the years after the crisis – the total loan portfolio shrank from US$5.4 billion in 2010 to $4.3 in 2011 (Mader 2015:181).

The crisis in Andhra Pradesh did not come out of nowhere, and despite efforts to attribute it to unregulated and unscrupulous practices by lenders and loan collectors, it reflected longer-term patterns of uneven development as well as shorter-term conjunctural developments in the province and in Indian microfinance. On the first point, as Taylor rightly notes, 'The ability of MFIs to scale up their operations in Andhra Pradesh rests in part upon the institutional infrastructure and culture of formal credit put in place through the social and development banking schemes of the 1970s and 1980s, alongside the expansion of the self-help group (SHG) model under the auspices of the state in the 1990s and 2000s' (2011:486). In general, despite the shift towards more explicitly market-oriented strategies implicit in the turn away from subsidised and state-backed forms of credit in the 1980s and 1990s, efforts to expand access to credit in rural India were longstanding, dating at least to the start of the twentieth century. Andhra Pradesh had long been an important focal point for these efforts. As noted in the previous chapter, this was exacerbated by the commercialisation of microfinance in the 2000s, as MFIs increasingly piled new speculative capital into expanding operations in areas where they had existing material and social infrastructures already in place.

Microlenders also found a ready market for microloans because they landed in the context of accelerating dispossession and agrarian distress, in which relations of indebtedness were already extensive. Farmer suicides in Andhra Pradesh had in fact been on the rise since the late 1980s, amidst a deepening crisis of agricultural production and social reproduction. There were several contributing factors (see Taylor 2011; 2013; Rao and Suri 2006). The liberalisation of agricultural prices did not, in fact, lead to an increase of farm gate prices (as neoliberal theorists, along with the World Bank and IMF, had expected; see Chapter 2). In the context of stalled land reform processes and continued population growth, there was a dramatic fragmentation of landholdings and a rapid increase in landless farmers. By 2000, holdings under two hectares represented nearly half of all agricultural land under cultivation in the area. In the context of falling and volatile prices, this created increased pressures for agricultural intensification and, as a result, for seasonal purchases of chemical pesticides and fertilisers. For farmers with limited resources, input purchases meant taking on debt. By the mid-2000s, Andhra Pradesh had the highest per-unit consumption of pesticides and the second-highest consumption of fertilisers in India, and the highest reliance on purchased seeds (Rao and Suri 2006:1547). The prices of these inputs spiraled in the 1990s and 2000s, a problem exacerbated because intensive pesticide and fertiliser use tended to degrade soil fertility, and hence require progressively heavy applications to maintain similar levels of productivity. In Taylor's words, these dynamics 'tied many into lopsided debt relations, in which the power of credit is used to lock producers into relationships with landed and merchant capital that manifestly favours the latter' (2011:495). It also prompted a push towards risky and expensive borewell drilling, largely by farmers seeking to enable dry-season cropping in a context where debts often consumed close to the entirety of income from wet-season harvests. The proliferation of wells and intensification led to increasing pressure on already-fragmented aquifers, ultimately driving the depletion of groundwater and exacerbating productivity pressures (Taylor 2013:703).

The microfinance boom in Andhra Pradesh, in short, took place in a context in which relations of indebtedness and insecurity were already accelerating, and in which the infrastructures necessary for microlending were already in place. The crisis sparked significant shifts in the sector in India. It sparked an inquiry by the Reserve Bank of India that led to a round of regulatory reforms – most notably, interest rate caps and individual limits on total indebtedness for lower-income borrowers (RBI 2011). In the aftermath of the crisis and regulatory reforms, Indian MFIs dramatically reoriented their focus towards the urban 'less poor' and towards closer integration with the financial system more broadly. These shifts also kicked off a round of consolidation in the microfinance sector, with the number of registered MFIs falling from more than 70 prior to the crisis to 56 by the end of 2016 (EY 2016:14). At places like CGAP, meanwhile, the Andhra Pradesh crisis largely reinforced the shifts already underway away from a narrow focus on microcredit and towards a wider suite of financial services under the guise of 'financial inclusion'. One brief published in the midst of the crisis would note that the ultimate conclusion from the crisis was that 'credit-only' models of microfinance provision had significant limits as development tools: 'As local markets mature, the delivery model for financial services for the poor must evolve to support healthy outreach and the growth of a broad range of products that poor people need' (CGAP 2010:6).

It's important to keep in view the longer-term context of microfinance failures. In the first place, the 'profit-outreach' tradeoff, and maybe especially the underlying diagnosis of transaction costs as the obstacle to extending services to the poorest, echoes a number of the dynamics discussed across previous chapters. The microfinance boom in Andhra Pradesh may indeed have been something of an exception in this respect, insofar as small landholders and landless farmers were expressly targeted by microlenders. Even in Indian microfinance, though, there has been a growing turn towards lending to urban, 'less-poor' borrowers in the aftermath of the collapse. It speaks, once again, to a longstanding tension between 'inclusion' and stratification embedded into the infrastructures of colonial and postcolonial financial systems. We could say the same about periodic crises of over-indebtedness. Microfinance initiatives have persisted in spite of these problems. This is no surprise in and of itself – where they are allowed to be grimly exploitative and have access to a pool of 'less poor' borrowers who are nonetheless being squeezed by rising living costs and in need of credit, MFIs can make a lot of money. There have been more localised cycles of boom and crisis, including most notably in Cambodia, in recent years (see Green 2019; Brickell *et al.* 2020). Microfinance has even been transported into new territories in the Global North (Gerard and Johnston 2019). Nonetheless, microfinance has increasingly, since 2010, been subsumed into a wider agenda of 'financial inclusion'.

ENTER 'FINANCIAL INCLUSION'

An important step in the solidification of 'financial inclusion' was the announcement of the 'G20 Principles for Innovative Financial Inclusion' in 2010 (AFI 2010) and the subsequent Maya Declaration on Financial Inclusion in 2011. For some authors, 'financial inclusion' is not much more than a relabelling of microcredit. Milford Bateman, for one, noted in 2012:

Diehard microfinance advocates saw the writing on the wall a few years back. They realised they had better quickly locate some other goal the microfinance movement could proclaim to be genuinely passionate about and diligently working towards, otherwise there would be real trouble – enter 'universal financial inclusion'. (Bateman 2012)

Insofar as it's many of the same agencies and experts involved in promoting microcredit who have segued into talking about 'financial inclusion', and insofar as the failures of the former have played a major role in paving the way for the latter, Bateman has a point. Indeed, much of the turn towards financial inclusion picked up elements of the rethinking of microcredit that had already been taking place, particularly the emphasis on consumption smoothing and poverty management rather than poverty reduction. That said, there are some ways in which 'financial inclusion' as a policy agenda does represent a substantial departure from the 'microcredit' agenda (see Mader 2018).

In the first instance, 'financial inclusion' shifts objectives away from poverty reduction *per se* and towards the extension of formal saving and lending to the poor in and of itself, whether or not it tangibly reduces poverty rates (see Taylor 2012). To an extent, this move was already underway among microfinance advocates well before the crises outlined above, particularly in the turn to arguments about consumption smoothing. Roodman's comments, quoted above, on the role of microfinance in 'giving poor families control over their finances' rather than reducing poverty are a good example. One CGAP publication in 2006, for instance, detected a tendency towards a broader understanding of 'inclusive financial systems': 'Today, there is a growing recognition that not all poor people are necessarily entrepreneurs, but all poor people do need and use a variety of financial services' (Helms 2006:17). But the push towards 'financial inclusion' as a policy agenda – in the sense of a shift towards an emphasis on the regulatory and infrastructural 'enabling environment' for a wider range of financial services embracing payments, savings, investment, and insurance alongside microcredit – did not take place in earnest until the early 2010s. The crises of commercial microfinance in particular and of global finance in general from 2008 to 2010 helped spur a much wider reconsideration.

'Financial sector deepening' is increasingly held to be necessary for the effective allocation of resources to enable 'inclusive growth' and for the management of risks on an individual level. This implies a rather more ambiguous and indirect relationship to poverty reduction. Indeed, financial inclusion advocates increasingly argue that poverty reduction and the facilitation of microenterprise are unrealistic goals (see El-Zogbhi 2019). The growing emphasis on 'financial inclusion' in this sense thus represents a kind of embrace of the 'consumption smoothing' effects of microfinance, or even just an argument that financial services make the lives of the poorest marginally more convenient. One CGAP staffer draws an analogy:

> many rigorous impact evaluations of water and sanitation interventions find little to no impact on diarrheal disease. Does that mean that there are no benefits of clean water or sanitation? Of course not. It does mean that the programs aren't fully dealing with the myriad sources of water contamination. That's a problem that needs solving, but it's not a reason to say that clean water and sanitation doesn't make a difference to poor households. (Ogden 2019)

It should go without saying that there are some problems with this analogy. A bank account is not unambiguously like indoor plumbing – which may not change anyone's income, or even eliminate all sources of water-borne illness, but will undoubtedly make their day-to-day life more convenient. It's even less clear that a microloan with usurious interest rates is likely to improve a borrower's life in a similar way.[14] Equally, 'will this make things better for direct beneficiaries in the short run?' can too easily be a way of evading uncomfortable questions about whether more radical solutions to poverty might be needed (cf. Mader 2018). But whether we accept the analogy isn't really the main issue here. The more general point is that we should read these rethinkings as attempts to rescue an intellectual case for poverty finance – if in a form with radically scaled-back ambitions. The aim of financial inclusion is no longer to reduce poverty levels or increase incomes, but to give people (financial) tools to cope with low and unpredictable incomes.

There is a wider shift implied here in terms of how the role of financial markets is understood. It is much less a question of allocating resources to entrepreneurs, and much more a means of developing markets for the provision of risk management. 'Financial inclusion' thus implies access to a wider range of financial tools beyond microcredit, especially including savings, payment systems, and insurance (AFI 2010:1). This is reflected directly in the founding documents of the financial inclusion agenda. The G20 Principles start by noting that 'Awareness is growing that access to a wider set of financial tools, such as savings products, payment services … and insurance (including microinsurance directed at the needs of the poor), provides poor people with much greater capacity to increase or stabilize their income, build assets, and become more resilient to economic shocks' (AFI 2010:1). It epitomises a wider shift towards 'risk management' as an objective of poverty reduction and development governance (see Best 2013; Sharma and Soederberg 2020). This has entailed significant efforts to build markets for other kinds of financial products, notably payment systems and insurance. As we'll see over the next two chapters, attempts to build the former have succeeded on their own terms, in some places. The latter have been almost entirely unsuccessful, despite considerable optimism at the start of the 2010s. There was, for a short while in the early 2010s, a real vogue for microinsurance – a development I'll return to in the next chapter. For the moment, though, I want to turn to a brief discussion of the specific mechanics by which global development agencies and consultants have sought to promote the spread of financial inclusion.

MECHANICS OF FINANCIAL INCLUSION

As noted in previous chapters, microfinance relied on building alternative financial infrastructures which used community solidarities to manage credit risk. MFIs were new institutions that were supposed to operate outside the spatial and institutional bounds of 'traditional' financial systems. Efforts at developing channels for investment in commercial microfinance sought to carve out new informational infrastructures, which might enable the movement of capital from metropolitan financial markets to impoverished farmers and informal workers in the periphery. Critically, these systems all still relied on MFIs distributing loans, group lending structures, and the mobilisation of social solidarity to minimise default risks. Advocates of commercialisation certainly sought to make MFIs more efficient, but in practice they mainly worked to mobilise capital for them. The turn to financial inclusion implied an emphasis on building infrastructures to enable the provision of financial services to the poorest. This was a continuation, by different means, of the effort at development as anticipatory spatial fix outlined in the previous chapter.

The G20 Principles and the Maya Declaration laid much of the groundwork for subsequent discussions about technology in relation to financial inclusion. The G20 Principles placed a heavy emphasis, yet again, on transaction costs as a limit on access to finance. On its first page, the AFI report outlining the G20 principles notes that 'As a general rule, transaction costs do not vary in direct proportion to a transaction's size. Thus serving the poor with small value services is simply not viable using conventional retail banking or insurance approaches' (AFI 2010:1). New technologies, especially mobile transactions, and 'innovation' more broadly, have been increasingly identified as key means of reducing these costs. A recent report from McKinsey and Company, for instance, argues that: 'Every step towards the full digitalization of financial services helps reduce costs, making it profitable for providers to serve a much larger range of customers' (McKinsey & Co. 2016:31).

New forms of mobile payment systems are perhaps the paradigmatic example here (see Maurer 2012). Most prominently, M-Pesa – a mobile payment system operated by South African telecoms provider Vodacom, first established in Kenya – has grown dramatically, expanding into conventional banking services, following its establishment in 2007. It was just starting to come to prominence by 2010. I will return to a closer examination of M-Pesa in Chapter 7. For the moment, it's worth underlining that M-Pesa is often explicitly cited as an example of good practice in promoting financial inclusion by lowering transaction costs, both in the AFI report itself and elsewhere (e.g. Suri and Jack 2016). The key claim here is that mobile technologies can enable the rapid and inexpensive extension of financial systems to populations that would normally be excluded from participation in mainstream financial markets due to physical barriers resulting in overly high transaction costs, particularly because cellular networks are comparatively easy to set up in remote areas. Indeed, a recent G20 report on financial inclusion notes explicitly: 'Digital technologies have reached developing countries much faster than previous technological innovations; this is illustrated by the fact that households in developing countries are more likely to own a mobile phone than to have access to electricity or improved sanitation' (GPFI 2017:9). There is a particular politics in these claims. As Maurer very aptly notes, these kinds of arguments about the benefits of mobile money also include, 'de facto, an argument for the privatisation of infrastructure development, as well as "regulatory flexibility", and often, a retreat of the regulatory state' (2012:593).

It's here that a second key point about the understanding of technology in the G20 Principles and the Maya Declaration becomes clear. The key mechanism through which 'innovation' is meant to take place is by allowing the 'regulatory space' for private sector experiments with new technologies and new modes of service delivery that might lower costs. This is explicit on the first page of the G20 Principles report (AFI 2010:1). It is also echoed in the Maya Declaration's commitment to create an 'enabling environment to harness new technology that increases access and lowers costs' (AFI 2011:2). There is an underlying commitment here to a kind of targeted deregulation – selective, bounded changes to regulatory requirements might encourage private investments in particular activities. Again, this particular logic echoes efforts to develop 'enabling environments' for microfinance in the 1990s and early 2000s, as discussed in the previous chapter. This logic has played a significant role in shaping the ways in which regulators have involved themselves in promoting microinsurance (see Chapter 6), and fintech applications (discussed further in Chapter 7).

The effort to construct such 'enabling environments' has nonetheless been a very different process than was the case with the licensing debates about microfinance in the early 2000s. For one thing, central banks and ministries of finance have been much more active players in developing 'financial inclusion' policies nationally and globally, with significant efforts to develop policy frameworks that are systematic in scope and national or regional in scale alongside targeted regulations for particular kinds of institutions. This is reflected in the rapid expansion of 'national financial inclusion strategies', and in the relatively important role of central banks and ministries of finance in articulating them. By 2017, there were 47 countries with a formal strategy in place, and another 22 at various stages of negotiation and preparation, the majority of which were led by central banks with almost all of the rest by ministries of finance (AFI 2018a:5). The drive towards formal financial inclusion strategies has been led in no small part by the World Bank. The Bank has participated in the formulation of national strategies in a number of countries, and has issued guidelines on their development. These guidelines are especially telling about the underlying understanding of the role of governance in shaping financial inclusion:

> *Financial inclusion is not a naturally occurring phenomenon.* Accelerating progress toward financial inclusion requires taking a holistic view to identify constraining factors – such as high transaction costs and informational asymmetries – as well as potential opportunities, such

as the market entry of new technology-driven providers or the digitization of government-to-person payments. (World Bank 2018a:4, emphasis added)

The role for governance here is in identifying obstacles to, and fostering the development of, markets for poverty finance. It's also worth noting the reiteration here of the emphasis on transaction costs as an obstacle and digital technology as a solution.

The development of formal or informal national financial inclusion strategies has played out in different ways in different countries. There are a number of critical studies of these processes in different countries, including Senegal (Bernards 2016), Kenya and Nigeria (Dafe 2020), Pakistan (Settle 2020), and Turkey (Güngen 2017). Most of these, albeit from different perspectives, emphasise how global agendas around financial inclusion have intersected with, and to an extent been warped by, particular challenges of neoliberal statecraft in postcolonial contexts. In some cases, countries that have been slow to adopt national framework strategies have nonetheless fostered particular elements of 'financial inclusion' in different ways. For present purposes, the details of these programmes probably matter less than what the fact of their existence and extent says (1) about the prominence of 'financial inclusion' as a development theme, and (2) about the mechanisms through which 'financial inclusion' as a policy agenda operates. To an extent, there's a parallel here with the shift in the 1980s away from targeted credit programmes for agriculture and housing and towards efforts to promote wider reforms of financial systems as a whole.

UNEVEN FINANCIAL INCLUSION

It's worth pointing out, finally, that the financial inclusion agenda has met with mixed results. The World Bank's series of 'Findex' surveys of global financial inclusion are the most comprehensive global measures of 'financial inclusion'. They do show a headline reduction in the estimated number of 'unbanked' people worldwide (measured specifically by whether or not they have a bank account) from 2.5 billion in 2011 to 2 billion in 2014, and 1.7 billion in 2017 (see Demirguc-Kunt and Klapper 2012; Demirguc-Kunt et al. 2015; 2018). However, such figures overstate the degree of progress. Significantly, the reduction in the number of 'unbanked' is largely offset by a notable growth of dormant bank accounts.

In the 2011 survey, the Bank estimated there were 150 million dormant accounts globally, roughly 10 percent of the global total (Demirguc-Kunt and Klapper 2012:21); by 2014, these numbered 460 million, and 15 percent of the global total (Demirguc-Kunt *et al.* 2015:18), and by 2018 they comprised 20 percent of accounts (Demirguc-Kunt *et al.* 2018:64).

Uneven progress is even more evident when we talk about credit. Borrowing from formal financial institutions continues to be heavily outweighed by borrowing from family and friends or informal lenders in most developing regions. As Table 5.1 shows, the growth of 'access' to formal credit has been slow, uneven, and even prone to reversals in particular cases. Indeed, in the aggregate, the estimated proportion of people borrowing from formal financial institutions in the two lowest income quintiles in lower and middle-income countries *fell* between 2011 and 2014, and had yet to return to 2011 levels in the latest survey in 2017. As we'll see further in the next chapter, this is even more the case when we talk about areas like microinsurance, which in theory epitomises the shift towards financial inclusion and 'risk management' as development logics, but has rarely amounted to much in practice.

There are a number of different ways we could interpret the uneven development of financial inclusion, but the conventional diagnosis, whose unfolding consequences I'll explore further in Chapters 6 and 7, is that it is down to the persistence of high transaction costs and weaknesses in existing credit information infrastructures. In the words of one group of consultants, in contexts where formal credit histories, employment records, and tax documentation are often absent, lenders 'are unable to properly understand their consumers and assess their risk, either forcing them to charge high interest rates to protect against unforeseen risk or discouraging them from serving new markets' (Insight2Impact 2016:4). The World Bank's *Doing Business* reports now regularly echo this diagnosis in pointing to a positive correlation between credit bureau coverage and private credit as a share of GDP (World Bank 2016:59). Advocates of financial inclusion, in short, are well aware that the infrastructures underlying everyday credit are highly uneven. Developing alternative means of credit scoring, drawing on Big Data or psychometric profiles (discussed further in Chapter 7), is presented as a relatively straightforward technical fix in response to the uneven progress of financial inclusion – rendering precarious or informal incomes into calculable credit risks. For instance, one report commissioned by the Inter-American Development Bank (IADB) notes that 'alternative analytics ... help develop more

Table 5.1 Indicators of financial inclusion in selected countries

Country	Percent of Poorest Two Income Quintiles with a Bank Account			Percent of Poorest Two Income Quintiles Borrowing from a Formal Financial Institution		
	2011	2014	2017	2011	2014	2017
Brazil	39.4	58.5	56.6	4.9	7.5	7.4
China	46.0	72.0	68.4	8.0	5.9	6.8
Colombia	13.3	23.4	35.0	8.3	6.4	9.0
El Salvador	6.1	21.6	19.3	3.6	13.5	6.6
India	27.3	43.8	77.1	7.4	4.9	5.6
Kenya	20.7	36.3	70.5	4.2	10.6	11.7
Malaysia	50.4	75.6	80.5	2.9	15.2	9.3
Mexico	11.9	28.6	25.8	5.3	6.5	4.0
Nigeria	12.8	33.8	24.5	1.8	6.5	2.8
Peru	5.2	18.4	27.0	8.6	7.4	7.3
Philippines	10.7	14.9	18.0	4.8	8.2	5.2
South Africa	38.8	56.5	62.6	4.7	4.2	7.1
Tanzania	7.5	11.3	37.3	2.7	4.0	3.1
Uganda	10.9	13.5	47.3	6.0	11.3	8.6
Zimbabwe	24.1	16.3	43.6	2.9	2.2	0.9
Low- and Middle-Income Countries Total	**29.1**	**44.8**	**54.2**	**7.7**	**6.8**	**7.5**

Source: World Bank Findex Data.

robust client risk profiles at a fraction of what it would cost to compile such information manually' (Hoder *et al.* 2016:18).

Both transaction costs and a lack of available information about potential borrowers are longstanding concerns for promoters of various forms of poverty finance, as we've seen throughout this book. Of course, attributing the uneven expansion of credit to these factors is a problematic, depoliticising diagnosis. As we've seen in previous chapters, these patterns of uneven development of financial infrastructures in the Global South have their origins in very specific colonial and postcolonial histories, which neoliberal interventions are systematically unable to confront. But there is an important kernel of truth to this diagnosis nonetheless; namely, the limits of financial inclusion are, in no small part, explained by the limits of existing credit infrastructures. This matters because it suggests that rather than representing the inexorable spread of the 'invitation to live by finance' (Martin 2002), financial inclusion, in its growing reliance on fintech innovations, might better be read as an effort to overcome some of the longstanding critical limits to financial accumulation.

There is more going on here than infrastructures alone. It is surely also part of the story that workers' incomes have become increasingly precarious over the last few decades (see Chapter 3), which has rendered certain kinds of financial accumulation more difficult. As noted in the introduction, poverty finance, like other forms of 'interest bearing capital', ultimately depends on workers' incomes for its realisation – on 'everything that goes on in between' the giving of credit and the repayment of interest, in Marx's terms. The possibilities for financial accumulation out of precarious livelihoods are, simply put, more restricted where those incomes themselves are more restricted. We'll see in further detail in Chapters 6 and 7 how this has undercut certain schemes for 'financial inclusion' through new technologies or innovative financial practices.

CONCLUSION

In this chapter, I've outlined the growing disillusionment with microcredit on the part of the global development mainstream. At best, microcredit has been seen to have limited impacts on poverty and livelihoods, including by ostensibly 'best practice' RCTs. At worst, microcredit booms have exacerbated grim crises of social and ecological reproduction, with lethal consequences, most notably in Andhra Pradesh. The response has been to move the goal posts (from 'poverty reduction' to 'convenience') and to double down on certain aspects of market-building interventions. CGAP, the World Bank, and others transitioned sharply after about 2010 towards the promotion of 'financial inclusion'. This entailed a move on the one hand towards the promotion of a wider range of financial services, including insurance and payment services alongside credit, and on the other towards more fine-grained efforts to construct new financial infrastructures. This was a shift in tactics and techniques, but not necessarily in modes of practice, from the earlier turn to the anticipatory spatial fix in the late 1990s and 2000s debates about microcredit. As shown in the final section above, this new approach wasn't any more successful than the previous ones, even on its own terms.

As with previous chapters, we should understand the rise of financial inclusion as an effort to adapt neoliberal development logics in the face of failure, and to respond to deeply embedded constraints inherited from colonial modes of financial practice, against the backdrop of persistent constraints on the mobilisation of public resources. Financial inclusion does indeed represent a widening of the 'invitation to live by finance' (Martin 2002) implicit in microcredit (Mader 2018). But it's worth bearing in mind that finance capital itself has had little direct involvement in this process. Instead, as with commercial microcredit in particular, the rise of 'financial inclusion' represents yet another series of efforts to coax finance capital into serving developmental ends. As the next two chapters will show, these efforts remain fraught. Efforts to promote the development of new financial markets have exacerbated existing patterns of uneven development, and often foundered on the fundamental problem of – to again use Marx's terms – what 'happens in between'.

PART III

Innovation to the rescue?

6
The forever-latent demand
for microinsurance

In the last chapter, I noted that one of the major shifts from commercial microcredit to the broader agenda of 'financial inclusion' was the explicit embrace of a wider range of financial services, particularly payments, savings, and especially insurance, alongside credit. In this chapter I explore the latter. In doing so, I pick up a thread left off in Chapter 3, where I examined how the promotion of small, simplified insurance contracts, targeting the poorest, was adopted in the 1990s, in parallel to microcredit, as a response to widespread precarity. Much like the transformations in microcredit discussed over the last two chapters, scaling up microinsurance without radically overhauling the structural inequalities inherent in the global financial system requires mobilising private finance capital. Much like microcredit, there have been a series of efforts to develop commercial bases for microinsurance markets. These were somewhat slower to get started; the earliest attempts to commercialise microinsurance through regulatory change came in the first years of the 2000s, and experiments to build new infrastructures began with the rising profile of microinsurance in the early 2010s. Both of these sets of efforts largely failed.

If microinsurance hasn't had the same deleterious impacts on precarious livelihoods in the Global South as, say, predatory microlending, it is nonetheless worth looking at. This is precisely because of the mismatch between the ambitions of its promoters, its ostensible centrality to the broader agendas of 'financial inclusion' and 'risk management', and its real outcomes. As I'll detail in the first section below, microinsurance markets never expanded at anything like the rate anticipated by promoters. Commercial microinsurance has also largely remined confined to a narrow range of products, primarily life insurance, which even advocates will typically admit carry less development potential than other areas like health or agricultural insurance. This chapter explores some of the reasons for these failures,[15] but focuses primarily on the reactions to them. It turns out, this is a story that in many ways looks quite a bit like the commercialisation of microfinance traced out in Chapter 4, with regulatory experiments increasingly complemented by various efforts to mobilise new market data and technologies in response to slow and uneven progress.

This chapter is organised into three main parts. In the first section below, I discuss the astronomic expectations for microinsurance development around the time of the emergence of the financial inclusion agenda, circa 2010, and the underwhelming practical results. In the second section, I show how efforts to develop new microinsurance markets initially turned on regulatory efforts at formalising existing informal mutuals and cooperatives. In the latter parts of this chapter, I map the ways that the networks of international organisations, consultants, philanthropies and donor agencies involved in promoting microinsurance have sought to respond to limited participation – both by finance capital and by target populations – in microinsurance markets. These interventions have generally sought to make 'second-best' forms of data and actuarial modelling techniques available to insurers in the absence of the highly elaborated data infrastructures built up around 'conventional' insurance in the Global North (see Ericson *et al.* 2000; McFall 2019). I examine two key areas of intervention here: (1) the mobilisation of alternative forms of data in assessing risks, particularly in index insurance, and (2) the dissemination of standardised actuarial techniques through a variety of physical documents and software packages. What's crucial here is that these interventions, as much as they seek to enable the profitable development of new financial markets, are being carried out by public or voluntary sector actors in the hopes of attracting the interest of financial capital.

I argue that these interventions make sense when we read them, and the microinsurance project in the first place, as reflective of the limits of neoliberalism and the relationship of neoliberal development projects to finance capital. Markets can't deliver adequate means of risk management to many, even most, of the poorest. Yet, the continued efforts to promote microinsurance are indicative of an inability to think beyond markets as a means of providing risk management. Tinkering with informational infrastructures in hopes of conjuring a 'marker' reflects, on the one hand, a neoliberal faith in the capacity of the 'market' to govern social relations (see Mirowski 2009; Peck 2010). But it also reflects structural constraints on state capacity – particularly fiscal constraints, which are felt particularly acutely in peripheral economies (see Alami 2018). The turn to market-based modes of managing risk is in important ways a response to the failure of redistributive models of risk management, both state and community-based, in the context of embedded and semi-permanent conditions of austerity across much of the Global South and the vastly uneven distribution of resources on a global scale.

FINANCIAL INCLUSION, RISK MANAGEMENT, AND MICROINSURANCE

Risk, vulnerability, and resilience are increasingly central to global debates about environmental change, poverty, and development. The turn from microcredit to financial inclusion was both reflective of this shift and a major element of it. A major part of the new emphasis on managing risks for development was a growing attention to the creation of new financial markets, and especially new forms of insurance. This is true at the macro-scale through the development of instruments like catastrophe bonds, but also increasingly in poverty finance interventions, especially those targeting dispersed individuals and communities through microinsurance (see Aitken 2015; Isakson 2015; Keucheyan 2018; Bernards 2018a; 2019c). The 2014 *World Development Report*, for instance, explicitly situates these individualised forms of insurance as a key component of risk management strategies (World Bank 2013:194–5). In this sense, appeals to insurance reflect a growing turn to 'risk management' discourses as crucial organising rubrics for global development practice more generally (Sharma and Soederberg 2020; Best 2013). Taylor argues (with little exaggeration) that 'Developing new forms of micro-insurance accessible by poor households has become a holy grail for the risk management agenda' (2016:239). Important promoters have included the ILO, with whom the concept was initially linked, but increasingly also the World Bank, CGAP and the International Association of Insurance Supervisors (IAIS); as well as bilateral donors, notably the UK and Germany; and major philanthropic organisations, especially the Gates Foundation and foundations linked to global reinsurers (see Aitken 2015; Bernards 2016, 2018a; da Costa 2013; Johnson 2013).

Expectations for the expansion of microinsurance markets were very high in the late 2000s and early 2010s. A 2010 report from Allianz on its existing and planned microinsurance operations noted, somewhat hyperbolically, that the market for microinsurance made up 'half the world':

> Four billion people live on incomes of less than eight dollars per day. 2.6 billion have to get by on less than two dollars per day. Besides suffering daily deprivations, the world's poor are often more exposed to risks ranging from disease to crop failures to the consequences of climate change … Microinsurance could help many of these people escape poverty. (Allianz 2010:1)

Ten years on, markets for microinsurance have not materialised as expected. Market expansion in Africa in terms of lives covered between 2011 and 2015, for instance, was in fact around 30 percent (MIC 2016) – not trivial, but far short of the doubling regional microinsurers had predicted (Matul *et al.* 2010), and achieved in no small part by registering existing informal mutuals and funeral insurance schemes (especially in South Africa; see below) rather than by making 'new' markets. The growth of microinsurance was also highly uneven: gross written premiums expanded overall but declined substantially in a number of countries including Nigeria, Senegal, and Ghana (MIC 2016). The proportion of people covered by microinsurance policies globally remains fairly small: an estimated 4.3 percent of the population in Asia (Mukherjee *et al.* 2014), 5.4 percent in Africa (MIC 2016), and 7.9 percent in Latin America and the Caribbean (MIC 2015). Equally concerning for advocates, microinsurance has remained primarily confined to life insurance, especially credit life (which pays an outstanding loan balance if the borrower dies), rather than in areas like health, property and agricultural insurance, all of which might be expected to have a much greater impact in terms of poverty reduction (Wipf *et al.* 2011). Allianz policies covered 55 million 'emerging customers' by 2016 – considerably more than a few years earlier, but still well shy of 'half the world'. Of these, moreover, 52.8 million (or 96 percent) held some form of life insurance policy (Allianz 2017), the overwhelming majority of whom (46 million) were covered by one group life insurance scheme in India (Allianz 2017:12).

Microinsurance thus clearly reflects broader trends in development governance emphasising poverty reduction through 'risk management' or 'resilience', often produced through participation in financial markets. It is also in demonstrable ways a failure, even on its own terms. It is not just that the creation of markets hasn't led to reductions in poverty, then;

it's that markets for microinsurance have simply failed to materialise on the scale or in the forms which promoters expected. Microinsurance is no less important for us to consider because of these limited 'real world' impacts. In fact, there's an argument to be made that the gap between expectations and real impacts is particularly revealing of the limits to neoliberal projects of marketisation in practice.

FORMALISING AND COMMERCIALISING RISK SHARING

As noted in Chapter 3, microinsurance, even more than microcredit, was initially articulated as an explicit alternative to both state and market alternatives for social protection. Yet, in common with related experiments with microcredit, there was a growing recognition by the late 1990s that it would be impossible to mobilise these kinds of systems at scale without the mobilisation of external resources. 'Microinsurance', in the guise articulated by Dror and Jacquier's article (1999), ran into essentially the same problem that state-backed initiatives for social protection had a decade earlier. Contributory systems didn't work for the poorest, but given embedded conditions of austerity across much of the Global South, the state wasn't a viable source of external resources. The emphasis was increasingly placed on commercialisation and marketisation as a means of expansion, as was the case with microcredit.

The IAIS has been a particularly important player in this regard. The IAIS was founded in 1995 with a secretariat hosted at the Bank for International Settlements in Basel. It is primarily an informal network of insurance supervisors, of which over 100 national and subnational regulatory bodies are members. The main regulatory mechanisms used by the IAIS are the 'Insurance Core Principles' (ICPs), coupled with the production of guidance on the application of the ICPs to specific issues. The shift to the IAIS has dovetailed with and reinforced a growing emphasis on developing commercial markets for microinsurance. Despite the overall dominance of commercialising imperatives, however, it proved difficult to separate microinsurance entirely from the debates about social protection for non-standard workers out of which it originated.

The first significant initiative towards developing global regulatory standards for microinsurance was the development and publication of an issues paper on microinsurance by the IAIS and the CGAP Working Group (IAIS 2007). The paper flags up the 'immense potential' of the microinsurance market 'if insurers can develop efficient and effective innovations' (2007:17). The paper explicitly refers to Pralahad's (2005) *Fortune at the Bottom of the Pyramid* and its arguments about the poor as a 'latent market', competition for which would drive poverty-reducing innovations. While there's a recognition throughout the paper that governments might, especially in the short term, be needed to help develop microinsurance schemes and even pay premiums, there's a clear emphasis on ensuring 'that the demarcation line between social security programmes and market-led approaches is clear, and subsidies do not inhibit market initiatives' (2007:15). The issues paper still pitches the development of microinsurance very much as a way of meeting the gaps left by conventional state and mainstream financial market coverage of risks: 'Of particular interest is the provision of coverage to persons working in the informal economy that do not have access to formal insurance nor social protection benefits paid by employers directly, or by the government through employers' (IAIS 2007:11). Insurance mechanisms are seen as a means of sidestepping the weaknesses of public provision. Drawing on ILO work in West Africa, the paper notes that for 'informal' workers, public redistributive systems rarely work, and that 'the only way for the poor to be covered is to set up microinsurance mutuals that are very inexpensive' (IAIS 2007:20). Nonetheless, the role of regulators is generally framed in terms of ensuring that microinsurers are run on a self-sustaining basis: 'Without an insurer's licence, the microinsurer is trapped in a vicious cycle: no licence and no reinsurance means greater risk of failure and the risk of being shut down by the regulator or police services' (IAIS 2007:27). The IAIS issues paper was followed up by the establishment of the Access to Insurance Initiative (A2ii) in 2009 as a joint venture of the IAIS, ILO, CGAP, the Deutsche Gesellschaft für Internationale Zusammenarbeit (GIZ), and FinMark Trust (FMT) (a public-private trust based in South Africa and funded by the UK Department for International Development). A2ii works largely in conjunction with the IAIS, but has a separate secretariat hosted by GIZ.

Developments in South Africa were particularly important in these early stages. Informal finance, and particularly informal funeral societies (*stokvels*), have long been widespread in the country. They developed primarily in the interstices of deliberately exclusionary systems of 'credit apartheid' (to use James and Rajak's [2014] phrase) discussed in Chapter 1. They have often been presented as static, 'traditional' practices, unregulated and prone to abuse in policy discussions around microinsurance and microcredit regulations. In reality, informal financial practices in South Africa have shifted in considerable ways in response to changing labour markets provoked by the end of apartheid and neo-liberalising reforms. Members are increasingly likely to be women, and the operations of *stokvels* and informal moneylending alike are increasingly interpolated with flows of grant income rather than wages, since the latter have become increasingly precarious (see Bähre 2007; 2011). Nonetheless, efforts to regulate these informal financial practices were formative developments in the articulation of global regulatory guidelines for microinsurance.

Microinsurance regulation in South Africa was initially developed primarily by the country's National Treasury Department, alongside efforts to develop global guidance at the IAIS, and in conjunction with FMT. The latter was the main direct institutional link between discussions at A2ii and CGAP and South African developments. An early example of FMT work on informal finance in South Africa (Bester *et al.* 2004) outlines a preliminary assessment of the scope for commercial microinsurance. Significantly, the report gives considerable attention to the intersections of microinsurance markets with public provision and 'informal' financial services. For FMT there was little doubt that commercial microinsurance should be not only a substitute for informal risk sharing, but indeed should replace certain kinds of state provision. The report notes, for instance, that 'Government provision of risk mitigation services tend to crowd out private provision. This is evident in that government is increasingly covering risks that were covered by the private sector in the past' (Bester *et al.* 2004:26). Meanwhile, the report also notes the widespread incidence of informal burial societies and funeral insurance, estimating that roughly 8 million people belonged to such organisations (2004:27). A follow-up report identifies the formalisation of *stokvels* as a key objective that could be advanced by the development of a distinct regulatory framework for microinsurance (Bester *et al.* 2005).

The National Treasury subsequently published an issues paper on regulating microinsurance in 2008, drawing heavily on these debates. Microinsurance regulation was explicitly 'intended to catalyse the market provision of risk management tools for poor households' (National Treasury 2008:vi). The paper's main proposal (closely mirroring IAIS proposals) was the creation of a separate licence for microinsurers, along with 'a special prudential regime commensurate to the risks applicable to microinsurance policies (National Treasury 2008:vi). Eligibility for microinsurance licences would be based on a number of criteria lowering prudential risk: the report proposed limiting cover to 'low-risk' events, as well as capping policy terms at 12 months and benefits at 50,000 rand (National Treasury 2008:36–7). For products meeting these criteria, the report suggests that existing regulations 'might prevent entry of possibly capable insurers' (National Treasury 2008:46) – suggesting that the capital adequacy ratios specified in existing insurance regulations were likely unnecessarily high for microinsurers, and also highlighting the requirement that insurers be publicly listed companies. Along with facilitating the entry of new microinsurers, the main benefit of this new 'regulatory space' was seen to be the possibility of formalising existing 'illegal' insurance schemes: 'not only will this provide the option for some … larger operations to be legalised, the streamlined regulation suggested also enables the formal sector to better compete with the illegal sector' (2008:62). Following a series of industry consultations on the 2008 discussion paper, the Treasury issued a policy document detailing a planned microinsurance policy framework in 2011 (National Treasury 2011). This document largely carried forward the main points of emphasis from the 2008 discussion paper. It again proposed a dedicated licensing regime for microinsurance, with modified prudential standards, which burial societies and funeral insurance schemes would need to adhere to if they were to offer guaranteed benefits to members. The basic objective of commercialising risk management through the extension of regulation to 'informal' operators is again explicit.

One of A2ii's first major initiatives, in conjunction with the IAIS, was to publish a follow-up issues paper on the regulation of mutuals and cooperatives in the provision of insurance, shortly after the publication of the first Treasury document in South Africa and echoing many of the themes raised in those debates (IAIS 2010). In general, the issues paper emphasises the desirability of bringing mutuals and cooperatives under the same regulatory frameworks as commercial insurers. It also clearly frames mutuals and cooperatives as 'stepping stones' towards the development of commercial insurance markets:

> Historically, when risks are too large for individuals to manage in their own right, they have looked to pool these risks. This pooling may start through relatively intuitive, informal risk pooling and later develops into more formalised products … and eventually, insurance products provided by formal insurers. (IAIS 2010:13)

Here the IAIS echoes a common refrain in discussions of 'financial inclusion' about the costly reliance of the poor on 'informal' financial practices for managing risks (World Bank 2013); but equally frames the development of effective markets as, essentially, a step-wise development out of informal forms of risk pooling, to be fostered by regulatory provisions encouraging the 'formalisation' of informal operations.

The general narrative in regulatory debates, then, was one in which formalisation and licensing would lead to the development of commercial microinsurance. We've seen already in the previous section what happened on a general basis – namely, very little. Of more interest in what follows are the responses to these failures.

DIAGNOSING MICROINSURANCE FAILURES

Efforts to troubleshoot the slow and uneven growth of microinsurance have increasingly focused on experimental means of more directly building the infrastructures needed for the assessment of risks. This has often entailed the development or application of new technologies or alternative sources of data, or the development of calculative practices that might work with more limited data.

In one sense, the failures of microinsurance could very much be read as financial markets doing exactly what they're supposed to – that is, allocating money and resources in the most profitable ways. The basic problem is the mismatch between the dynamics of really-existing financial accumulation and the kinds of risk management that microinsurance advocates hope financial markets will provide. One review puts it quite simply: 'Only if microinsurance products are profitable will it be attractive for insurance companies to offer them in significant volumes' (Clarke and Grenham 2013:s90). The conditional terms in which this statement is couched are telling. Beyond 'bottom of the pyramid' platitudes and sweeping statements about 'half the world' as a potential market, there have always been serious doubts about the profitability of microinsurance.

There is a good case to be made that, in common with many of the other themes discussed in this book, the reason why the poor are held to need greater access to insurance is precisely the same reason why they are unprofitable insurance clients. They have low and unpredictable incomes coupled with heightened vulnerability to accidents, illness, or bad weather. We might argue that a basic, unavoidable problem is that the constitution of profitable new markets for microinsurance is difficult or impossible where underlying streams of income are limited and irregular (see Bernards 2018a; 2020a). Indeed, this contradiction may be even more pronounced in the case of insurance, which depends on an upfront payment from the insured as opposed to repayments in the future from the debtor in the case of a loan. A recent report on the potential contributions of insurance markets to economic development in sub-Saharan Africa concludes that incomes and employment levels remain too low across the region to support the development of extensive insurance markets (Chamberlain *et al.* 2017). Promoters of microinsurance have clearly been aware that this is a problem for some time. Some micro-insurers sought, not entirely successfully, to navigate this problem by adopting variable payment schedules to cope with the 'irregular and unpredictable cash flows' of potential clients even in the early 2000s (see Wipf *et al.* 2006:156). It's this crucial contradiction – between the logics of profit-maximization through which markets are meant to operate and the social purposes which neoliberal modes of development practice seek to serve through the construction of markets – that the interventions described below seek to cut through by tinkering with underlying technical infrastructures.

One important area of intervention has been efforts to promote demand for microinsurance. The failure to translate supposedly 'implicit' demand into actual purchases of microinsurance has led to a proliferation of studies on the determinants of microinsurance demand (e.g. Kouame and Komenan 2012; Eling *et al.* 2014; Stein 2016; Platteau *et al.* 2017) and a growing emphasis on the promotion and marketing of microinsurance to potential clients, especially through efforts at promoting insurance 'literacy' (Cole 2015; Fonseca 2016). Efforts to engineer demand through behavioural interventions of course speak to a wider tendency in neoliberal development interventions towards 'nudging' (see Berndt 2015). Demand interventions, though, don't get to the heart of the problem of profitability in the way that other interventions targeting insurance infrastructures and risk management frameworks have, so the following pages focus primarily on the latter.

Here it's worth pointing out that a longstanding diagnosis of the underlying problems of profitability in microinsurance has been a lack of available data. As with wider claims about limited information hindering financial inclusion, there's a kernel of truth here. Metropolitan insurers depend on a highly elaborated infrastructure, produced historically

through long-running processes of development of statistical and actuarial techniques from the nineteenth century onwards. As Ewald notes,
'insurance has two bases: first, the statistical table or graph that testi-
fies to the regular occurrence of certain events; second, the calculation
of probabilities that are then applied to these statistics so that one can
evaluate the possibility of these same events' (1990:142). These dynamics
have been amplified in more recent times. Ericson *et al.* (2000:534), now
twenty years ago, noted a trend towards the 'unpooling' of risks in private
insurance, as insurers are able to further segment categories of risk with
the emergence of 'increasingly detailed risk information (e.g. financial,
medical) which is available to actuaries and underwriters, both concerning individual insureds and concerning trends in populations'. This
tendency is increasingly reflected in the widespread, if contradictory,
adoption of personalised risk pricing through, for instance, self-tracking
(see McFall 2019). In short, mainstream insurance techniques have
entailed the development of an increasingly dense and complex infrastructure of statistical methods, a growing array of instruments, and
surveillance techniques, coupled with actuarial expertise, aimed at quan-
tifying risks in increasingly fine-grained detail.

The contrast here is identified explicitly in the 2007 IAIS guidelines: 'Even when there are relevant longevity, mortality and morbidity
data, which is infrequent, these tables do not typically reflect the risk
of low-income households that are more exposed to a wider variety of
risks' (IAIS 2007:13). For agricultural insurance in particular, concerns
about the lack of appropriate data and the expense involved in collecting
it by conventional means are frequently flagged as major concerns (e.g.
Brown *et al.* 2011:213). As with discussions of data problems in financial
inclusion examined at the end of the last chapter, this is a depoliticising,
ahistorical diagnosis, which nonetheless hits on part of the problem. But
the uneven development of insurance infrastructures is neither acciden-
tal nor natural.

Insurance infrastructures were not developed in colonised parts of
the world, for reasons that have much to do with the place of insurance
in the colonial histories traced elsewhere in this book. Indeed, colonial
insurance ventures represented perhaps an even more extreme version
of the banking systems discussed in Chapter 1. The development of
insurance was intimately linked with the expansion of empire. The rise
of Lloyd's of London and other maritime insurers was intimately linked
with both the rise of British merchant capital to global prominence in

the nineteenth century (Cain and Hopkins 2016:78–89) and with the Atlantic slave trade (see Baucom 2005). Yet insurance for colonised subjects was rarely directly considered. Even as themes of risk and risk management, with important parallels to contemporary concerns, dominated discussions about agricultural production and volatile ecological hazards (see Bernards 2019c), policy solutions (discussed in Chapter 1) tended towards the promotion of 'thrift' and '*prévoyance*' through cooperative-like structures. In a discussion with a London-based insurer about offering a limited life insurance scheme in colonial Ghana, even at the eve of independence and as banks were expanding their branch networks across the colonised world, one British official felt compelled to reassure the firm that government clerks were 'excellent risks', and that 'You will not be asked to insure men in the bush who wear loin-cloths and lion skins having several wives and dozens of children and relatives who would kill them off if they knew they would get some money'.[16] Public or nationalised insurance schemes had been introduced as adjuncts to efforts to promote agricultural modernisation or as elements of social security in many territories in the aftermath of decolonisation, but these were generally early casualties of structural adjustment – whether directly, through retrenchment and privatization, or indirectly, through the effects of currency devaluations. In Uganda, where the currency had been devalued by 99 percent in 1987, a CGAP report relays a possibly apocryphal, but nonetheless realistic, story: 'One insurer relates the story of a man who had a well-endowed whole life policy pre-1987. When he came during the 1990s to collect the proceeds, he spent more for the taxi ride to get to the insurance company than he collected as his benefits' (McCord *et al.* 2005:4). The point is that the material and institutional infrastructures necessary to provide insurance were never developed to the same extent in colonised spaces because of the particular relationship of insurance to colonial capitalism. Postcolonial reforms did seek to compensate, to an extent, but the alternative structures that were built up in the 1960s and 1970s were decimated by structural adjustment. Data problems for insurers in the Global South, in short, are embedded in the historical patterns of uneven development mapped throughout this book.

At the same time, the historical reasons for their absence in postcolonial contexts notwithstanding, the centrality of data and fine-grained calculations of risk to insurers' profits does make the uneven development of data infrastructures into an important obstacle for the expansion of insurance. As Christophers (2016: 337–8) rightly notes, insurance profits depend on the conversion of concrete hazards into abstract financial risks through the exchange of streams of premium income from insurees for protection against those hazards. In a useful twist on Marx's value theory, he notes that insurers' realisation of surplus value in this context depends precisely on the fact that the 'price' (in the form of promised payouts) that insurers are required to pay for peoples' capacity to generate risk bears no necessary relation to the value those risks themselves produce for insurers (that is, the flows of premium income they generate and the return on investing them). This introduces a notable reliance of insurers both on elaborate estimations of risk and on squeezing potential payouts (Christophers 2016:338). Where this point is relevant for the present discussion is that insurers' profits are rooted in two preconditions. One is the presence of reliable streams of income from which streams of premia can be drawn – or, in other words, the production of 'abstract' risks out of concrete ones is still dependent on the livelihoods of working classes (broadly understood). The second precondition is an infrastructure enabling fine-grained calculations of premia and payouts, dependent on reams of data. Uncalculable risks can't be subjected to this process of abstraction and exploitation. Responses to the failures of microinsurance market construction have sought, in essence, to draw in finance capital by creating the second of these preconditions for the realisation of profits through the production of new, alternative calculative infrastructures. The basic logic of the anticipatory spatial fix is plainly visible. These are efforts at creating infrastructures through which over-accumulated finance capital might be circulated.

INDEX INSURANCE AND SATELLITE DATA

Here and in the next subsection, I'm going to explore some specific examples of efforts to create the bases for profitable microinsurance operations through interventions making new forms of data available. In this section, I look at the troublesome rise of index insurance as a form of agricultural insurance. Index insurance, strictly speaking, is a form of derivative rather than insurance policy (see Clarke 2011; Johnson 2013). Index insurance contracts do not indemnify clients against specific losses, but rather specify a set payment triggered by an underlying event, which is used as a proxy for likely damages. In theory, index insurance premiums and claims are calculable based on historical weather, crop, or other such data. Proposals for index insurance in agriculture in the Global South date to the early 2000s, where they were very often framed as a potential complement, or even an alternative, to collateral for agricultural microcredit (e.g. Skees and Barrett 2006). They were given increasing institutional support towards the end of the 2000s, with the World Bank and USAID, in particular, providing prominent support for the development of market infrastructures.

Index insurance has significant limitations, from the perspective of the smallholding farmers it is ostensibly targeted towards. The derivative character of index insurance instruments leaves borrowers subject to so-called 'basis risk' – the possibility that the cover provided fails to fully compensate for losses (Clarke 2011; Johnson 2013). There are more fundamental questions that some authors have raised about the value of index insurance based in narrowly technical conceptions of, say, weather risk that ignore the broader patterns of social and ecological relations through which the very uneven exposure of agrarian populations to such risks are produced (see Isakson 2015; Taylor 2016; da Costa 2013; Johnson 2013; Bernards 2019c). These limitations do a lot to explain weaker than expected 'demand' among target populations for index insurance (da Costa 2013; Taylor 2016). They intersect in this respect with the patterns of deepening precarity traced in various places in this book. One critic of index-based agricultural insurance, for instance, usefully notes that

> The better-off farmers will have little demand for insurance because they are already sufficiently well insured via their informal mechanisms ... On the other hand, the poor farmers could benefit from agricultural insurance, but are too poor and credit constrained to translate the potential benefit into effective demand. (Binswanger-Mkhize 2012:193)

Existing index insurance schemes have, as a result, often remained heavily reliant on subsidies. By some distance, the largest existing index insurance scheme, the Weather Based Crop Insurance Scheme in India, is a publicly subsidised, compulsory programme (see Clarke et al. 2012). Beyond subsidisation, though, it's difficult to envision a solution to the problems posed by precarious incomes without abandoning index insurance altogether.

Promoters of index insurance have sought to resolve the failure to develop working markets by focusing on the 'supply' side of index insurance. They have often attempted to do so by means I've described elsewhere in terms of the 'anticipatory spatial fix' – by preparing infrastructures into which capital might be circulated.

One way of doing this has been to tinker with the means of setting indices. One possible approach to index insurance is to select a relevant variable correlated with crop losses – rainfall is most common, where either drought or flooding would be a threat to farm output. This has often raised the fact that the kind of reliable and fine-grained local weather data that would allow the calculation of appropriate indices and thresholds simply isn't always available. Index insurance 'cannot reliably scale up if it only works in areas covered by existing rain gauges, which lack extensive historical weather data records at least two decades long' (Mann *et al.* 2014:1). Evaluations of several schemes have identified 'spatial basis risk' as a particular problem – where a plot of land is too far from the physical weather station in which a given weather index is measured, and regional differences mean that crops are lost but the index is not triggered (see GIZ 2019). In practice, this has meant that index insurance schemes often have been accompanied by efforts at constructing a rather mundane infrastructure of rain gauges. As Angeli Aguiton (2021) shows particularly clearly in an analysis of index insurance programmes in Senegal, this is often a fraught, expensive, and labour-intensive process. Rain gauges need maintenance and checking. They can be automated to report data to a central server through a mobile connection, but doing so is only possible where mobile network coverage is available, and subject to service interruptions (including from inclement weather!).

Another significant challenge here is that – even setting aside the historical and structural embeddedness of environmental hazards – the risks faced by smallholder farmers are typically not limited to weather alone but also include, for instance, pests and disease. An alternative approach, then, has been to develop 'area-yield insurance' products. Here the index is based on the historical average of crop yields, with payouts when yields fall below historical averages by a set threshold. Area yield insurance holds some advantages for farmers relative to weather indices – by definition, it covers a wider range of risks. But it is also expensive to administer. Typically, indices and area yields have been calculated by site visits. One CGAP project in Nigeria, for instance, notes that 'the field sampling required by insurers to determine average yields in each community or unit of area insured is costly and imposes a heavy logistical burden – it entails sampling campaigns at different times in different regions for different crops – to scale coverage nationwide' (Hernandez *et al.* 2018:2).

In both cases, experiments with satellite data have been held out as possible solutions (Black *et al.* 2018). Remote sensing of rainfall and soil moisture is increasingly seen as a means of addressing the lack or unreliability of weather-station data, and vegetation indices are seen as possible substitutes for site visits in area-yield insurance (see Mann *et al.* 2014). As one review notes: 'In many developing countries there are limited ... data for index design e.g., limited crop yield data or rain gauge networks. One method of overcoming this is to use remotely sensed data from satellites' (Greatrex *et al.* 2015:25). Experiments in this area, notably, have been substantially underpinned by the World Bank, CGAP, and International Fund for Agricultural Development (IFAD). IFAD, in particular, carried out an extensive study on remote sensing and index insurance in Senegal, which played a significant role in articulating the global shift towards remote sensing (IFAD 2017).

Yet spatial resolution issues – the 'relationship between the farm and the pixel' (Mann *et al.* 2014:3) – have posed ongoing problems. Basis risk, as the IFAD report notes, 'can be influenced by the spatial resolution of the satellite images, where index measurements may be in the form of single pixels or groups of pixels that are aggregated to form the unit area of insurance' (IFAD 2017:15). Put simply, satellite imagery can be used to estimate yields only over fairly wide areas, raising renewed problems of spatial basis risk. As the summary of one recent expert conference notes,

> remotely sensed rainfall is only a proxy for actual rainfall ... Aggregation over space as well as over time generally improves skill ... It is important, however, that indices represent the local conditions experienced by the policyholders. It is therefore necessary to balance the improvements in skill gained by aggregating against the loss of representativity of local conditions ... (Black *et al.* 2018:202)

Remote sensing, then, is nominally a cheaper and more precise infrastructure for index insurance, but introduces challenges of its own (cf. Angeli Aguiton 2021).

This has had implications for what remote sensing can actually do in practice. The above-mentioned project run by CGAP and start-up Pula in Nigeria, for instance, sought initially to use satellite data to reduce costs of on-farm visits (see Hernandez *et al.* 2018). The project found that satellite data was too poor a predictor of yield variation at the level of individual farms to usefully substitute for site visits, as it only correlated sufficiently closely with average crop losses at higher levels of aggregation. The project ultimately wound up cutting costs by allowing Pula to replace government administrative districts with a smaller number of larger areas, in which yields were found to be more closely intercorrelated and normally distributed, as the basis for ground-level monitoring: 'Instead of using satellite data to predict individual farm yields, we focused on using these data to define the boundaries of units of area insured that are much larger than the [Local Government Area] and that have a common yield distribution' (Hernandez *et al.* 2018:3). Or, in short, on a basic level remote sensing has considerable limits, which have dogged efforts to substitute it for costly-to-assemble insurance data infrastructures; where it has been used, it has been as a means of refining some elements of existing ones.

The point here is that the persistent failure of efforts to construct markets for index insurance has been met with efforts to develop new market infrastructures through the application of new technologies, particularly through the deployment of remote sensing. Remote sensing can, at best, offer cheaper and more precise measures of rainfall or vegetation indices (and current evidence is ambivalent about even this). It does not resolve the more fundamental limits to index insurance from the perspective of smallholders or landless farmers. The narrow technical conception of climate risk contained in index insurance glosses the socially and historically embedded nature of those risks. Equally, the rising precarity of the very populations targeted by index insurance, compounded by the accelerating effects of climate breakdown, mean that few – even among those who might hypothetically benefit from index insurance – can afford it. Index insurance has consistently foundered on the wider patterns of uneven development revealed throughout this book, many of which have their origins in colonial histories (see Bernards 2019c). The response has been to double down on market-oriented responses to those risks, seeking to construct more effective infrastructures through which insurance risks might be calculated, in the hopes of attracting the more active involvement of finance capital.

TWEAKING FIRMS: CIRCULATING SPREADSHEETS
AND ACTUARIAL PRACTICES

The second area of intervention has revolved around firm-level calculative practices. Beyond index insurance, efforts to promote health insurance, or even just to ensure the spread of life insurance policies, have entailed building new calculative systems that can be cheaply and quickly adapted to different contexts. We can observe a series of initiatives aimed at developing alternative actuarial practices suitable for microinsurance operations. These have emerged out of the diagnosis of microinsurance's limited spread as being rooted in the absence of data highlighted above. For instance, officials from the ILO's Impact Insurance Facility note, beyond the problems posed by the novelty and limited experience of microinsurance operators, that 'programmes often face the difficulty of collecting quality data due to lack of management information systems. Many programmes still collect data on a manual basis, or use systems that have not been appropriately designed to collect microinsurance data' (Wrede and Phily 2015).

Interventions promoting the development of actuarial skills have been carried out by a network of public and private authorities, including the IAIS, professional associations (most notably the International Actuarial Association [IAA]), private consultancies, and a number of donor-funded organisations working on microinsurance (including the Microinsurance Centre [MIC]). The IAA developed an issue paper on actuarial functions in microinsurance at the request of the IAIS, which was eventually published in 2014 (IAA 2014). The report emphasises different options through which actuarial personnel can be incorporated into microinsurance operations, although it notes that 'microinsurance providers may have fewer needs in some of the traditional core actuarial areas due to the nature, scale, and scope of the products offered and therefore it would be appropriate to apply proportionality when setting regulations' (IAA 2014:8); and further that a significant challenge in hiring and retaining certified actuaries in microinsurance operations, or in bringing them in as consultants, is that they represent a relatively high cost for enterprises whose profitability is largely premised on minimising costs. One of the important solutions to these issues noted in the paper is the development of 'formula-based approaches' to actuarial calculations, in which 'standard factor-based formulas for calculating solvency capital and certain types of technical provisions would minimize the need for actuaries within the overall microinsurance market' (IAA 2014:27). These reduced requirements, the report notes, are expected to be coupled with regulatory restrictions (which have been advocated by the IAIS) limiting microinsurance operations to relatively low-risk activities.

In practice, the development of such formula-based actuarial models has been the most significant area of activity. The IAA facilitated the production of a simplified pricing model for credit-life insurance schemes, in cooperation with the UK Actuarial Profession (UKAP) in 2012 (UKAP 2012). A similar model for health microinsurance, designed in conjunction with actuarial-service firm Milliman, was released in 2016 (Milliman 2016). Both models share three critical features. First, they use readily available software platforms rather than the more specialised actuarial programs typically preferred by commercial insurers. Both models are downloadable for free as Microsoft Excel files. Second, they substitute publicly available epidemiological and mortality data – from national statistical agencies and/or the World Health Organization – for data derived from historical claims experiences. Third, both models are careful to insist that they are primarily intended for 'educational' or 'illustrative' purposes and that organisations choosing to use the models directly do so at their own risk.

The ILO's Impact Insurance Facility has also produced training modules and guidelines on pricing in microinsurance operations aimed at fulfilling a similar function. The ILO training guide on pricing, released in 2015 (Wrede and Phily 2015), is somewhat more general than the IAA-sponsored models in that it offers some basic principles and formulae rather than actual spreadsheets with built-in pricing models, but does operate along the same lines as the above initiatives. The guide emphasises the need to supplement claims experience with a number of different data sources, including (depending on the type of insurance offered) mortality tables and health statistics from the WHO and/or national authorities, and even from published epidemiological research and service providers in the case of health insurance (Wrede and Phily 2015:53–4). It also recommends developing measures of the willingness and ability of subscribers to pay based on pilot-tests, interviews, and focus groups (2015:61–3). As with the actuarial models produced by the IAA and its partners, then, the ILO guide emphasises drawing on publicly available data sources to substitute for the lack of historical claims data on which to price policies.

Excel sheets with embedded macros don't have the same sheen of technological sophistication as remote sensing applications, but their deployments in the context of microfinance are similar in important respects. They are intended to substitute quick, cheap, and available data for the complex, increasingly personalised and fine-grained data infrastructures on which insurance profits increasingly rely. Mortality statistics or epidemiological publications are – much like remote sensing data – proxies for highly elaborated calculative infrastructures through which insurance profits might be realised. They can, of course, only address half the problem, at best. The more fundamental, and intractable, problem is very similar to the fundamental problem with poverty finance identified in the introduction. Namely, the basic reason why peripheral workers are held to need microinsurance – their disproportionate exposure to health and mortality hazards (much like the disproportionate exposure of smallholders and landless farmers to climate risks) – is rooted in the same conditions that make it hard for them to purchase insurance.

CONCLUSION

One key conclusion of the above discussion is surely that markets can't deliver adequate means of risk management to many of the poorest, and arguably that they can only do so to a small minority at best. Yet the continued efforts to promote the development of microinsurance are indicative of an inability to think beyond markets as a means of providing risk management. Markets are increasingly a 'default' mode of development intervention, paradoxically even in the persistent absence of interest on the part of finance capital in actually providing them. The experiments traced above have, notably, been driven by professional associations, consultants, academics, philanthropies, and international organisations, rather than by metropolitan finance capital *per se*. This chapter has sought to explain these dynamics by situating recent experiments with the technical infrastructures underpinning microinsurance in the longer history of neoliberal efforts to develop social protection systems for the poorest.

Thus, we should read the continued push to engineer markets not exactly as an indication of the pervasive spread of financial logics, but more of the structural power of finance capital in development. It is reflective of a wider dynamic of development-by-anticipatory spatial fix, which I have traced in the latter chapters in this book. The wider dynamic of attempting to mobilise finance capital by developing informational infrastructures needed to smooth its movement is a continuation of the dynamics highlighted in the discussion of the commercialisation of microfinance in Chapter 4. As noted in the previous chapter, the turn to 'financial inclusion' also entailed a partial shift in these strategies towards more fine-grained engagements with credit and insurance data 'on the ground' in the Global South, away from efforts to build channels for capital. In the next (and final) chapter, we'll see how similar dynamics are reflected in the latest fad for 'fintech'.

7
Fintech and its limits

I started out this book with a discussion of the ostensibly miraculous powers of fintech for reducing poverty. One of the chief aims of this book has been to put this hype in perspective, showing how it reflects recurrent, failure-prone efforts to deal with underlying patterns of uneven development through poverty finance. We're in a position, now, to return to a critical discussion of fintech itself. In doing so, I want to challenge both the somewhat fantastical claims about the benefits of fintech and some readings of its ill-effects, which at times lean too heavily on understandings of fintech as an element of processes of financialisation. I'll show, instead, how the embrace of fintech is an uneven and error-prone response to the deeply embedded limits of financial infrastructures and the challenges of engineering markets in the context of precarious incomes. New fintech applications in global development are profoundly political interventions: they represent efforts, much like those traced in the previous three chapters, at developing more fine-grained market infrastructures in the hopes of attracting mobile finance capital.

Emergent financial technologies have often been understood as governmental techniques aimed at producing particular kinds of market subjects amenable to participation in financialised models of accumulation. Here, recent critical contributions on fintech from IPE scholars (e.g. Aitken 2017; Gabor and Brooks 2017) follow a longer tradition of research that treats consumer credit scoring as a disciplinary technology, shaping and constituting the subjectivities of target populations (Leyshon and Thrift 1999; Jeacle and Walsh 2002; Marron 2007; Langley 2014). Previous assessments along these lines have tended to emphasise the disciplining and stratifying tendencies implicit in new modes of credit scoring (Roderick 2014; Fourcade and Healy 2017). Generally speaking, these studies have focused on the contents of models and algorithms and the behavioural expectations they mobilise – references to James Scott's (1998) concept of 'legibility' are very common (e.g. Gabor and Brooks 2017; Aitken 2017; Fourcade and Healy 2017). Gabor and Brooks, for instance, note that in a context where data about patterns of mobile phone use can increasingly be deployed in credit scoring through the activities of groups like start-up Cignifi, 'A mobile phone ... would become a new Panopticon for self-regulating behaviour in ways that preserve mobile-data based credit scores' (2017:430). Aitken (2017) similarly argues that, while the 'unbanked' are typically understood in terms of their exclusion from financial markets, experiments with new forms of credit data show a wider effort to constitute the 'unbanked' as a social category and make them legible to financial capital. Drawing in particular on Leyshon and Thrift (2007), Aitken describes these activities as a kind of 'prospecting' for streams of income that can be assembled into financial assets. Other authors draw somewhat more optimistic assessments emphasising the possibilities for new forms of resistance and agency implicit in emergent financial technologies (e.g. Kremers and Brassett 2017; Kear 2017; Maurer 2012; Langley 2014). In either case, though, credit scores and other fintech applications are widely treated as forms of hyper-individualised and responsibilising governmentality – as (neo)liberal modes of governing economic activity through the 'self-regulating capacities of subjects' (Miller and Rose 1990).

Assimilating these developments into wider narratives of 'financialisation', however, can implicitly ascribe a unidirectional, even teleological, nature to the development of fintech (see Bernards 2019a; 2019b).[17] This is problematic in the first instance because it can lead us to overlook the very limited progress of financial inclusion in practice. In particular, as we have seen in previous chapters, despite a considerable number of global and national policy frameworks promoting 'financial inclusion', actual progress in terms of 'access' to credit for the poorest has been highly uneven. Borrowing from formal financial institutions continues to be heavily outweighed by borrowing from family and friends or informal lenders in most developing regions. As discussed at the end of Chapter 5, the growth of formal credit has been slow, uneven, and fragile, and – as Chapter 6 showed – we can tell much the same story with respect to insurance. This is in no small part because, as Mader (2018:477) accurately notes, private capital has continued to prefer high-interest loans targeted primarily to the 'urban, employed, "less poor"'. When set in the context of the uneven progress of the 'financial inclusion' agenda, growing attention to technology appears to reflect a further revision of neoliberal understandings of market-building. Where the promotion of commercial microfinance and the early promotion of financial inclusion tended to emphasise the construction of institutional vehicles to facilitate access to global capital markets and standardised forms of information, the 'turn to technology' represents a shift towards engagements with the minute, material elements of the devices needed to mobilise information and set prices. But we are nonetheless dealing with a further iteration of development practice as anticipatory spatial fix.

This chapter traces the rise of fintech in global development, showing how it represents a continuation of the dynamics highlighted earlier in this book. The chapter is split into four parts. The first section gives a short discussion of Kenya's mobile money boom. As already intimated in Chapter 5, the success of M-Pesa in Kenya did much to popularise the idea that new technological systems might lower transaction costs and enable wider access to credit, and indeed that the latter could be developed by the private sector. The second section traces the growing consensus around the value of fintech for financial inclusion among leading agencies in global development. The third section gives a short overview of new techniques for credit scoring based around deploying alternative data. The final section considers some of the key limits to fintech applications and how these reproduce the fundamental patterns of uneven development traced throughout this book.

A FINTECH SUCCESS STORY? KENYA'S MOBILE MONEY BOOM

In Chapter 5, I made note of the frequent tendency to refer to Kenya's M-Pesa system as a kind of model for how technology-enabled financial inclusion might be brought about. This story is worth exploring in more detail here, both because it provides important context for the wider embrace of fintech and because it illustrates quite clearly some of its pathologies.

M-Pesa is a mobile money service launched by Safaricom (a Kenyan affiliate of Vodafone) in 2005.[18] Users deposit and withdraw funds in M-Pesa accounts through designated agents, and transfer money between user accounts via mobile phone. It was initially a pilot project funded by the UK Department for International Development, which was launched commercially in 2007. Importantly, while M-Pesa is often framed as a 'disruptive' new technology, it is in practice intimately linked to the existing financial system. The Central Bank of Kenya (CBK) played an important role in ensuring close links between M-Pesa and the existing financial system (see Dafe 2020). Concerned that mobile payments could 'create' alternative money, the CBK required each 'digital shilling' to be matched by an equivalent shilling in a commercial bank account owned by Safaricom. Indeed, while there was some early resistance from commercial banks to the development of M-Pesa, this was largely allayed in the early 2010s as banks were encouraged, by the CBK in particular, to adopt mobile money systems as a means of lowering transaction costs (see Dafe 2020:516).

The growth of M-Pesa, and mobile money more generally, was dramatic. By early 2020, the Kenya Central Bank counted just under 60 million mobile money user accounts – slightly more than one per person in Kenya. Users may have multiple accounts and the CBK provides no estimates of the number of dormant accounts, but it is hard to argue that the vast majority of adults in Kenya now use mobile money accounts regularly. At the peak in December of 2019, there were nearly 55 million mobile money transactions, with a total value of KSh 382 billion (about US$3.6 billion).[19] In the World Bank's most recent Findex survey in 2017, 72 percent of adults in Kenya reported having a mobile money account. It's worth underlining that Kenya has considerably higher measures of mobile money use as compared to anywhere else in Africa (as a region, Africa has the highest rates of mobile money use by some distance; see, e.g., Sahay *et al.* 2020). The only other country where that figure reached 50 percent was neighbouring Uganda. The figure across sub-Saharan Africa as a whole was 21 percent.[20] Mobile money in Kenya was also considerably more intimately important to peoples' livelihoods: Kenya had the highest rates of mobile money use both for wage payments and domestic remittances, at 33 percent of wage recipients and 94 percent of remittance senders and receivers respectively. We should keep in mind that the relative depth of Kenya's financial system, itself rooted in the country's history as a territory of white settlement and capitalised large-scale agriculture and a nexus of sub-regional commercial capital (see Chapter 1), had a role to play in the expansion in Kenya of 'disruptive' mobile money. These patterns of uneven development are replicated in the roll-out of fintech elsewhere, as will be shown later on in the chapter.

For the moment, though, the key point is how and why M-Pesa has been so widely celebrated in global development. The claim is frequently made that mobile money has allowed Kenya to 'leapfrog' developmental constraints posed by its existing financial sector: 'new technologies solve problems arising from weak institutional infrastructure and the cost structure of conventional banking' (Aron 2017:4). Perhaps the most notable study touting the benefits of mobile money in Kenya is an article published in *Science* in 2016, estimating that the spread of M-Pesa had directly resulted in 194,000 Kenyan households (or 2 percent of the country's population) being lifted out of poverty, disproportionately in female-headed households (Suri and Jack 2016). The authors suggest that access to mobile payments enabled 'a more efficient allocation of labor, savings, and risk' (2016:1292) among households – for instance, by enabling informal risk sharing mechanisms to operate over a wider geographical area, making internal migration and remittances easier, and especially by allowing easier access to remittances that might be used to set up small enterprises. These conclusions, particularly the 194,000 households (or 2 percent) figure, seem to have obtained something of a 'common-sense' status in global development circles. Suri and Jack's estimate of M-Pesa's impacts has been cited widely, including in a major inter-agency report from the United Nations on 'financing for international development' (United Nations 2018), as well as in World Bank policy frameworks for other countries including Côte D'Ivoire (World Bank 2019a), Uganda (World Bank 2019b), and Zambia (World Bank 2020a). Kenya's digital finance boom, in short, is politically relevant well beyond Kenya itself.

More skeptical assessments of M-Pesa, and of mobile money more broadly, suggest that narratives of entrepreneurial growth enabled by fintech mask new patterns of exclusion and stratification (Bhagat and Roderick 2020; Natile 2020). Bateman *et al.* (2019) issued a direct rebuttal to Suri and Jack. They argue that to attribute poverty reduction to the reallocation of labour from agriculture to microenterprise, one of the central mechanisms that Suri and Jack (2016) highlight, ignores high rates of business failure in the latter sector and the possibility that new businesses may simply displace others in already oversaturated and highly competitive informal markets. Recent analyses have also criticised the wider developmental claims made on behalf of Kenyan fintech. Natile (2020) situates M-Pesa in the longer trajectory of colonial dispossession and development intervention in Kenya, highlighting how the language of 'inclusion' and 'opportunity' surrounding M-Pesa obscures deeply rooted and strongly gendered inequalities.

Kenya's apparent success, though, emerging as it has in the context of deeply uneven progress in promoting financial inclusion, has helped to deepen and lend credence to the wider hopes that fintech will provide a way around what are seen as the chief obstacles to the spread of formal finance: high transaction costs and limited credit information. Mobile money also has the advantage of being less overtly exploitative than, say, a usurious microloan – although it does still depend on collecting fees from users, and, as we'll see further below, can provide the basis for the expansion of other financial services. But mobile money also threatens to create new kinds of exclusions. In the first instance, the use of mobile or digital means to, say, send and receive remittances does not, in itself, change the volume or frequency of those payments themselves – as Guermond (2020:15) aptly notes of mobile money services in Senegal and Ghana. Equally, mobile payments don't really reduce the costs of making payments so much as shift them onto users, who are not all equally able to bear them. Mobile money does reduce the need to carry physical cash and hence some transaction costs for banks. However, at a minimum, a mobile money account requires the user to have access to a mobile phone and to be able to pay for airtime. More elaborate digital apps require a yet-more expensive smartphone and access to data. These are not trivial concerns. Recent evidence from Southern and Eastern Africa suggests that poorer users are eschewing existing fintech applications specifically because of the impossibility of using them without paying for phones and carrier plans (see Chetty *et al.* 2019). Nonetheless, the example of M-Pesa underpins much of the enthusiasm for the development of fintech solutions to financial exclusion.

FINTECH FOR FINANCIAL INCLUSION:
AN EMERGING (NEOLIBERAL) CONSENSUS

The general enthusiasm for fintech and 'innovation' in promoting financial inclusion, reflected in the hype around M-Pesa, is increasingly being cemented in global policy. One of the flagship outcomes of the World Bank and the IMF's Joint Annual Meetings for 2018 was the 'Bali Fintech Agenda' (BFA) (World Bank and IMF 2018). The BFA was launched, with considerable fanfare, by a panel featuring Bank of England Governor Mark Carney, IMF President Christine Lagarde, World Bank President Jim Yong Kim, South African Reserve Bank Governor Lesetja Kganyago, Indonesian Finance Minister Sri Mulyani, and Indonesian President Joko Widodo. The BFA follows a number of similar pronouncements. Notably, the Alliance for Financial Inclusion (AFI), a network of central banks and finance ministries, announced the 'Sochi Accord on Fintech for Financial Inclusion' the previous month (AFI 2018b), and the G20 published a set of 'High-Level Principles for Digital Financial Inclusion' (HLPs) in 2016 (GPFI 2016). Taken together, the BFA, the Sochi Accord, and the HLPs point to an emerging consensus around a set of potential benefits of fintech and emergent risks and areas for regulatory intervention. Three key points are worth underlining here.

First, the BFA, the HLPs, and the Sochi Accord are non-binding statements of principles. The background paper to the BFA, for instance, is explicit that it does not 'aim to provide specific guidance or policy advice at this stage' (World Bank and IMF 2018:10). These documents are, in this sense, reflective of a wider use of 'soft law' and informal 'best practices' in setting regulatory standards for the promotion of financial inclusion (see Soederberg 2013, also Chapter 5).

Second, and maybe more importantly, the BFA, the HLPs, and the Sochi Accord are reflective of a growing regulatory emphasis on fintech as both a source of new risks and a key means of securing wider participation in financial markets by the so-called unbanked. The sense throughout these guidelines is of fintech as a Janus-faced beast which might enable ever-wider access to ever-more-efficient financial markets, yet create new risks and regulatory challenges in so doing. The core appeal of fintech is very much pitched in terms of its ostensible capacity to extend access to financial services – for instance, a press release to accompany the announcement of the BFA quotes then-World Bank President Kim: 'Countries are demanding deeper access to financial markets, and the World Bank Group will focus on delivering fintech solutions that enhance financial services, mitigate risks, and achieve stable, inclusive economic growth' (World Bank 2018b). The first point of the BFA identifies the key (potential) benefits of the expanded use of fintech primarily in terms of 'inclusion', access, and 'deepening' of financial activity: 'increasing access to financial services and financial inclusion; deepening financial markets; and improving cross-border payments and remittance transfer systems' (World Bank and IMF 2018:7).

All three statements of principles identify emergent challenges, primarily in terms of financial stability and integrity. The BFA suggests that fintech enables financial activity to blur national boundaries, and that 'These developments could lead to increased multipolarity and interconnectedness of the global financial system, potentially affecting the balance of risks for global financial stability' (World Bank and IMF 2018:9). In the HLPs in particular, a key emphasis is placed on limiting the potential for criminal activity, fraud, and other threats to 'financial integrity', noting that the monitoring of risks is necessary to 'build cyber resilience into financial markets and safeguard the financial system from illicit activities' (GPFI 2016:9). This is echoed in the Sochi Accord, which notes that 'leveraging fintech for financial inclusion creates new regulatory challenges and poses cybersecurity, data privacy, money laundering and consumer protection-related risks' (AFI 2018:2). The underlying argument is centred on the need for regulators to balance emergent risks against the need to minimise regulatory barriers to entry for new firms. A key technique for doing so has been to carve out time-bound or product-specific regulatory exceptions for experiments with new activities targeting the poor. So-called 'regulatory sandboxes' for fintech applications – time-limited, product-specific licences for particular companies to conduct 'experiments' with 'innovative' practices and technologies – are a good example (see Brown and Piroska 2021). The World Bank and the G20, together with a number of central banks and financial regulators in both the Global North and South, have also increasingly promoted and coordinated targeted regulatory frameworks for fintech applications aimed at promoting 'access' to finance for the 'unbanked'. Recently, CGAP in particular has promoted regulatory sandboxes (see Jenik and Lauer 2017). The concept was first implemented by the Consumer Financial Protection Bureau in the US in 2012. Sandboxes have since been announced or implemented primarily in low or middle-income countries including Malaysia, India, Mauritius, Brazil, Mexico, Jordan, Kenya, Sierra Leone, China, and Thailand.

Third, another area of growing consensus is on the importance of the physical infrastructures of financial markets. Point II of the BFA and Principle 4 of the HLPs both focus specifically on improving the quality of ICT infrastructure. This could be read in the first instance as a recognition by policymakers of the materiality of markets – of the breadth of physical and informational substrates needed to enable financial transactions. But underlying both documents is a particular theory of how to deepen and strengthen those infrastructures, namely: if left the regulatory space to do so, markets will develop infrastructures on their own. This is somewhat belied by the very active role that donors and the IFIs have actually taken in promoting the development of these infrastructures. Donor support for the early development of M-Pesa is one obvious example. Another increasingly important form of support has been providing financial and in-kind support to particular fintech firms. The Entrepreneurial Finance Lab (EFL), for instance, a key fintech firm developing 'psychometric' credit scoring practices (discussed further below), was developed out of a 2006 research initiative at the Harvard Kennedy School. It was incorporated as a private company in 2010 and subsequently attracted funding from a number of different bilateral and multilateral development agencies. In 2013, the project was funded by the G20's 'SME Finance Challenge' (SME Finance Forum 2014). Subsequent pilot studies were sponsored by the Inter-American Development Bank (IADB) and the World Bank and carried out in Latin America. The IADB facilitated and published studies co-authored by EFL staff which tested models developed in the project discussed above with SME borrowers in Argentina (Klinger *et al.* 2013a) and Peru (Klinger *et al.* 2013b). World Bank staff did likewise in Peru in 2012 (Arráiz *et al.* 2015).

Underlying these developments is, increasingly, an idea of fintech as a set of means for expanding the uneven infrastructures of financial markets, in order to mobilise finance capital for lending to the 'unbanked'. The logic of the anticipatory spatial fix is again evident.

WHAT CAN FINTECH DO?

It might be useful here to highlight the kinds of technologies that have emerged in this context. 'Alternative' forms of credit data are especially salient. Here, two major developments are notable: applications of 'Big Data' and the mobilisation of new kinds of what might be called 'small data' (Kitchin and Lauriault 2015). 'Small' data refer to conventional data collection processes using controlled sampling techniques limiting scope, timeframe, size, and variety. Big Data, by contrast, are produced continually, in high volume and variety, and often as a by-product of the normal operation of information technologies rather than through direct investigative processes (see Kitchin and Lauriault 2015). The analysis of such mass volumes of data is made possible by the application of computerised algorithms, which are distinguished from the static 'models' used in traditional statistical analyses by their dynamic and recursive character (Beer 2016). In either variety, though, applications of alternative credit data seek to replace direct assessments of creditworthiness based on income with indirect measures of the 'character' of borrowers. In so doing, they introduce important pathologies. They are ultimately dependent on being able to 'plug in' to existing credit infrastructures (to use Star's [1999] term), and wind up replicating wider patterns of uneven development as a result.

Big Data

Big data applications have proliferated, if unevenly, in recent years in global finance (see Campbell-Verduyn *et al.* 2017). Credit scoring applications targeting the so-called unbanked have been a particularly important focus here. Big Data, especially in the context of growing mobile phone and internet use in developing countries, are seen as a vital source of alternative credit scoring for 'unbanked' consumers:

> The increased use of digital technologies … is generating a wealth of new data that can be used to … assess creditworthiness, and manage risk more effectively. A growing number of financial technology companies … are developing innovative tools to do precisely this. (Hoder *et al.* 2016:7)

A notable example here is the start-up Cignifi, which aims to produce alternative credit scores on the basis of potential borrowers' mobile phone use. Cignifi developed a proprietary algorithm that uses a behavioural model drawing on data on calls and texts received per day, along with patterns of web and social network usage, to assess the creditworthiness of mobile users who can then be selectively targeted for financial products. This is licensed out to telecommunications operators and financial service providers (see Aitken 2017).

Similar algorithms based on social media usage and social networks have also been rolled out, notably by another start-up firm, Lenndo (see Langevin 2019). Lenndo often directly invokes microcredit's reliance on social networks to assess credit risk – arguing that by mobilising social network data, it is able to incorporate information about the 'character' and behaviour of borrowers, along with social pressures, at scale in a way that conventional credit scores are not able to do. One of the firm's founders, for instance, described the process of developing the firm's algorithms in an interview with Forbes: 'We talked to anthropologists, behavioral economists and we talked to psychologists and tons of microfinance finance professionals to get our arms around the social dynamic that resulted in good loans' (quoted in Groenfeldt 2015). Algorithms scraping social media activity are described explicitly as a means of approximating those dynamics: 'Our analytics transform their social media interactions into a rich relationship' (quoted in Groenfeldt 2015). A recently-published study jointly authored by Lenndo staff and

Belgium-based academics, and drawing on data provided by Lenndo, likewise concluded by arguing that 'The good predictive performance of the generated models allows to automate the credit scoring process for microfinance to massive settings, *mainly thanks to the ability to include the difficult concept of character*' (de Cnudde *et al.* 2019:362). Big Data credit scoring, in short, seeks to pull off much the same trick as MFIs did in the 1990s and 2000s, substituting social networks 'on the ground' for thinly developed credit infrastructures, but on a much larger scale.

One of the main problems here, as Langevin has compellingly argued, is that these systems of scoring credit risk bear little direct relation to the incomes and assets of borrowers: 'self-learning algorithms … do not allow for the productive aspects of micro-entrepreneurial activities, nor of those related to credit in general, to be included in the equation that determines credit scores' (2019:794). Propensity to repay and available resources are separate (if related) categories. A credit score based on, for instance, how a borrower's social media contacts or their phone metadata correlates with credit repayment, measures the former almost to the exclusion of the latter. An algorithm trained on this data can only identify traits of people who are more likely to repay their loans. It can't tell whether they are repaying because they can afford to or because they're more vulnerable to pressures to prioritise paying debts over buying food.

This is a set of concerns with a long lineage. Indeed, they can be slotted into a longer history of critical questions raised about statistical credit-scoring techniques when these were pioneered in the US in the 1970s. Present-day Big Data-enabled credit scores are able to process exponentially larger and more diverse data sets than older computer applications, including data produced and collected indirectly, but they still rely on the same underlying logic as longer-running practices of credit scoring. They produce predictive scores for individual borrowers based on correlates of credit performance in the wider population. As one critic noted in 1982 of then-relatively-new statistical credit scores:

> since prediction is the sole criterion for acceptability, any individual characteristic that can be scored, other than obviously illegal characteristics, has potential for inclusion in a statistical credit scoring system … Few of these variables bear an explanatory relationship to credit performance. At best they might be statistical indicators whose rela-

tionship to payment performance can exist only through a complex chain of intervening variables. (Capon 1982:84)

Capon was one among many participants in these debates who called for regulatory restrictions limiting credit scoring to factors with a direct explanatory effect on credit performance – primarily repayment history and income and employment variables (1982:90). These and similar calls were all but ignored in the US and elsewhere (see Roderick 2014). This nonetheless matters because this dynamic – in which logics of correlation and brute empiricism are prioritised over causation and explanation – is only enhanced by algorithmic credit scores (see Roderick 2014; Aitken 2017). Indeed, Big Data credit scores based on the by-products of peoples' phone or internet usage rely almost exclusively on data that lacks a direct explanatory link to repayment. Promoters would likely argue that this is the whole point, as Big Data credit scoring is mostly meant as a 'second-best' substitute for conventional data where the latter is absent. However, as we'll see further in the example of digital over-indebtedness in Kenya discussed below, this dynamic has in practice often created new sources of vulnerability and dispossession.

Psychometric credit scoring

There have also been efforts to develop alternative forms of 'small' data for evaluating credit in the absence of formal credit histories and employment or property records. Most prominent, perhaps, are so-called 'psychometric' credit scores (see Bernards 2019a; Aitken 2017). Psychometric tests in general aim to quantify cognitive attributes for the purpose of screening individuals' suitability for certain tasks. They originated out of efforts to develop 'scientific' techniques for hiring, primarily in the US. One of the highest-profile applications of such systems for credit scoring was developed by EFL. EFL developed a test drawing on measures of intelligence and 'integrity' to be administered to potential borrowers lacking detailed credit histories (see Klinger et al. 2013c). As I'll discuss further shortly, questionnaires are heavily rooted in applied psychology literature, often initially developed in human resources applications to help large firms with hiring decisions. Different firms use different formulae, but psychometric tests for the purpose of credit scoring generally consist of a mix of cognitive tasks (such as asking respondents to recall a series of numbers), questions aimed at assessing personality type (for example,

'I feel comfortable around people', 'I get chores done right away') and measures of honesty. Tests are normally administered by computer in a bank branch or retail outlet, but some companies have developed online and mobile versions in some settings as well. Psychometric credit scoring firms have often claimed that administering tests on computers or digital devices also enables testers to track mouse movements and response times for signs of indecision, distraction, or dishonesty (e.g. *The Economist* 2016). Different models vary, but I'll explain in more detail below what went into EFL's system, along with a discussion of its key limits.

As with Big Data applications, the basic point is that adopting alternative forms of credit data – assessing the psychological character of borrowers rather than their more opaque economic circumstances – is framed as a way of diminishing collateral requirements and interest rates that might otherwise disqualify informal workers and businesses from formal borrowing. Psychometric credit scores are often promoted by drawing a direct analogy to the use of personal credit scores in the US for small business loans: 'Unfortunately this rich-country solution cannot be directly applied to emerging markets, because the long and detailed personal credit histories that are available in the United States are not available for most small business owners around the world' (Klinger *et al.* 2013a:10). Psychometrics are thus explicitly framed as a cheap and quick second-best option, allowing financial institutions to approximate the modes of calculating credit risk available in the Global North through alternative forms of data.

On the surface, psychometrics have somewhat more direct bearing on the livelihoods of borrowers insofar as they mobilise the quasi-mythical figure of the informal worker as risk-taking 'entrepreneur' at the root of 'self-help' stories about housing finance and microcredit. This is, first of all, a deeply ideological vision of informal livelihoods. The figure of the informal workers as 'entrepreneur' can usefully be situated in what Breman and van der Linden (2014:927) have aptly described as a longer-term 'policy of informalization', in which the World Bank and others have coupled pressures for the removal of protective institutions with efforts to develop training and credit facilities and to formalise property rights, in order to promote self-employment and entrepreneurial livelihoods. The point here is that the claim that psychometrics actually measures the income and productive activities of borrowers depends in the first instance on the transposition of a romanticised, de Soto-esque vision of 'entrepreneurial' activity onto real informal economies – which are often better understood as forms of 'survivalist improvisation' (Davis 2006) carried out by vulnerable and dispossessed actors in marginal sites. This matters in terms of the efficacy of psychometrics because there are good reasons to suspect that assessments of static individual intelligence and personality traits are deeply limited in the context of really-existing informal economies, which are suspended in various institutional networks, sets of power relations, and structures of accumulation (see Phillips 2011; Meagher 2016). The intensely individualising thrust of psychometric methods, by default, is inattentive to the structural forms of vulnerability that underpin informality – and which render notions of 'entrepreneurship' and 'success' problematic. As I'll note in relation to the case of India below, whatever improvements psychometric tests might make to default rates can be quickly overwhelmed by the instability of informal earnings in contexts marked by widespread precarity and poverty. Psychometrics, in short, are inattentive to the messy and highly varied complex of gendered, ethnic, racial, and other forms of social differentiation through which the array of survivalist activities making up 'informal' economies are typically mediated in practice. They are largely blind to 'everything that happens in between' borrowing and repayment, to again return to Marx's words.

Moreover, actually implementing this understanding of informal workers as potentially more or less successful entrepreneurs in psychometric tests has not proven entirely straightforward. The model developed by EFL draws on a number of widely used tests of intelligence and personality traits drawn from a growing literature in applied psychology, which has explored linkages between intelligence, personality traits, and 'entrepreneurial success' (e.g. Baum and Locke 2004). The basic premise is, ostensibly, that 'entrepreneurs' with greater aptitude will more likely be able to repay a loan. None of this literature, however, was directly concerned with default risk. The first problem in applying psychometrics to credit scoring was thus quite simply the need to figure out what factors might actually predict default. An early technical note from EFL suggested that 'unlike building a model based on typical socio-demographic characteristics, psychometric questions have not been asked on past applications nor are client answers present in large bureaus, and therefore psychometric information represents new data that must be collected.' (EFL 2012:2). There is a critical slippage implicit here: despite the continual references to promoting 'entrepreneurship', in tailoring and testing the model to account for default risk, EFL's scoring methods in fact turn less on predicting the entrepreneurial success of borrowers than on predicting their likelihood of making loan repayments. This is underlined by the subsequent development of the model.

The first iteration of the EFL model was tested in a research project conducted in Kenya, South Africa, Nigeria, and Peru. Tests were administered to existing clients of a number of banks, and psychometric scores were tested against default rates and self-reported profit levels (Klinger et al. 2013a). The tests were scored along three dimensions: personality type, intelligence, and honesty. Measures of personality drew on a series of publications in psychology about the relationships between the so-called 'big five' personality traits and entrepreneurship (see Zhao and Seibert 2006; Ciavarella et al. 2004). Intelligence was measured through 'digit span recall' tests (in which participants are shown a string of digits for five seconds, the digits are hidden for five seconds, and then the test-taker is asked to enter the number) as well as Ravens Progressive Matrices (which present test-takers with a series of incomplete geometric patterns and ask them to choose from among eight possible options to complete the pattern) (Klinger et al. 2013a:16–17). Both tests had previously been used in published studies on predictors of success in entrepreneurship (de Mel et al. 2008). They also incorporated an assessment of 'honesty and integrity' drawn from a questionnaire originally developed to screen potential convenience store employees in the US for their propensity for theft (Bernardin and Cooke 1993), based on an adapted version of the 'Honesty' subscale of the London House Personnel Selection Inventory (Klinger et al. 2013a:17–18). Notably, this measure of 'honesty' was explicitly incorporated as a measure of *credit risk* rather than entrepreneurial aptitude. Indeed, it is noted that the impacts of 'honesty and integrity' on entrepreneurship are unstudied and likely ambiguous: 'Are dishonest entrepreneurs more likely to fail at business because they cannot generate the trust needed for relationships? Or are honest entrepreneurs more likely to fail because they will be taken advantage of in the cut-throat marketplace?' (Klinger et al. 2013a:18).

Psychometric credit scores also necessarily give a static picture of borrowers. They 'fix' in place an assessment of the credit risk attached to an actor with a capacity for reflexivity and agency, and engaged in livelihood activities that are themselves embedded in complex relations of dispossession, exploitation, and improvisation. A snapshot of a potential borrower's character traits might struggle to capture those elements, but this static character of psychometric tests is also necessary to their

ability to plug into existing financial infrastructures. They are administered in roughly 30-minute-long computerised tests, mostly carried out
on site in bank branches or retail outlets. This trade-off is important.
Because they are short tests administered in a particular time and place,
they are relatively easy to slot into existing credit infrastructures based
primarily on face-to-face evaluation of credit applications in brick and
mortar branches. But as a result, psychometrics do very little to 'disrupt'
or to actually extend credit to 'excluded' people far removed from those
infrastructures.

In short, Big Data and psychometric credit scoring have important
dynamics in common. Indeed, they operate in a sufficiently similar
institutional landscape that in 2017, Lenndo merged with EFL. Both
psychometric and big data credit scoring exist in a slightly awkward relationship with the patterns of 'real' economic activity from which they
seek to abstract streams of financial income. There is also already something of a contradiction at work here with respect to inclusion. The
tension highlighted throughout this book between promises of inclusion and logics of segmentation, stratification, and exclusion – of sorting
out those able to profitably participate in credit markets from those 'too
risky' to do so – are especially present in the development of alternative
forms of credit data (Aitken 2017:291).

These hints about the limits of the turn to technology as a means of promoting inclusion are made more evident by considering them in context
of the wider trajectory outlined in this book. New forms of stratification
seem unlikely to overcome the underlying 'profit-outreach tradeoff' that
hampered the development of microfinance markets for the poorest in
the previous decade (Cull *et al.* 2009). Indeed, as Mader (2018) rightly
argues, financial capital has continued to 'cherry-pick' its engagements
with the agenda of financial inclusion, primarily through high-interest
loans to the urban, 'less poor'. Fintech applications ultimately promise,
at best, more fine-grained forms of cherry-picking, and indeed they
operate primarily by contracting out their proprietary scoring systems
to existing lenders. Lenndo, for instance, piloted its algorithm on a small
pool of borrowers in the Philippines and Colombia before selling its loan
portfolio in 2015 to a mobile-based savings bank in the Philippines, in
order to concentrate on licensing its algorithm to other financial institutions (Balea 2015). The majority of EFL's actual applications are not
in fact for small business loans but for microloans or, even more likely,
for retail credit (see Bernards 2019a:827). They don't help to solve the

more fundamental underlying problem, which is simply that irregular and precarious incomes are exceedingly difficult to convert into predictable income streams amenable to financial speculation. Alternative forms of credit data have thus tended only to exacerbate the tendencies towards uneven development highlighted throughout this book. This trajectory is usefully understood in terms of the ongoing confrontation between neoliberal logics of perpetually re-engineered marketisation, particularly the emphasis on markets as processors of information, and everything 'that happens in between' (Marx 1991) in terms of productive activity and livelihoods in order to enable commodified, fetishised market activities. The turn to technology in efforts to promote financial inclusion thus represents a continuation of particular regulatory logics implicit in previous interventions to promote microfinance and financial inclusion, without addressing the underlying challenges that have hampered these projects.

FINTECH AND UNEVEN DEVELOPMENT: TWO BRIEF EXAMPLES

In this final section, I want to turn to a brief inspection of the commercial roll-out of fintech-enabled credit. This turns out to reveal fast-unfolding and fraught efforts, both by private businesses and by policymakers, to navigate the broader contradictions of neoliberalising reforms.

The uneven rollout of digital credit in Kenya

The rise of digital credit, starting with Safaricom's 2012 launch of M-Shawari, has proven rather more controversial than M-Pesa. Media reports, both in Kenya (e.g. Singh 2018) and beyond (Donovan and Park 2019) have highlighted concerns about the rapid rise of over-indebtedness facilitated by digital lending apps. Even erstwhile promoters of mobile money, including CGAP, have raised concerns about digital credit and over-indebtedness (e.g. Izaguirre et al. 2018).

It matters here that the development of digital finance in Kenya has largely reinforced existing patterns of financial activity. Digitally-enabled loans are concentrated on urban, employed borrowers, and dominated by existing banks. The most recent national 'FinAccess' survey in Kenya, run jointly by Financial Sector Deepening Kenya, the KCB, and the Kenya National Bureau of Statistics, found overall rates of 'financial inclusion' – referring to access to formal financial services of any kind, including mobile money – that ranged from 96 and 94 percent in Nairobi and Mombasa, respectively, to 57 and 64 percent in the peripheral Northern Rift Valley and Upper Eastern regions (FinAccess 2019:11). Equally, although mobile money use in general had expanded in rural areas, there was still a persistent gap between rural and urban residents in terms of formal 'financial inclusion', with 91.2 percent of urban residents, against 77.3 percent of rural residents, accessing formal financial services. Previous research has also found much heavier concentrations of mobile money agents in Nairobi in particular, and the surrounding metropolitan area in general, than in the rest of the country (Barboni 2015:70, 77).

These differences are even more pronounced when we start to look at credit in particular rather than 'financial inclusion' in general. Table 7.1 shows usage rates of mobile lending services (like M-Shawari) and digital lending apps for rural and urban populations in the country as a whole, based on the underlying data from the FinAccess survey. In general, among rural residents, 6.6 percent of respondents currently or had previously made use of mobile lending services, and 6.4 percent reported the same of digital lending apps. The corresponding figures among urban residents were 17.2 and 11.4 percent, respectively. This pattern is broadly replicated in other studies (e.g. Kaffenberger *et al.* 2018).

Table 7.1   Mobile and digital borrowing, urban and rural residents, Kenya. Author calculations based on 2019 Kenya FinAccess Survey data

Residency	Total Respondents	Number accessing credit through mobile money (past or present)	Percentage of urban/ rural residents accessing credit through mobile money	Number accessing credit through digital apps (past or present)	Percentage of urban/rural residents accessing credit through digital apps
Urban	3 611	621	17.2	411	11.4
Rural	5 058	336	6.6	326	6.4
Total	8 669	957	11.0	737	8.5

Even among urban centres, access to digital credit is highly uneven. Table 7.2, drawing on the same underlying data, compares the prevalence of mobile and digital borrowing among urban areas in Kenya, highlighting the disparity between the two major historic financial and commercial centres – Nairobi and Mombasa – and the rest of the country. The proportion of survey respondents in those cities (and the wider metropolitan area, in the case of Nairobi) reporting past or present borrowing using both mobile money services (25 percent) and digital lending apps (18.2 percent) is more than double the respective rate of use of mobile (12.3 percent) and digital borrowing (7.1 percent) in other urban settings.

Table 7.2   Mobile and digital borrowing, urban residents by county. Author calculations based on 2019 Kenya FinAccess Survey data

County	Total respondents with urban residence	Number accessing credit through mobile money (past or present)	Percentage accessing credit through mobile money	Number accessing credit through digital apps (past or present)	Percentage accessing credit through digital apps
Nairobi	703	191	27.2	63	9.0
Mombasa	231	42	18.2	62	26.8
Kiambu	156	72	46.2	68	43.6
Nairobi Metro/ Mombasa total*	**1395**	**349**	**25.0**	**254**	**18.2**
Kisumu	98	15	15.3	1	1.0
Nakuru	98	10	10.2	7	7.1
Uasin Gishu	64	11	17.2	3	4.7
Meru	70	11	15.7	3	4.2
All other urban total**	**2216**	**272**	**12.3**	**157**	**7.1**

*   Includes all counties in Nairobi Metropolitan Area (Nairobi, Kiambu, Murang'a, Kajiado, Machakos)
** Urban residents from all counties except Mombasa and Nairobi Metro

These are patterns with clear parallels to the geographic distribution of the financial sector in colonial Kenya. Up to about 1950, bank branches in Kenya were predominantly located in Mombasa and Nairobi (Morris 2016:652; Engberg 1965:190; Upadhyaya and Johnson 2015:18–20; Bostock 1991), and virtually all in European-dominated 'White Highland' areas near the East African Railway running from Mombasa to Lake Victoria. As Morris notes, 'of the 20 areas of Kenya where the three major banks (Barclays, Standard and National and Grindlays) were represented in 1950, only two (Kisii and Bungoma) were not dominated by European enterprise' (2016:652). Subsequent expansion in the last decade of colonial rule did see the extension of branch infrastructures outside of these cities themselves, but banking assets have remained heavily concentrated near these two commercial centres.[21]

There has unquestionably been a boom in indebtedness among Kenyan urban residents. And this has certainly been facilitated by the amount of money poured into digital lending applications. Like with microfinance in Andhra Pradesh, though, the boom in digital lending in Kenya is the result of the confluence of sharp increases in the precarity of livelihoods with a spatially restricted boom in speculative capital available for lending. The close integration of mobile money and digital lending platforms with the existing formal banking sector in Kenya appears to also be a significant contributor to the rise of indebtedness in Kenya. Donovan and Park (2019) rightly link the rise of digital indebtedness in Kenya to the wider precarity of livelihoods in urban settings, noting the widespread 'zero-balance economy'. The concept of 'informal' work was initially popularised in relation to Kenya in the 1970s (see Bernards 2018b), and reliance on informal incomes has ballooned in the neoliberal era (see Budlender 2011). Livelihood insecurities have equally been exacerbated by the privatisation of key utilities and the rapid expansion of informal housing.

There is growing criticism in Kenya of some of the more general dynamics highlighted in the discussion of Big Data credit scores above, notably that they measure propensity rather than borrowers' income or assets: 'An inherent flaw in these models is that they are built on data reflecting a consumer's willingness to repay rather than their ability to repay. This is a crucial distinction representing the difference between a client that is willing to skip meals or borrow from other lenders to repay the original loan and a client that can afford the loan without experiencing such debt stress' (Kessler 2020). Indeed, one of the most important things which it turns out Big Data credit scoring *does* enable is a range of aggressive debt collection practices. There has been a boom in debt collection firms alongside the boom in digital credit, and the availability of information about borrowers' contacts and social networks has facilitated coercive collection tactics. One former debt collector interviewed by the *Financial Times*, for instance, explains: 'If I have a phone number that has borrowed [from] Branch, Tala and Opesa, the [debt agency's] system has three accounts linked to the same phone or ID number … Collection is challenging, so sometimes, because you really want the commission, you have to figure out a way to get a customer to pay' (quoted in Roussi 2020). Big Data credit scores are, in essence, mobilising the capacity to further squeeze borrowers' already strained and precarious incomes. They increasingly represent a kind of digital-ised hyper-exploitation.

There are several key dynamics intersecting the digital credit boom in Kenya, then. In the first instance, the relative depth of Kenya's pre-existing financial system and attendant infrastructures has clearly played a key role both in marking the country out as a site at which spatially fixing capital has been concentrated, and in directing a disproportionate share of credit towards urban spaces. The relatively extensive and intensive development of financial infrastructures in colonial Kenya is an impor-tant piece of background context. Second, the inability of Big Data credit scores to accurately assess 'everything that happens in between' has been attenuated, for the moment, by the capacity of digital lending systems to mobilise social pressures to repay. This is a notable instance of a pattern discussed elsewhere in this book – where poverty finance has attracted substantial interest from finance capital.

Navigating crises in microcredit: India

A number of other significant applications of psychometric credit scores are intimately linked to patterns of crisis and regulatory change in microfinance markets – including the partnership between EFL and microlender Janalakshmi Financial Services (JFS) in India. In Chapter 5 I made note of the wider shifts in the Indian microfinance sector after the RBI introduced a number of restrictions on microlending activity in the aftermath of the Andhra Pradesh crisis. Microlending shifted increasingly towards larger loans, urban residents, and loans to individ-uals rather than groups.

As Table 7.3 makes clear, JFS – which, unlike most Indian MFIs in the 2000s, was already targeting urban borrowers and aimed to offer a wider range of financial services on an individual basis – was well-positioned to capitalise on these shifts. It is worth noting here that JFS activities are explicitly oriented towards people engaged in informal activities, who make up the considerable majority of India's population (see Agarwala 2013). After the collapse of the rural microfinance sector, this popula-tion was explicitly targeted by the segments of financial capital that had rushed into Andhra Pradesh in the decade prior. The rapid expansion of JFS's loan portfolio was underwritten by several rounds of venture capital funding as well as by subsequent investments from a range of global institutional investors after 2013. JFS was subsequently given regulatory permission to operate as a bank rather than an MFI in early 2017. The role of EFL here was as part of a wider bundle of 'innovative' technologies deployed to manage credit risks and to simplify interactions with borrowers in these settings, with psychometric tests incorporated into a set of systems, notably including biometric identification and a tiered system of loan provision, in which borrowers who established reliable credit histories in group loans or with small sums were offered larger loans (EFL n.d.:2–3). This is a useful illustration of the point raised in the section above about the tendency of psychometrics to reinforce existing patterns of uneven development, due to the need to plug alternative forms of data into existing credit infrastructures. But, more importantly, the realisation of financial profits through this emergent infrastructure shows signs of being undercut by shifts in the patterns of informal economic activity through which interest and repayments needed to be realised.

Table 7.3 Janalakshmi Financial Services: Unsecured credit portfolio. Source: JFS annual reports (various years)

Year	Credit Outstanding (INR)	Overdue (INR)
2013	8 192 885 770	8 516 242
2014	18 636 385 622	69 571 173
2015	36 608 860 652	266 356 370
2016	90 660 844 896	180 137 266
2017	117 747 500 000	817 600 000

One of the most notable developments here was the Indian government's experiment with 'demonetisation' in late 2016 (see Chandrasekhar and Ghosh 2018). With less than four hours' notice, notes with values from 500 rupees to 1000 rupees were withdrawn from circulation. Early analyses showed considerable job losses in the aftermath of demonetisation, including a drop of the 'economically active' population by roughly 1.5 million (Vyas 2017). These impacts were disproportionately felt by informal economies, where cash transactions have continued to predominate and the adoption of digital payment systems is liable to be costly (requiring, for instance, equipment purchases to enable point of sale payments) and slow (see Chandrasekhar and Ghosh 2018). Given that urban informal economies remain the main targets for JFS lending, this 'liquidity crunch' had an outsized impact. In this context, at JFS measures of portfolio at risk – the proportion of credit accounts more than 30 days past due, a commonly used measurement of asset quality for MFIs – spiked from 0.95 percent in the 2015–16 fiscal year to 35.31 percent in 2016–17 (JFS 2017:40). The impact of the demonetisation push was perhaps primarily a short-term problem for lenders like JFS, but it does nonetheless show the fragility of the extension of financial accumulation through the abstraction of precarious livelihoods enabled (in part) by psychometrics.

Navigating the limits of financial accumulation

The point of these brief discussions is to highlight the fact that practical applications of psychometrics often appear to be driven fundamentally by efforts to cope with the contradictions of neoliberal development strategies and broader patterns of uneven development. In the case of JFS in India, we can point to the rapid expansion of the company's credit portfolio after 2010, into which EFL scoring was plugged after 2014. JFS was well positioned here to capitalise on a wider movement of financial capital towards individual loans, increasingly to urban borrowers, in the aftermath of the Andhra Pradesh crisis and regulatory reforms in India's microcredit system. As informal livelihoods have increasingly come under strain, partly as a result of demonetisation policies, however, there are signs of increasing distress. There are few signals of imminent collapse in Kenya, although there is growing pressure for regulatory restrictions on digital lending, and the ability of Big Data credit scores to mobilise social pressures to repay seems to play a key role in keeping creditors afloat.

In either case, narratives of financialisation, with their attendant implications of increasingly pervasive financial logics, fail to capture the complex and contradictory landscapes of accumulation into which psychometric credit scores have been rolled out. Fintech seems, from this perspective, less like a further step towards the all-encompassing financialisation of the global economy and more one means, amongst others, through which private companies and international regulatory agencies have sought (with limited success) to navigate the complex and contradictory landscape of precarious livelihoods wrapped up in processes of neoliberalisation. Equally, and critically, in both cases discussed here there are indications of rising distress, including defaults and deteriorating returns on credit in the case of JFS – an indication that abstracted predictions of default risk do not enable financial capital to escape the patterns of concrete activity needed to enable repayment. Seen from this angle, fintech looks like an *ad hoc* effort to convert irregular, precarious incomes into predictable, calculable asset streams in the context of shifting patterns of livelihoods and regulatory change. They point us towards a reading of the turn to fintech as a sign of the fragile and uneven nature of financial accumulation at the margins.

CONCLUSION

In this chapter, I've returned to the fintech hype with which I started this book. The chapter examined the growing turn to fintech as a solution to the challenges encountered in previous efforts to promote access to finance for the poorest. The rollout of fintech applications represents yet another iteration of the cycle of failure and adaptation in neoliberal development frameworks. Promoters of financial inclusion have increasingly engaged in efforts to develop markets at the level of tinkering with the fine-grained infrastructures needed to assess credit risk, administer payments, and the like. These efforts, importantly, share much of the logic of the anticipatory spatial fix identified in previous chapters, and have served to reinforce the tensions and patterns of uneven development described throughout this book. In short, for all the hype about the disruptive power of fintech, it appears to reproduce the pathologies and limits of poverty finance more generally.

It has been common to discuss the development of fintech applications for financial inclusion, much like the wider agenda of financial inclusion itself, in terms of processes of financialisation. In assimilating experiments with fintech into a wider narrative of financialisation, existing analyses have often missed some of the key drivers of such developments and some of the fundamental contradictions and limits therein. This suggests that some caution is probably in order around the ways in which the concept of financialisation is used in these debates. As Christophers (2015:194) has aptly noted, 'narratives of financialization tend implicitly to become one-sided, even teleological scripts of linear, uninterrupted, ineluctable development'. Slotting experiments with fintech into such narratives without exploring the wider complex of underlying relations through and into which such devices are necessarily rolled out can lead to critiques that fail to engage with important political dynamics of such processes.

Conclusion

The preceding chapters have sketched a series of efforts to promote wider access to formal financial services. Most of these have failed on their own terms; virtually all have failed to deliver substantial benefits; none have unambiguously delivered significant, large-scale reductions in poverty. This is a history replete with what Best has called, in a different context, 'quiet failures' – failures of policy interventions to produce expected results, continually 're-narrated ... as a kind of inevitable success' (2020:597).

We can usefully understand the recurrent failures of neoliberal development governance, in which poverty finance interventions have virtually always played a central role, as fraught attempts to confront the limits posed by colonial financial infrastructures and wider patterns of dispossession and uneven development, some of which I described in Chapter 1, to a project of marketisation and commodification. I showed in Chapter 2 how struggles to reform agricultural and housing finance in the 1970s and 1980s were central to the initial articulation of neoliberalism in global development. The turn to microfinance in the 1990s traced in Chapter 3 was, in part, a direct response to the failures of these programmes. It was part of a wider move to adjust and rehabilitate neoliberal development frameworks after the catastrophic impacts of structural adjustment, without breaching the limits imposed by semi-permanent conditions of austerity. The push to 'scale-up' microcredit and microinsurance schemes, in the context of these constraints, led increasingly to efforts to develop new infrastructures that might link microfinance to global circuits of capital accumulation in the 2000s, outlined in Chapter 4 here. In Chapter 5, I showed how this project largely failed, driving a broader rethink of the role of finance in development, encapsulated in the rise of the 'financial inclusion' agenda in the early 2010s. Here, too, the financial inclusion agenda has met with limited success, both on its own terms – in expanding access to finance – and more generally, in terms of reductions in poverty. In Chapters 6 and 7, I examined a series of responses to these failures, which have broadly taken on the form of increasingly close engagements, on ever-more fine-grained terms, with the construction of new financial infrastructures in insurance and wider financial markets. Poverty finance would seem, from the history outlined above, fundamentally incapable of overcoming the underlying patterns of uneven development towards which it is addressed.

In concluding here, I want to briefly do two things. The first is to trace developments in poverty finance in the context of the current pandemic and the associated global economic crisis. The second is to sketch some of the implications of the narrative traced across this book.

POVERTY FINANCE IN PANDEMIC TIMES

I've written much of this book in 2020 and 2021, in the midst of a global pandemic which has prompted the worst economic crisis in decades. Given the scope of disruption and change over the last year, it makes sense to give over part of this concluding chapter to a postscript about poverty finance in the context of the multifaceted COVID-19 crisis.

The early months of 2020 were very bad for many microfinance institutions (MFIs) and fintechs. There were numerous reports of fintech lenders in distress (Ruehll and Sender 2020; Findlay 2020; Ruehll and Findlay 2020). This had knock-on effects for other firms not directly exposed to credit risk. LenndoEFL, for instance, was bankrupt by August of 2020 (Goh 2020). Things were, and remain, even worse for borrowers. A survey in Pakistan found that 90 percent of borrowers expected to struggle to make payments, and MFIs expected to collect only 34 percent of payments due in April 2020 (Malik *et al.* 2020). In Cambodia, where the microcredit sector was already well into crisis territory before the pandemic, with an average microloan debt per borrower of US$3,804 (roughly double the country's GDP per capita), the situation is simply dire (see Brickell *et al.* 2020). Already heavily indebted borrowers now face the loss of incomes, and potentially of land, homes, and businesses if they are unable to repay.

There are two things worth underlining about the present crisis. First, the crisis has brought to light key problems with the basic modalities of most 'fintech' applications. As noted in Chapter 7, fintechs promise to extend access to credit to 'excluded' borrowers through a hyper-individualised approach to assessing credit risk. The claim is that by scraping mobile phone data or developing novel measures of personality, and developing algorithms to analyse that data, they can provide accurate measures of the creditworthiness of informal sector workers lacking conventional documentation like pay stubs, income tax receipts, property titles, or credit histories. This approach remains 'dangerously hermetic', in Langevin's (2019:810) terms, to the actual productive capacities and economic situation of borrowers. A mix of hype, over-accumulated capital, and occasional examples of profitable deployment has encouraged an influx of venture capital investment in fintech firms. It can work for lenders when times are good and income opportunities are available, though it remains unclear, at best, whether fintechs actually provide borrowers with opportunities to increase incomes that might not have existed otherwise. But the over-extension of credit on terms only loosely linked to borrowers' material capacity to repay is a bad system for anyone during a downturn. Previous national slowdowns have resulted in arrears and missed payments, much like we're seeing at the moment. I recapped the example of JFS in India in the previous chapter (cf. Bernards 2019a). Sporadic crises of over-indebtedness have also long been endemic in digital lending and microfinance – previous chapters traced notable crises in Bolivia, in Andhra Pradesh, and in Kenya. What's different right now isn't really the problem itself, but the global nature of the crisis.

Second, and more fundamentally, the current crisis throws into sharp relief how impoverished the conception of poverty reduction underlying financial inclusion really is (see Bernards 2021d). For all the grim brutality of the pandemic's impacts across much of the Global South, these developments mark continuations of longer-term processes. Responses to COVID-19 seem likely to exacerbate and entrench conditions of austerity. While the IMF has trumpeted its 'unconditional' rescue packages for developing countries, the fine print on these suggests that the IMF has simply shifted from *ex post* to *ex ante* conditionality. That is, rather than compelling policy reforms in exchange for loans, the fund is granting loans only to countries that have already put in place what the IMF considers 'very strong' policy frameworks. Analysis from Oxfam suggests that the vast majority of IMF loans made in 2020 (76 of 91) have required spending cuts (Martin 2020).

All of this suggests that the pandemic has at once rendered the situation for fintech and microcredit lenders and borrowers in the Global South extremely precarious, and that responses to it have exacerbated these conditions. Recent advocates of 'financial inclusion' have unquestionably pushed a more sophisticated set of arguments than the myths about bootstrap entrepreneurialism that accompanied the microcredit fad in the 1990s and 2000s. The emphasis more recently has been on financial services as tools for 'risk management', enabling the poor to be 'resilient' to shocks and hence able to take advantage of opportunities to increase incomes. Yet, if we weren't already aware, the pandemic is revealing or underlining a lot about how risk and vulnerability are distributed systemically in the global economy. We urgently need alternatives to asking individuals to develop their own tools to manage risks. Risks and vulnerabilities in the global political economy are both systemic and disproportionately borne at the margins. Addressing these will require systemic change. Yet responses to the pandemic, and indeed to the wider ecological crisis of contemporary capitalism looming in the background, seem primed at the moment to double down on these trends.

'Risk management' and 'resilience' are very much at the core of responses to the COVID-19 pandemic. The Managing Director of the IMF wrote in September of 2020: 'Perhaps first among the many lessons of 2020 is that the notion of so-called black swan events is not some remote worry. These purportedly once in a generation events are occurring with increasing frequency' (Georgieva and Selassie 2020). The chief lesson taken from the pandemic, here, is that policymaking needs to shift towards more pre-emptive, preparatory modes of dealing with 'shocks', which will come ever more frequently with accelerating climate change. But when we look at what measures might actually promote 'resilience' here, we see, among other things, the adoption of rainwater harvesting techniques in Chad, 'climate smart agriculture' by way of better mobile phone networks (and hence access to better weather information), new 'digital skills', and expanded access to electricity through 'small, off-grid, solar powered energy plants' financed through 'pay-as-you-go' models, and broadening access to finance (Georgieva and Selassie 2020). 'Financial inclusion' narratives are also receiving renewed emphasis in this context, with CGAP, the wider World Bank, and the IMF insisting that emergency assistance to the poorest in the midst of lockdown present a prime opportunity to expand digital payment systems (see Bernards 2020b; 2021d).

Responses from microlenders and promoters to pandemic distress have so far, unsurprisingly, indicated very little willingness to rethink their basic operating model. A number of major MIVs agreed joint guidelines for rescheduling payments from distressed MFIs. The heavy emphasis is on rescheduling rather than providing relief to MFIs (and by extension their borrowers) (BlueOrchard *et al.* 2020). CGAP explicitly warned in the early days of the pandemic against debt relief or renewed subsidies for distressed micro-borrowers, urging that efforts to grapple with the crisis work to maintain 'payment discipline' (Tarazi 2020). Promoters of financial inclusion and fintech are also doubling down on calls to expand mobile and digital payment systems. There are renewed calls to expand the use of mobile and digital payments to administer emergency income support (Rutkowski *et al.* 2020). The theory is that digital payments can minimise physical contact and so are preferable to physical cash during a pandemic, and could potentially facilitate more rapid distribution of emergency aid. The World Bank is currently even describing reducing taxes on mobile transactions as itself a 'social protection' measure (World Bank 2020b:69).

In short, as the grim inadequacy of the last decade's worth of neoliberal buzzwords – 'financial inclusion', 'risk management', 'resilience' and the like – is being revealed in vivid detail by the pandemic, the World Bank, the IMF and others are doubling down on them. They are also doubling down on the reproduction of the conditions of quasi-permanent austerity that have profoundly shaped their rollout. Attention to the longer history within which such efforts are embedded, and the particular colonial patterns of uneven development that they reproduce, thus seems particularly urgent. The resort to depoliticising solutions which download the cost of and responsibility for dealing with risks onto peripheral workers, reflected in direct responses to the pandemic and in efforts to articulate a post-pandemic agenda for global development, is shaped in no small part by enduring conditions of austerity. But the last year has made grimly clear that it will likely be increasingly difficult to substantively address pressing development challenges in this way. Individualised modes of 'resilience' are wholly inadequate in the face of the widespread structural patterns of dispossession underlined by the pandemic.

BEYOND POVERTY FINANCE

What might an alternative development agenda look like? The history presented in the previous chapters isn't exactly a 'how-to' guide. Any effort to build an alternative social and economic order, it's fair to say, will come about largely because of the struggles of working class and peasant movements, which fall somewhat outside the scope of this book (see Ajl 2018; Bailey 2019; Pradella and Marois 2015; Selwyn 2017). But a few points about what a genuine effort to confront the realities of poverty and dispossession might require are nonetheless in order.

It's worth noting that poverty finance has persistently, and usually explicitly, been a way of avoiding public provision or redistribution. This is certainly true of contemporary experiments with financial inclusion, as critics have repeatedly pointed out (e.g. Bateman 2010; Mader 2018; Soederberg 2014). But this is also a dynamic cutting across all of the interventions discussed in this book. Even when, as was the case in the colonial period, credit and 'thrift' interventions have been directed by the state and mobilised state resources in support of poverty finance, the aim has always been to shift costs and responsibilities onto targeted populations. 'Self-help' housing provision, microinsurance, and index insurance were all likewise explicit alternatives to socialised provision of housing, healthcare, and mitigation against climate risks. The language of limited public resources has consistently been mobilised to justify turning to the market or to self-financing by the poor. But this has always been a constructed scarcity born of an unwillingness to confront colonial patterns of uneven development and overaccumulation. As Marx famously notes, 'accumulation of wealth at one pole simultaneously acts as the accumulation of misery, the torment of labour, slavery, ignorance, brutalization and moral degradation at the other side of the pole' (Marx 1990:799). To talk about limited public resources as an ahistorical fact is to reify existing patterns of accumulation. Trying to reduce poverty without confronting these dynamics is self-defeating.

This tendency to naturalise and evade confrontation with existing patterns of accumulation and power is unfortunately epitomised in the approaches to development as anticipatory spatial fix traced in the latter chapters here. The anticipatory spatial fix seeks to mobilise finance capital by creating the infrastructural conditions for its profitable deployment. The weight of evidence considered here suggests that poverty finance interventions have persistently shifted the costs of coping with poverty and precarious livelihoods onto precisely the people with, by definition, the least resources with which to meet these costs. The hope of mobilising private finance profitably in these contexts has often been a vain one as well. Sometimes these interventions have been directly harmful; sometimes they've simply done very little to change things. But they've virtually always been an explicit alternative to substantial public provision of food and shelter, or other redistributive measures.

Relatedly, the long history of failures traced in this book suggests that access to finance itself will do little to address poverty or climate vulnerability. I noted in the introduction that the basic reason why the poorest are held to need access to finance – namely, low and unpredictable incomes – is precisely the same reason why they are generally considered bad credit risks. It's equally a reason why access to credit or savings won't alter relations of poverty. Having a bank account doesn't make up for not having enough money to buy food or pay rent in the first place. Having access to credit often means being subjected to intensified exploitation in the future (see Soederberg 2014; Bernards 2019c). Having a low income makes buying insurance to hedge against climate uncertainty vastly more difficult. As noted in Chapter 6, larger farmers who can afford index insurance have better means of protecting against risks, while those who might benefit would struggle to afford it (see Binswanger-Mkhize 2012). Poverty finance solutions to poverty, precarity, and climate vulnerability have in common a tendency to download costs and risks of ameliorating those circumstances onto the people least able to afford them, and often least culpable for the creation of those circumstances in the first place.

As a result, poverty finance can deepen and further entrench precarity and dispossession. There is notable tendency in more explicitly 'marketised' approaches to poverty finance towards spatially and temporally delimited crises of over-indebtedness driven by a rush of finance capital into particular infrastructures (as in Andhra Pradesh, or more recently, Cambodia and Kenya). But more often it's simply difficult or impossible to mobilise financial capital to provide services to the poorest, for the same basic reason that they are held to need expanded access to formal credit – that is, the basic condition of precarious livelihoods in the first place. These conditions themselves, as well as the material infrastructures of global finance, which remain deeply inflected by colonial histories, militate against the deployment of finance capital. In many of the interventions discussed in this book, this has manifested itself as a tension between 'inclusive' rhetorics and practices of stratification. Poverty finance interventions increasingly take the form of attempts to build infrastructures to allow finance capital to more accurately differentiate good from bad credit risks.

Indeed, this speaks to a wider problem facing the growing emphasis on mobilising private finance for development (on which see Gabor 2021; Tan 2021; Mawdsley 2018). Finance, as noted in the introduction, is risk-averse and profit-oriented. The history of poverty finance shows especially clearly that trying to mobilise private finance for development purposes means development where, when, how, and for whom it is relatively low risk and relatively profitable. It also shows the fallacy of hoping to foster development by preparing the ground for finance capital. Doing so has generally meant the clustering of investments in particular places where the conditions for profitability are greatest and where infrastructures for the deployment and circulation of finance capital are already in place. This has led to a pattern of short-lived cycles of boom and bust in places, amidst general disinterest in most places and populations in the Global South. As techniques mirroring, for instance, the use of guarantee funds, investment vehicles, securitisation, or constructing new measures of creditworthiness, are increasingly central to climate mitigation and broader developmental efforts, the results of these dynamics in poverty finance are worth bearing in mind. An expanded role for private finance in development is likely to deepen and exacerbate dynamics of uneven development.

In short, the mobilisation of private finance to bring about development is a neoliberal fantasy, and one which remains dangerously oblivious to the historical conditions in which efforts to produce new financial markets take place. Confronting poverty means much more directly democratising control over the global economy. It means, at a minimum, social provision of basic needs – housing, food, water, care – and actively seeking reparative justice for the continued damage of colonial dispossession and extractive development across much of the colonised world. Access to finance in and of itself, without these conditions, will likely continue to do little at best and to exacerbate relations of dispossession at worst. It is beyond the scope of this book to explain how these fundamental transformations in the global political economy might be brought about. I hope, though, that the history traced here has helped to underline why such changes are *necessary*.

Notes

1. For similar perspectives focused on financial markets, see Bernards (2019a; 2021a), Christophers (2014), and more generally Castree (2002), Kirsch and Mitchell (2004).
2. S. Himsworth to W. G. Hulland, 28 November 1953, in British National Archives (BNA) CO 1025/8.
3. P. Selwyn to W. G. Hulland, 4/1/1954, in BNA CO 1025/8.
4. Minute, Burridge to Newsom, 25 February 1951, in BNA CO 533/561/10.
5. See Thurston (1987) and Shipton (1992) on the history of the Swynnerton Plan and its significance.
6. Press Release no. 633/53 from the Information Services Dept. Accra, 9 May 1953, p. 1, in BNA CO 554/692, emphasis in original.
7. Ibid, p. 2.
8. See Bernards (2019c) for a more detailed discussion.
9. Critically, both the disproportionate riskiness of agricultural incomes and the urban focus of bank branch infrastructures are naturalised in McKinnon's argument. In reality, as argued in the previous chapter, these were distinct products of colonial modes of development.
10. On agricultural 'modernisation', see Bernstein (1990); Woodhouse (2012).
11. The following is outlined in further detail in Bernards (2021c).
12. My calculations are based on research reported in Bernards (2021c).
13. Clarke (2019) makes a similar argument about the rise of digitally-enabled peer-to-peer lending in recent years.
14. We might also note that improvements to water and sanitation that don't pay sufficient attention to localised patterns of property relations, exploitation, and accumulation can have downsides for some intended beneficiaries. Many people in informal settlements are renters, and upgrades to infrastructure can displace poorer tenants if they enable landlords to command higher rents than current tenants can afford (see Desai and Loftus 2012).
15. For more detailed explanations of the failures of microinsurance markets, see Binswanger-Mkhize 2012; da Costa 2013; Isakson 2015; Johnson 2013; Taylor 2016; Bernards 2018a; 2019c.
16. Appendix to Kathleen Owen letter to J. L. Keith, esq., 23 October 1947, p. 2; in BNA CO 554/160/4.
17. See Christophers (2015) for a similar argument about the concept of 'financialisation' more broadly.
18. See, e.g., Morawczynski (2009), Maurer (2012), and Dafe (2020) for more detailed histories.
19. Data from Kenya Central Bank, available at www.centralbank.go.ke/national-payments-system/mobile-payments/.

20. Data from World Bank Findex Survey, available at https://databank.world-bank.org/reports.aspx?source=global-financial-inclusion.
21. This argument is developed at further length in Bernards (2022).

Bibliography

Aagard, P. (2011) 'The global institutionalization of microcredit', *Regulation and Governance* 5(4):465–79.

Abrams, J. (2012) *Global microfinance ratings comparability*, Washington: Multilateral Investment Fund.

Adams, D. W. (1971) 'Agricultural credit in Latin America: A critical review of existing external funding policy', *American Journal of Agricultural Economics* 53(2):163–72.

AFI (2010) *Innovative Financial Inclusion: Principles and Report on Innovative Financial Inclusion from the Access through Innovation Sub-Group of the G20 Financial Inclusion Experts Group*. Seoul: G20.

—— (2011) *A Quick Guide to the Maya Declaration on Financial Inclusion*, available www.afi-global.org/sites/default/files/publications/afi_maya_quick_guide_withoutannex_i_and_ii.pdf.

—— (2018a) *National financial inclusion strategies: Current state of practice*, Kuala Lampur: Alliance for Financial Inclusion.

—— (2018b) *Sochi Accord: Fintech for Financial Inclusion*, available: www.afi-global.org/sites/default/files/publications/2018-09/Sochi_FS18_AW_digital.pdf.

Agarwala, R. (2013) *Informal Labour, Formal Politics, and Dignified Discontent in India*, Cambridge: Cambridge University Press.

Aitken, R. (2013) 'The Financialization of Microcredit', *Development and Change* 44(3):473–99.

—— (2015) *Fringe Finance: Crossing and Contesting the Boundaries of Global Capital*, London: Routledge.

—— (2017) '"All Data is Credit Data": Constituting the Unbanked', *Competition & Change*, 21(4):274–300.

Ajl, M. (2018) 'Delinking, food sovereignty, and populist agronomy: notes on an intellectual history of the peasant path in the global south', *Review of African Political Economy* 45(155):64–84.

Alami, I. (2018) 'On the terrorism of money and national policy-making in emerging economies', *Geoforum* 96:21–31.

Albers, T. N. H., M. Jerven, and M. Suesse (2020) 'The fiscal state in Africa: Evidence from a century of growth', *African Economic History Network Working Paper no. 55*.

Allianz (2010) *Learning to Insure the Poor: Microinsurance Report, Allianz Group*, Munich: Allianz SE.

—— (2017) *Emerging Consumers (Formerly Microinsurance) Full-Year Report 2016*, Munich: Allianz SE.

Amin, S. (1976) *Unequal Development: An Essay on the Social Formations of Peripheral Capitalism*, Hassocks: Harvester Press.

Angeli Aguiton, S. (2021) 'A market infrastructure for environmental intangibles: the materiality and challenges of index insurance for agriculture in Senegal', *Journal of Cultural Economy* 14(5):580–95.

Aron, J. (2017) '"Leapfrogging": a survey of the nature and uses of mobile money', *Centre for the Study of African Economies Working Paper WPS/2017-02*, Oxford: CSAE.

Arráiz, I., M. Bruhn, and R. Stucchi (2015) 'Psychometrics as a Tool to Improve Screening and Access to Credit', *World Bank Policy Research Working Paper 7506*.

Atim, C. (1998) *The Contribution of Mutual Health Organizations to Financing, Delivery, and Access to Health Care: Synthesis of Research in Nine West and Central African Countries*, Geneva: ILO.

Austen, R. (1987) *African Economic History*, London: James Currey.

Bähre, E. (2007) *Money and Violence: Financial Self-Help Groups in a South African Township*. Leiden: Brill.

—— (2011) 'Liberation and Redistribution: Social Grants, Commercial Insurance, and Religious Riches in South Africa', *Comparative Studies in Society and History* 53(2):371–92.

Bailey, D. (2019) 'Extra-capitalist impulses in the midst of crisis: perspectives and positions outside of capitalism', *Globalizations* 19(4):371–85.

Bair, J. (2009) 'Taking aim at the New International Economic Order', in P. Mirowski and D. Plehwe (eds.), *The road from Mont Pèlerin: The making of the neoliberal thought collective*, Cambridge: Harvard University Press, 348–85.

Bajaj, V. (2010) 'Microlender, first in India to go public, trades higher', *New York Times*, 16 August, available: www.nytimes.com/2010/08/17/business/global/17micro.html.

Balea, J. (2015) 'Lenndo stops lending, now helps clients determine customer creditworthiness', *Tech in Asia*, 26 January, available: www.techinasia.com/lenddo-customer-trustworthiness.

Bamberger, M. (1983) 'The role of self-help housing in low-cost shelter programmes for the Third World', *The Built Environment* 8(2):95–107.

Banaji, J. (2016) 'Merchant Capitalism, Peasant Households and Industrial Accumulation: Integration of a Model', *Journal of Agrarian Change* 16(3):410–31.

Bannerjee, A., E. Duflo, R. Glennerster, and C. Kinnan (2015) 'The miracle of microfinance? Evidence from a randomized evaluation', *American Economic Journal: Applied Economics* 7(1):22–53.

Barboni, G. (2015) 'The geography of financial services providers in Kenya', in A. Heyer and M. King (eds.), *Kenya's Financial Transformation in the 21st Century*, Nairobi: FSD Kenya, 63–106.

Barclays DCO (1937) *A banking centenary: A history of Barclays Bank (Dominion, Colonial, and Overseas)*, Plymouth: W. Brendan and Sons.

Bassett, C. (2018) 'Africa's next debt crisis: regulatory dilemmas and radical insights', *Review of African Political Economy* 44(154):523–40.

Basu, S. (2005) 'Securitization and the challenges faced in microfinance', *Centre for Micro Finance Research Working Paper Series*, Chennai: Institute for Financial Management and Research.

Bateman, M. (2010) *Why Doesn't Microfinance Work? The Destructive Rise of Local Neoliberalism*, London: Zed Books.

—— (2012) 'Let's not kid ourselves that financial inclusion will help the poor', *The Guardian*, 8 May, available: www.theguardian.com/global-development/poverty-matters/2012/may/08/financial-inclusion-poor-microfinance.

—— (2017) 'The political economy of microfinance', in M. Bateman and K. Maclean (eds.), *Seduced and betrayed: Exposing the contemporary microfinance phenomenon*, Albuquerque: University of New Mexico Press, 17–31.

—— (2020) 'Moving from "developmental" to "anti-developmental" local financial models in East Asia: Abandoning a winning formula', *Geoforum*, DOI: 10.1016/j.geoforum.2020.11.009.

Bateman, M., M. Duvendack, and N. Loubere (2019) 'Is fintech the new panacea for poverty alleviation and development? Contesting Suri and Jack's M-Pesa findings published in *Science*', *Review of African Political Economy* 46(161):480–95.

Baucom, I. (2005) *Specters of the Atlantic: Finance Capital, Slavery, and the Philosophy of History*, Durham: Duke University Press.

Bauer, P. T. (1971) *Dissent on Development: Studies and Debates in Development Economics*, London: Weidenfield & Nicholson.

—— (1976) *Western Guilt and Third World Poverty*, Washington, DC: Georgetown University, Ethics and Public Policy Center.

Baum, J. R. and E. A. Locke (2004) 'The Relationship of Entrepreneurial Traits, Skill, and Motivation to Subsequent Venture Growth', *Journal of Applied Psychology* 89(4):587–98.

Beckman, B. (1976) *Organising the Farmers: Cocoa Politics and National Development in Ghana*, Uppsala: Scandinavian Institute of African Studies.

Bédécarrats, F., I. Guérin, and F. Roubaud (2019) 'All that glitters is not gold: The political economy of randomized evaluations in development', *Development and Change* 50(3):735–62.

Beer, D. (2017) 'The social power of algorithms', *Information, Communication, and Society* 20(1):1–13.

Bennett, D. (2009) 'Small change: Billions of dollars and a Nobel Prize later, it looks like microfinance doesn't do much to fight poverty', *Boston Globe*, 20 September, available: http://archive.boston.com/bostonglobe/ideas/articles/2009/09/20/small_change_does_microlending_actually_fight_poverty/.

Berman, B. J. and J. M. Lonsdale (1981) 'Crises of accumulation, coercion, and the colonial state: The development of the labour control system in Kenya, 1919–1929', *Canadian Journal of African Studies* 14(1):55–81.

Bernardin, H. J. and Cooke, D. K. (1993) 'Validity of an Honesty Test in Predicting Theft among Convenience Store Employees', *Academy of Management Journal* 36(5):1097–108.

Bernards, N. (2016) 'The International Labour Organization and the ambivalent politics of financial inclusion in Francophone West Africa', *New Political Economy* 21(6):606–21.

—— (2018a) 'The Truncated Commercialization of Microinsurance and the Limits of Neoliberalism', *Development and Change* 49(6):1447–70.

—— (2018b) *The Global Governance of Precarity: Primitive Accumulation and the Politics of Irregular Work*, London: Routledge.

—— (2019a) 'The poverty of fintech? Psychometrics, credit infrastructures, and the limits of financialization', *Review of International Political Economy* 26(5):815–38.

—— (2019b) 'Tracing mutations in neoliberal development governance: "Fintech", failure, and the limits of marketization', *Environment and Planning A: Economy and Space* 51(7):1442–59.

—— (2019c) '"Latent" surplus populations and colonial histories of drought, groundnuts, and finance in Senegal', *Geoforum*, DOI: 10.1016/j.geoforum.2019.10.007.

—— (2020a) 'Centring labour in financialization', *Globalizations* 17(4):714–29.

—— (2020b) 'The Covid-19 crisis should force a rethink of "financial inclusion" in Global Development', *Global Policy Blog*, available: www.globalpolicyjournal.com/blog/06/07/2020/covid-19-crisis-should-force-rethink-financial-inclusion-global-development.

—— (2021a) 'Child Labour, Cobalt, and the London Metal Exchange: Fetishes, Fixing, and the Limits of Financialization', *Economy and Society*, DOI: 10.1080/03085147.2021.1899659.

—— (2021b) 'Poverty finance and the durable contradictions of colonial capitalism: Placing "financial inclusion" in the long run in Ghana', *Geoforum* 123: 89–98.

—— (2021c) 'The World Bank, agricultural credit, and the rise of neoliberalism in global development', *New Political Economy*, DOI: 10.1080/13563467.2021.1926955.

—— (2021d) 'COVID-19 and the international political economy of risk and resilience', *Global Perspectives* 2(1):23665.

—— (2022) 'Colonial financial infrastructures and Kenya's uneven fintech boom', *Antipode*, DOI: 10.1111/anti.12810.

Bernards, N. and M. Campbell-Verduyn (2019), 'Understanding technological change in global finance through infrastructures', *Review of International Political Economy* 26(5):773–89.

Bernards, N. and S. Soederberg (2020) 'Relative Surplus Populations and the Crises of Contemporary Capitalism: Reviving, Revisiting, Recasting' *Geoforum*, DOI: 10.1016/j.geoforum.2020.12.009.

Berndt, C. (2015) 'Behavioural economics, experimentalism, and the marketization of development', *Economy and Society* 44(4):567–91.

Bernstein, H. (1977) 'Notes on Capital and Peasantry', *Review of African Political Economy* 4(10):60–73.

—— (1979) 'African peasantries: a theoretical framework', *Journal of Peasant Studies* 6(4):421–43.

—— (1990) 'Agricultural "modernisation" and the era of structural adjustment: Observations on sub-Saharan Africa', *Journal of Peasant Studies* 18(1):3–35.

—— (2010) *Class Dynamics of Agrarian Change*, Halifax: Fernwood Press.

Best, J. (2013) 'Redefining Risk as Poverty and Vulnerability: Shifting Strategies of Liberal Economic Governance', *Third World Quarterly* 34(1):109–29.

—— (2014) *Governing Failure: Provisional Expertise and the Transformation of Development Finance*, Cambridge: Cambridge University Press.

—— (2016) 'When crises are failures: contested metrics in international finance and development', *International Political Sociology* 10(1):39–55.

—— (2020) 'The quiet failures of early neoliberalism: from rational expectations to Keynesianism in reverse', *Review of International Studies* 46(5):594–612.

Bester, H., D. Chamberlain, R. Hawthorne, S. Malherbe, and R. Walker (2004) *Making Insurance Markets Work for the Poor in South Africa: Scoping Study*, Johannesburg: Genesis Analytics.

Bester, H., D. Chamberlain, R. Short, and R. Walker (2005) *A Regulatory Review of Formal and Informal Funeral Insurance Markets in South Africa*, Johannesburg: Genesis Analytics.

Bhagat, A. and L. Roderick (2020) 'Banking on refugees: racialized expropriation in the fintech era', *Environment and Planning A: Economy and Space* 52(8):1498–515.

Bigger, P. and S. Webber (2021) 'Green structural adjustment in the World Bank's Resilient City', *Annals of the American Association of Geographers* 111(1):36–51.

Binswanger-Mkhize, H. P. (2012) 'Is there too much hype about index-based agricultural insurance?', *Journal of Development Studies* 48(2):187–200.

Black, E., H. Greatrex, M. Young, and R. Maidment (2018) 'Incorporating satellite data into weather index insurance', *Bulletin of the American Meteorological Society* 97(10):ES203–ES206.

Blaisdell, T. C., E. K. Bauer, H. E. Erdman, I. F. Davis (1953) *Farm credit in underdeveloped areas: A summary report of the International Conference on Agricultural and Cooperative Credit*, Berkeley: University of California, Foreign Operations Administration and Department of State.

BlueOrchard, MicroVest, Developing World Markets, ResponsAbility, OikoCredit, Symbiotics, Triodos Investment Management, Incofin Investment Management and Triple Jump (2020) *Coordination among MIVs in response to Covid 19*, available: www.oikocredit.org.uk/k/n6727/news/view/321524/88434/oikocredit-and-other-impact-investors-agree-coronavirus-coordination-principles.html.

Bond, P. (1998) *Uneven Zimbabwe: A Study of Finance, Development, and Underdevelopment*, Trenton: Africa World Press.

—— (2004) 'Bankrupt Africa: Imperialism, sub-imperialism, and the politics of finance', *Historical Materialism* 12(4):145–77.

—— (2013) 'Debt, Uneven Development and Capitalist Crisis in South Africa: From Moody's Macroeconomic Monitoring to Marikana Microfinance Mashonisas', *Third World Quarterly* 34(4):569–92.

Bonizzi, B., C. Laskaridis, and J. Griffiths (2020) *Private lending and debt risks of low-income developing countries*, London: Overseas Development Institute.

Boone, C. (1992) *Merchant Capital and the Roots of State Power in Senegal, 1930–1985*, Cambridge: Cambridge University Press.

Bostock, F. (1991) 'The British overseas banks and development finance in Africa after 1945', *Business History* 33(3):157–76.

Botero, F., C. Churchill, M. J. McCord and Z. Qureshi (2006) 'The future of microinsurance', in C. Churchill (ed.), *Protecting the poor: a microinsurance compendium*, Geneva: ILO, 583–603.

Boudillon, A. (1911) *La Question Foncière et l'Organisation du Livre Foncier en Afrique Occidentale Française*, Paris: Librairie Maritime et Coloniale.

Bowker, G. C. and S. L. Star (1996) 'How things (actor-net) work: Classification, magic, and the ubiquity of standards', *Philosophia* 25(3–4):195–220.

Brading, D. A. and H. E. Cross (1972) 'Colonial silver mining: Mexico and Peru', *The Hispanic American Historical Review* 52(4):545–79.

Breman, J. and M. van der Linden (2014) 'Informalizing the Economy: The Return of the Social Question at a Global Level', *Development and Change* 45(5):920–40.

Brenner, N., J. Peck, and N. Theodore (2010a) 'Variegated Neoliberalism: Geographies, Modalities, Pathways', *Global Networks* 10(2):182–222.

—— (2010b) 'After Neoliberalization?', *Globalizations* 7(3):327–45.

Bresnyan, E. (2004) 'The Consultative Group to Assist the Poor', *Addressing Challenges of Globalization: An independent evaluation of the World Bank's approach to global programmes*, Washington: World Bank Operations Evaluation Department.

Brickell, K., F. Picchioni, N. Natarajan, V. Guermond, L. Parsons, G. Zanello, and M. Bateman (2020) 'Compounding crises of social reproduction: Microfinance, over-indebtedness and the COVID-19 pandemic', *World Development* 136:105087.

Brown, E. and D. Piroska (2021) 'Governing fintech and fintech as governance: The regulatory sandbox, riskwashing, and disruptive social classification', *New Political Economy*, DOI: 10.1080/13563467.2021.1910645.

Brown, M. E., D. E. Osgood, and M. A. Carriquiry (2011) 'Science-based insurance', *Nature Geoscience* 4:213–14.

Bryan, D. and M. Rafferty (2006) *Capitalism With Derivatives: A Political Economy of Financial Derivatives, Capital and Class*, New York: Palgrave Macmillan.

—— (2010) 'Deriving Capital's (and Labour's) Future', in L. Panitch, G. Albo, and V. Chibber (eds.), *Socialist Register 2011: The Crisis This Time* 47:196–223.

Budlender, D. (2011) 'Statistics on informal employment: Kenya', *WIEGO Statistical Brief no. 5*, Manchester, WIEGO.

Buyske, G. (2014) *Microfinance ratings market assessment*, Washington: Multilateral Investment Fund.

Byström, H. N. E. (2008) 'The microfinance collateralized debt obligation: A modern Robin Hood?', *World Development* 36(11):2109–26.

Cahill, D. (2020) 'Market analysis beyond market fetishism', *Environment and Planning A: Economy and Space* 52(1):27–45.

Cain, P. (1985) 'J. A. Hobson, financial capitalism and imperialism in Late Victorian and Edwardian England', *Journal of Imperial and Commonwealth History* 13(3):1–27.

Cain, P. and A. G. Hopkins (2016) *British Imperialism, 1688–2015*, 3rd edition, London: Routledge.

Cammack, P. (2004) 'What the World Bank Means by Poverty Reduction and Why it Matters', *New Political Economy* 9(2):189–211.

Campbell-Verduyn, M., M. Goguen, and T. Porter (2017) 'Big Data and algorithmic governance: The case of financial practices', *New Political Economy* 22(2):219–36.

—— (2019) 'Finding fault lines in long chains of financial information', *Review of International Political Economy* 26(5):911–37.

Capon, N. (1982) 'Credit Scoring Systems: A Critical Analysis', *Journal of Marketing* 46(2):82–91.

Capps, G. (2018) 'Custom and exploitation: rethinking the origins of the modern African chieftancy in the political economy of colonialism', *Journal of Peasant Studies* 45(5–6):969–93.

Castree, N. (2002) 'False Antitheses? Marxism, Nature, and Actor-Networks', *Antipode* 34(1):111–46.

CFAO (1900) *Rapport adressé à M. E. Cotelle, consellier d'état*, president de la Comission des Concessions Coloniales, Marseille: Imprimerie Marsellaise.

CGAP (1996) 'Regulation and supervision of micro-finance institutions: Stabilizing a new financial market', *CGAP Focus Note no. 4*, Washington: World Bank Group.

—— (1997) 'The challenge of growth for micro-finance institutions: the BancoSol experience', *CGAP Focus Note no. 6*, Washington: World Bank Group.

—— (1998a) 'The Consultative Group to Assist the Poorest: A microfinance program', *CGAP Focus Note no. 1*, Washington: World Bank Group.

—— (1998b) 'Commercial banks in microfinance: New actors in the microfinance world', *CGAP Focus Note no. 12*, Washington: World Bank Group.

—— (1999) *CGAP Annual Report, July 1998–June 1999*, Washington: World Bank Group.

—— (2000) 'The rush to regulate: Legal frameworks for microfinance', *CGAP Occasional Paper no. 4*, Washington: World Bank Group.

—— (2007) 'Microfinance investment vehicles', *CGAP Brief*, Washington: World Bank Group.

—— (2010) 'Andhra Pradesh 2010: Global Implications of the Crisis in Indian Microfinance', *CGAP Focus Note no. 67*, Washington: World Bank Group.

—— (2011) 'Trends in cross-border funding', *CGAP Brief*, Washington: World Bank Group.

Chamberlain, D., A. Camargo, and W. Coetze (2017) *Funding the Frontier: The Link Between Inclusive Insurance Market, Growth, and Poverty Reduction in Africa*. Cape Town: CENFRI and FinMark Trust.

Chandrasekhar, C. P. and J. Ghosh (2018) 'The Financialization of Finance? Demonetization and the Dubious Push to Cashlessness in India', *Development and Change* 49(2):420–36.

Chemonics International (2000) *USAID/Mexico microenterprise strategy*, Washington: USAID.

Chetty, K., J. Josie, B. Siswana, E. Mashotala, K. Kariuki, C. Johnson, D. Saunders, H. Smit, S. Ben, Z. Wang, E. Brient, W. Li, and M. Luo (2019) 'Review of fintech strategies for financial inclusion in Sub-Saharan Africa', *Working Paper, T-20 Japan*, available: https://t20japan.org/wp-content/uploads/2019/03/t20-japan-tf2-10-fintech-strategies-financial-inclusion-sub-saharan-africa.pdf.

Christen, R. P., T. Lyman, and R. Rosenberg (2003) *Microfinance consensus guidelines: Guiding principles on regulation and supervision of microfinance*, Washington: CGAP.

Christophers, B. (2014) 'From Marx to Market and Back Again: Performing the Economy', *Geoforum* 57:12–20.

—— (2015) 'The Limits to Financialization', *Dialogues in Human Geography*, 5(2):183–200.

—— (2016) 'Risking value theory in the political economy of finance and nature', *Progress in Human Geography* 42(3):330–49.

Ciavarella, M. A., A. K. Buchholtz, C. M. Riordan, R. D. Gatewood, and G. S. Stokes (2004) 'The Big Five and Venture Survival: Is There a Linkage?', *Journal of Business Venturing* 19(4):465–83.

Clapp, J. and S. R. Isakson (2018) *Speculative Harvests: Financialization, Food, and Agriculture*, Halifax: Fernwood Press.

Clarke, C. (2019) 'Platform lending and the politics of financial infrastructures', *Review of International Political Economy* 26(5):863–85.

Clarke, D. J. (2011). 'A Theory of Rational Demand for Index Insurance', *Oxford University Department of Economics Discussion Paper Series, no. 572*.

Clarke, D. J. and D. Grenham (2013) 'Microinsurance and Natural Disasters: Challenges and Options', *Environmental Science and Policy* 27 (supplement): s89–s98.

Clarke, D. J., O. Mahul, K. N. Rao, and N. Verma (2012) 'Weather Based Crop Insurance in India', *World Bank Policy Research Paper 5985*, Washington: World Bank.

Cole, S. (2015) 'Overcoming Barriers to Microinsurance Adoption: Evidence from the Field', *Geneva Papers on Risk and Insurance* 40(4):720–40.

Collier, P. and D. Lal (1980) 'Poverty and growth in Kenya', *World Bank Staff Working Paper no. 389*, Washington: World Bank Group.

Cooper, F. (1996) *Decolonization and African Society: The Labor Question in French and British Africa*, Cambridge: Cambridge University Press.

—— (2011) 'Reconstructing Empire in British and French Africa', *Past & Present* 210 (supp. 6): 196–210.

—— (2014) *Africa in the World: Capitalism, Empire, Nation-State*, Cambridge: Harvard University Press.

Copley, J. and A. Moraitis (2021) 'Beyond the mutual constitution of states and markets: On the governance of alienation', *New Political Economy* 26(3):490–508.

Coquéry-Vidrovitch, C. (1975) 'L'Impact des Interets: SCOA at CFAO dans l'Ouest Africain, 1910–1965', *Journal of African History* 16(4):595–621.

—— (1977) 'Mutation de l'Impérialisme Français dans les Années 30', *African Economic History* 2(4):103–52.

Cowen, D. (2020) 'Following the infrastructures of empire: notes on cities, settler colonialism, and method' *Urban Geography* 41(4):469–86.

CPK (1950) *Report of the Committee on Agricultural Credit for Africans*, Nairobi: Government Printer.

CPK (1954) *A plan to intensify the development of African agriculture in Kenya*, Nairobi: Government Printer.

Cuevas, C. V. (1996) 'Enabling environment and microfinance institutions: lessons from Latin America', *Journal of International Development* 8(2):195–209.

Cull, R., A. Demirgüç-Kunt, and J. Morduch (2009) 'Microfinance Tradeoffs: Regulation, Competition, and Financing', *World Bank Policy Research Working Paper 5086*, Washington: World Bank Group.

—— (2018) 'The microfinance business model: Enduring subsidy and modest profit', *World Bank Economic Review* 32(2):221–44.

Da Costa, D. (2013) 'The "Rule of Experts" in Making a Dynamic Micro-insurance Industry in India', *The Journal of Peasant Studies* 40(5):845–65.

Dafe, F. (2020) 'Ambiguity in international finance and the spread of financial norms: the localization of financial inclusion in Nigeria and Kenya', *Review of International Political Economy* 27(3):500–24.

Dalgic, U. K. (2007) 'International expert organizations and policy adoption: The World Bank and microcredit in the 1990s', *Cultural Dynamics* 19(1):5–38.

Darling, M. L. (1928) *The Punjab peasant in prosperity and debt*, 2nd ed., London: Oxford University Press.

Davis, L. and R. A. Huttenback (1985) 'The export of British finance, 1865–1914', *Journal of Imperial and Commonwealth History* 13(3):28–76.

Davis, M. (2006) *Planet of Slums*, London: Verso.

De Cnudde, S., J. Moeyersoms, M. Stankova, E. Tobback, V. Javaly, and D. Martens (2019) 'What does your Facebook profile reveal about your creditworthiness? Using alternative data for microfinance', *Journal of the Operational Research Society* 70(3):353–63.

De Goede, M. (2021) 'Finance/security infrastructures', *Review of International Political Economy* 28(2):351–68.

De Mel, S., D. McKenzie, and C. Woodruff (2008) 'Returns to Capital in Micro-enterprises: Results from a Field Experiment', *Quarterly Journal of Economics* 123(4):1329–72.

Demirguc-Kunt, A. and L. Klapper (2012) 'Measuring Financial Inclusion: The Global Findex Database', *World Bank Policy Research Working Paper 6025*, Washington: World Bank Group.

Demirguc-Kunt, A., L. Klapper, D. Singer, and P. Van Oudheusen (2015) 'The Global Findex Database 2014: Measuring Financial Inclusion around the World', *World Bank Policy Research Working Paper 7255*, Washington: World Bank Group.

Demirguc-Kunt, A., L. Klapper, D. Singer, S. Ansar, and J. Hess (2018) *Global Findex Database 2017: Measuring Financial Inclusion and the Fintech Revolution*, Washington: World Bank Group.

Desai, V. and A. Loftus (2012) 'Speculating on slums: Infrastructural fixes and informal housing in the global south', *Antipode* 45(4):789–808.

Donovan, K. P. (2018) 'The rise of the randomistas: on the experimental turn in international aid', *Economy and Society* 47(1):27–58.

Donovan, K. and E. Park (2019) 'Perpetual debt in the Silicon Savannah', *Boston Review*, 20 September, available: http://bostonreview.net/class-inequality-global-justice/kevin-p-donovan-emma-park-perpetual-debt-silicon-savannah.

Dror, D. and C. Jacquier (1999) 'Micro-insurance: Extending Health Insurance to the Excluded', *International Social Security Review* 52(1):71–97.

Dugan, M. (2005) 'Donors succeed by making themselves obsolete: Compartamos taps financial markets in Mexico', *CGAP Case Studies in Donor Good Practices no. 19*, Washington: World Bank Group.

Duménil, G. and D. Lévy (2004) *Capital Resurgent: Roots of the Neoliberal Revolution*, Cambridge, MA: Harvard University Press.

Dunkerley, J. (1984) *Rebellion in the Veins: Political Struggle in Bolivia 1952–82*, London: Verso.

Duvendack, M., R. Palmer-Jones, J. G. Copestake, L. Hooper, Y. Loke, and N. Rao (2011) *What is the evidence of the impact of microfinance on the well-being of poor people?* London: EPPI-Centre, University of London.

The Economist (2014) 'Livestock insurance in Kenya: No Risk, No Reward', *The Economist*, 17 April 2014, available: www.economist.com/baobab/2014/04/17/no-risk-no-reward.

—— (2016) 'Tests of Character: How Personality Testing Could Help Financial Inclusion', *The Economist*, 1 October, available: www.economist.com/news/finance-and-economics/21707978.

—— (2020) 'How digital financial services can prey upon the poor', *The Economist*, 30 January, available: www.economist.com/finance-and-economics/2020/01/30/how-digital-financial-services-can-prey-upon-the-poor.

Edwards, P. (2003) 'Infrastructure and modernity: Force, time, and social organization', in T. J. Misa, P. Brey, and A. Feenberg (eds.), *Modernity and Technology*, Cambridge: MIT Press, 185–226.

EFL (2012) *Technical Note: EFL Modeling Methodology*, Cambridge, MA: Entrepreneurial Finance Lab.

—— (n.d.) 'EFL Case Study – Controlling Risk in a Microfinance Graduation: Janalakshmi Financial Services – India', available: www.eflglobal.com/resources/case-studies/.

Eling, M., S. Pradhan, and J. T. Schmit (2014) 'The Determinants of Microinsurance Demand', *The Geneva Papers on Risk and Insurance* 39(2):224–63.

El-Zogbhi, M. (2019) 'Is poverty reduction the right outcome for financial services?', *CGAP*, available: www.cgap.org/blog/poverty-reduction-right-outcome-financial-services.

Engberg, H. L. (1965) 'Commercial banking in East Africa, 1950–63', *Journal of Modern African Studies* 3(2):175–200.

Engberg, H. L. and W. A. Hance (1969) 'Growth and dispersion of branch banking in Tropical Africa, 1950–1964', *Economic Geography* 45(3):195–208.

Enns, C. and B. Bersaglio (2020) 'On the coloniality of "new" mega-infrastructure of East Africa', *Antipode* 52(3):101–23.

Ericson, R., D. Barry, and A. Doyle (2000) 'The Moral Hazards of Neoliberalism: Lessons from the Private Insurance Industry', *Economy and Society* 29(4):532–58.

EY (2016) *Evolving Landscape of Microfinance Institutions in India*, New Delhi: ASSOCHAM and Ernst & Young.

Ewald, F. (1990) 'Norms, Discipline, and the Law', *Representations* 30(1):138–61.

FinAccess (2019) *2019 FinAccess Household Survey*, Nairobi: FSD Kenya, CBK, KNBS.

Findlay, S. (2020) 'Indian fintechs face big test as economy feels the heat', *Financial Times*, 21 April, available: www.ft.com/content/200d394e-5c67-11ea-ac5e-df00963c20e6.

Fine, B. (2013) 'Financialization from a Marxist perspective', *International Journal of Political Economy* 42(4):47–66.

Fine, B. and A. Saad-Filho (2017) 'Thirteen things you need to know about neoliberalism', *Critical Sociology* 43(4–5):685–706.

Fonseca, C. (2016) *Helping Farmers Understand Index Insurance: Guidelines for Consumer Education Interventions*, Geneva: ILO.

Foster, J. B. (2015) 'The new imperialism of globalized monopoly-finance capital: an introduction', *Monthly Review* 67(3):1–22.

Fourcade, M. and K. Healy (2017) 'Seeing like a Market', *Socio-Economic Review* 15(1):9–29.

Frankel, C., J. Ossadón, and T. Pallesen (2019) 'The organization of markets for collective concerns and their failures', *Economy and Society* 48(2):153–74.

French, S. and A. Leyshon (2004) 'The new, new financial system? Towards a conceptualization of financial reintermediation', *Review of International Political Economy* 11(2):263–88.

Frimpong Boahmah, E. and N. S. Murshid (2019) '"Techno-market fix"? Decoding wealth through mobile money in the global South', *Geoforum* 106:253–62.

Froud, J., S. Johal, J. Montgomerie, and K. Williams (2010) 'Escaping the tyranny of earned income? The failure of finance as social innovation', *New Political Economy* 15(1):147–64.

Gabor, D. (2021) 'The Wall Street Consensus', *Development and Change*, DOI: 10.1111/dech.12645.

Gabor, D. and S. Brooks (2017) 'The Digital Revolution in Financial Inclusion: International Development in the Fintech Era', *New Political Economy* 22(4):423–36.

Gauthé, B. (1997) 'Sécurité Sociale pour le Secteur Informel au Bénin', in W. van Ginneken (ed.), *Social Security for the Informal Sector: Investigating the Feasibility of Pilot Projects in Benin, India, El Salvador, and Tanzania*, Geneva: ILO, 15–32.

Georgieva, K. and A. A. Selassie (2020) 'Charting a path for a resilient recovery in sub-Saharan Africa', *IMFBlog*, available: https://blogs.imf.org/2020/09/15/charting-a-path-for-a-resilient-recovery-in-sub-saharan-africa/.

Gerard, K. and M. Johnston (2019) 'Explaining microfinance's resilience: the case of microfinance in Australia', *Globalizations* 16(6):876–93.

Gill, S. (1992) 'Economic Globalization and the Internationalization of Authority: Limits and Contradictions', *Geoforum* 23(3):269–83.

—— (1995) 'Globalisation, Market Civilisation, and Disciplinary Neoliberalism', *Millennium* 24(3):399–423.

—— (1998) 'New Constitutionalism, Democratisation, and Global Political Economy', *Pacifica Review* 10(1):23–38.

GIZ (2019) *INFOCUS: Rural Insurance Services Programme (RISP) – Innovation & Technology – India*, Berlin: Federal Ministry for Economic Cooperation and Development.

Goh, M. (2020) 'LenndoEFL could face bankruptcy over $600k in unpaid fees', *TechinAsia*, 14 August, available: www.techinasia.com/lenddoefl-face-bankruptcy-600k-unpaid-fees.

Gokhale, K. (2009) 'A global surge in tiny loans spurs credit bubble in a slum', *Wall Street Journal*, 13 August, available: www.wsj.com/articles/SB125012112518027581.

Gold Coast Government (1951) *Report on Banking Conditions in the Gold Coast and on the Question of Setting Up a National Bank*, Accra: Government Printer.

Gonzalez-Vega, C., M. Schreiner, R. L. Meyer, J. Rodriguez, and S. Navajas (1996) 'BANCOSOL: The challenge of growth for microfinance organizations', *Economics and Sociology Occasional Paper no. 2332*, Columbus: Ohio State University.

Gould, H. (2015) 'What you should know about fintech and its positive powers', *The Guardian*, 3 February, available: www.theguardian.com/sustainable-business/2015/feb/03/what-you-should-know-about-fintech-positive-powers-banking.

Government of India (1931) *The Indian Central Banking Enquiry Committee, Part I – Majority Report, vol. 1*, Calcutta: Government Printer.

GPFI (2016) *G20 High Level Principles for Digital Financial Inclusion*, Chengdu: G20 Global Partnership for Financial Inclusion.

—— (2017) *2017 Financial Inclusion Action Plan*, Hamburg: G20 Global Partnership for Financial Inclusion.

Greatrex, H., J. Hansen, S. Garvin, R. Diro, M. Le Guen, S. Blakeley, K. Rao, and D. Osgood (2015) 'Scaling up index insurance for smallholders: Recent evidence and insights', *CCFAS Report, no. 14*, Copenhagen: Consultative Group on International Agricultural Research.

Green, W. N. (2019) 'From rice fields to financial assets: Valuing land for micro-finance in Cambodia', *Transactions of the Institute of British Geographers* 44(4):749–62.

Grimes, O. F. (1976) *Housing for low-income urban families: Economics and policy in the developing world*, Baltimore: Johns Hopkins University Press.

Groenfeldt, T. (2015) 'Lenndo creates credit scores using social media', *Forbes*, 29 January, available: www.forbes.com/sites/tomgroenfeldt/2015/01/29/lenddo-creates-credit-scores-using-social-media/?sh=45d7552d2fde.

Gruffydd-Jones, B. (2012) 'Bankable slums? The global politics of slum upgrading', *Third World Quarterly* 33(5):769–89.

Guermond, V. (2020) 'Contesting the financialization of remittances: Repertoires of reluctance, refusal, and dissent in Ghana and Senegal', *Environment and Planning A: Economy and Space*, DOI: 10.1177/0308518X20976141.

Güngen, A. R. (2017) 'Financial inclusion and policy-making: Strategy, campaigns, and microcredit *a la Turca*', *New Political Economy* 23(3):331–47.

Hall, S. (2012) 'Geographies of money and finance II: Financialization and financial subjects', *Progress in Human Geography* 36(3):403–11.

Harford, T. (2009) 'Perhaps microfinance isn't such a big deal after all', *Financial Times*, 5 December, available: www.ft.com/content/ae4211e8-dee7-11de-adff-00144feab49a.

Harold, R. P. (1966) *The Philippine challenge for thrift and homeownership: A report to the Agency for International Development, Department of State, USA on the future development of the savings and loan systems in the Republic of the Philippines*, Washington: International Union of Building Societies and Savings Associations.

Harris, K. and B. Scully (2015) 'A Hidden Counter-Movement? Precarity, Politics, and Social Protection Before and Beyond the Neoliberal Era', *Theory and Society* 44(5):415–44.

Harvey, D. (2003) *The New Imperialism*, Oxford: Oxford University Press.

—— (2004) 'The "New" Imperialism: Accumulation by Dispossession', *Socialist Register* 40:63–87.

—— (2006) *The Limits to Capital*, London: Verso.

Helleiner, E. (1994) *States and the Reemergence of Global Finance: From Bretton Woods to the 1990s*, Ithaca: Cornell University Press.

—— (2014) *The Status Quo Crisis: Global Financial Governance After the 2008 Meltdown*, Oxford: Oxford University Press.

Helms, B. (2006) *Access for All: Building Inclusive Financial Systems*, Washington: CGAP.

Hernandez, E., R. Goslinga, and V. Wang (2018) 'Using satellite data to scale smallholder agricultural insurance', *CGAP Brief*, Washington: CGAP.

Hesketh, C. (2020) 'Between Pachakuti and passive revolution: The search for post-colonial sovereignty in Bolivia', *Journal of Historical Sociology* 33(4):567–86.

Hesketh, C. and A. D. Morton (2013) 'Spaces of uneven development and class struggle in Bolivia: Transformation or *trasformismo*?' *Antipode* 46(1):149–69.

Hilferding, R. (1981) *Finance Capital: A study of the latest phase of capitalist development*, London: Routledge.

Hoder, F., M. Wagner, J. Sguerra, G. and Bertol (2016) *Harnessing the FinTech Revolution: How Digital Innovations are Revitalizing MSME Finance in Latin America and the Caribbean*, New York: Oliver Wyman.

Hoque, M. and Z. U. Ahmed (1989) 'A review of microenterprise credit programs in Bangladesh', *Economics and Sociology Occasional Paper no. 1589*, Columbus: Department of Agricultural Economics and Rural Sociology, Ohio State University.

Hudson, P. (2017) *Bankers and Empire: How Wall Street Colonized the Caribbean*, Chicago: University of Chicago Press.

IAA (2014) *Issues Paper: Addressing the Gap in Actuarial Services in Inclusive Insurance Markets*, Ottawa: IAA.

IAIS (2007) *Issues in Regulation and Supervision of Microinsurance*, Basel: IAIS.

—— (2010) *Issues Paper on the Regulation and Supervision of Mutuals, Cooperatives and Other Community-Based Organizations in Increasing Access to Insurance Markets*, Basel: IAIS.

IFAD (2017) *Remote sensing for index insurance: Findings and lessons learned for smallholder agriculture*, Rome: IFAD.

ILO (1977a) *Improvement and harmonisation of social security systems in Africa*, Geneva: ILO.

—— (1977b) *Iran – Project Findings and Recommendations: Social Security*, Geneva: ILO.

—— (1980) *Malaysia – Social Security for Farmers and Fishermen: Project Findings and Recommendations*, Geneva: ILO.

—— (1982) *Rapport au Gouvernement de la République Gabonaise sur la Réstructuration et l'Extension de la Protection Sociale*, Geneva: ILO.

—— (1989) *Rapport au Gouvernement de la République Camerounaise sur l'Extension de la Protection Sociale aux Populations non-Salariées*, Geneva: ILO.

Inikori, J. (2002) *Africans and the Industrial Revolution in England: A Study in International Trade and Economic Development*, Cambridge: Cambridge University Press.

Insight2Impact (2016) *Client Insight Note – Now You See Me: How Alternative Data is Unlocking New Markets for Financial Services*, Cape Town and Johannesburg: CENFRI and FinMark Trust.

Isakson, S. R. (2015) 'Derivatives for Development? Small-Farmer Vulnerability and the Financialization of Risk Management', *Journal of Agrarian Change* 15(4):569–80.

Izaguirre, J. C., M. Kaffenberger, and R. Mazer (2018) 'It's time to slow digital credit's growth in Kenya', *Consultative Group to Assist the Poor*, available: www.cgap.org/blog/its-time-slow-digital-credits-growth-east-africa.

Jafarov, E., R. Maino, and M. Pani (2019) 'Financial repression is knocking at the door, again. Should we be concerned?', *IMF Working Paper WP/19/211*, Washington: IMF.

Jafri, J. (2019) 'When billions meet trillions: impact investing and shadow banking in Pakistan', *Review of International Political Economy* 26(3):520–44.

Jain, S. and D. Gabor (2020) 'The rise of digital financialization: the case of India', *New Political Economy* 25(5):813–28.

James, D. and D. Rajak (2014) 'Credit Apartheid, Migrants, Mines, and Money', *African Studies* 73(3):455–76.

Jeacle, I. and E. J. Walsh (2002) 'From Moral Evaluation to Rationalization: Accounting and the Shifting Technologies of Credit', *Accounting, Organizations and Society* 27(8):737–61.

Jenik, I. and K. Lauer (2017) 'Regulatory Sandboxes and Financial Inclusion', *CGAP Working Paper*, Washington: World Bank Group.

JFS (2017) *Janalakshmi Annual Report 2016-2017*, Bangalore: Janalakshmi Financial Services.

Johnson, L. (2013) 'Index Insurance and the Articulation of Risk-Bearing Subjects', *Environment and Planning A* 45(11):2663–81.

Joslin, D. (1962) *A Century of Banking in Latin America*, London: Oxford University Press.

Kaffenberger, M., E. Totolo, and M. Soursourian (2018) 'A digital credit revolution: Insights from borrowers in Kenya and Tanzania', *CGAP Working Paper*, Washington: Consultative Group to Assist the Poor.

Kamenov, N. (2019) 'Imperial cooperative experiments and global market capitalism, c.1900–c.1960', *Journal of Global History* 14(2):219–37.

—— (2020) 'The place of the "cooperative" in the agrarian history of India, c.1900–1970', *Journal of Asian Studies* 79(1):103–28.

Karasti, H., F. Millerand, C. M. Hine, and G. C. Bowker (2016) 'Knowledge infrastructures: Part I', *Science and Technology Studies* 29(1):2–12.

Karlan, D. and J. Zinman (2011) 'Microcredit in theory and practice: Using randomized credit scoring for impact evaluation', *Science* 332(6035):1278–84.

Kear, M. (2017) 'Playing the Credit Score Game: Algorithms, "Positive" Data, and the Personification of Financial Objects', *Economy and Society* 46(3–4):346–68.

Kentikelenis, A., T. H. Stubbs, and L. P. King (2016) 'IMF conditionality and development policy space, 1985–2014', *Review of International Political Economy* 23(4):543–82.

Kessler, A. (2020) 'It's time to protect Kenyans from a digital lending laboratory', *Center for Financial Inclusion Blog*, 26 February, available: www.centerforfinancialinclusion.org/its-time-to-protect-kenyans-from-a-digital-lending-laboratory.

Keucheyan, R. (2018) 'Insuring climate change: new risks and the financialization of nature', *Development and Change* 49(2):484–501.

Khandker, S. R., B. Khalily, and Z. Khan (1995) *Grameen Bank: Performance and Sustainability*, Washington: World Bank Group.

Kidder, T. (1997) 'Macro debates at the Micro-Credit Summit', *Development in Practice* 7(4):432–35.

Kimari, W. and H. Ernestson (2020) 'Imperial remains and imperial invitations: Centring race within the contemporary large-scale infrastructure of East Africa', *Antipode* 52(3):825–46.

Kirsch, S. and D. Mitchell (2004) 'The nature of things: Dead labour, non-human actors, and the persistence of Marxism', *Antipode* 36(4):687–705.

Kitchin, R. and T. Lauriault (2015) 'Small Data in an Era of Big Data', *Geojournal* 80(4):463–75.

Kiwara, A. D. (1999) 'Health Insurance for the Informal Sector in the Republic of Tanzania', in W. van Ginneken (ed.), *Social Security for the Excluded Majority: Case Studies of Developing Countries*, Geneva: ILO, 117–44.

Kiwara, A. D. and F. Heijnis (1997) 'Health Insurance for Informal Sector Workers: Feasibility Study on Arusha and Mbeya, Tanzania', in W. van Ginneken (ed.), *Social Security for the Informal Sector: Investigating the Feasibility of Pilot Projects in Benin, India, El Salvador, and Tanzania*, Geneva: ILO, 73–94.

Klinger, B., L. Castro, P. Szenkman, and A. Khwaja (2013a) 'Unlocking SME Finance in Argentina with Psychometrics', *Inter-American Development Bank Technical Note no. IDB-TN-532*.

Klinger, B., A. I. Khwaja, and J. LaMonte (2013b) 'Improving Credit Risk Analysis with Psychometrics in Peru', *Inter-American Development Bank Technical Note no. IDB-TN-587*.

Klinger, B., A. Khwaja, and C. del Carpio (2013c) *Enterprising Psychometrics and Poverty Reduction*, New York: Springer.

Knafo, S. (2020) 'Rethinking neoliberalism after the Polanyian turn', *Review of Social Economy*, DOI: 10.1080/00346764.2020.1733644.

Koddenbrock, K. (2020) 'Hierarchical multiplicity in the international monetary system: from the slave trade to the CFA Franc in West Africa', *Globalizations* 17(3):516–31.

Koddenbrock, K., I. H. Kvangraven, and N. S. Sylla (2020) 'Beyond financialisation: the need for a *longue durée* understanding of finance in imperialism', https://doi.org/10.31219/osf.io/pjt7x.

Kouame, E. B. H. and A. N. Komenan (2012) 'Risk References and Demand for Microinsurance under Price Uncertainty: An Experimental Approach for Cocoa Farmers in Côte d'Ivoire', Microinsurance Innovation Facility Research Paper no. 13, Geneva: ILO.

Kremers, R. and J. Brassett (2017) 'Mobile Payments, Social Money: Everyday Politics of the Consumer Subject', *New Political Economy* 22(6):645–60.

Kvangraven, I. H. (2020) 'Nobel rebels in disguise: Assessing the rise and rule of the Randomistas', *Review of Political Economy* 32(3):305–41.

—— (2021) 'Beyond the stereotype: restating the relevance of the dependency research programme', *Development and Change* 52(1):76–112.

Langevin, M. (2019) 'Big data for (not so) small loans: technological infrastructures and the massification of fringe finance', *Review of International Political Economy* 26(5):790–814.

Langley, P. (2014) 'Equipping Entrepreneurs: Producing Credit and Credit Scores', *Consumption, Markets, and Culture* 17(5):448–67.

Langley, P. and A. Leyshon (2020) 'The platform political economy of fintech: reintermediation, consolidation, and capitalisation', *New Political Economy*, DOI: 10.1080/13563467.2020.1766432.

Lapavitsas, C. (2013) *Profiting Without Producing: How Finance Exploits Us All*, London: Verso.

Leão, L. d. S. and G. Eyal (2020) 'Searching under the streetlight: A historical perspective on the rise of the randomistas', *World Development* 127:104781.

Lecoq, J. (1903) *Les Sociétés Indigènes de Prévoyance de Secours et de Prêts Mutuels des Communes d'Algérie*, Paris: A. Pedone.

Leyshon, A. and N. Thrift (1999) 'Lists Come Alive: Electronic Systems of Knowledge and the Rise of Credit Scoring in Retail Banking', *Economy and Society* 28(3):434–66.

—— (2007) 'The Capitalization of Almost Everything: The Future of Finance and Capitalism', *Theory, Culture & Society* 24(7–8):97–115.

Li, T. M. (2009) 'To Make live or let die? Rural dispossession and the protection of surplus populations', *Antipode* 41(S1):66–93.

Lockwood, E. (2015) 'Predicting the Unpredictable: Value-at-risk, Performativity, and the Politics of Financial Uncertainty', *Review of International Political Economy* 22(4):719–56.

Lonsdale, J. and B. Berman (1979) 'Coping with the contradictions: The development of the colonial state in Kenya, 1895–1914', *Journal of African History* 20(4):487–505.

Lutz, E. and P. L. Scandizzo (1980) 'Price distortion in developing countries: A bias against agriculture', *European Review of Agricultural Economics* 7(1):5–27.

Luxemburg, R. (2003) *The Accumulation of Capital*, New York: Routledge.

Maclean, K. (2013) 'Gender, Risk, and Microfinancial Subjectivities', *Antipode* 45(2):455–73.

Mader, P. (2015) *The Political Economy of Microfinance: Financializing Poverty*, New York: Palgrave Macmillan.

—— (2018) 'Contesting Financial Inclusion', *Development and Change* 49(2):461–83.

Mahoney, J. (2010) *Colonialism and Postcolonial Development: Spanish America in Comparative Perspective*, Cambridge: Cambridge University Press.

Maldonado, C. (1989) 'The Underdogs of the Urban Economy Join Forces: Results of an ILO Programme in Mali, Rwanda, and Togo', *International Labour Review* 128(1):65–84.

Malik, K., M. Meki, J. Morduch, T. Ogden, S. Quinn, and F. Said (2020) 'COVID-19 and the Future of Microfinance: Evidence and Insights from Pakistan', *Oxford Review of Economic Policy* 36(S1):S138–S168.

Mann, B., T. Dinku, and H. Greatrex (2014) 'Data for Index Insurance', *Global Index Insurance Facility Knowledge Notes*, Washington: World Bank Group.

Mann, G. and J. Guyer (1999) 'Imposing a Guide on the *Indigène*: The Fifty-Year Experience of the *Sociétés de Prévoyance* in French West and Equatorial Africa', in E. Stiansen and J. Guyer (eds.), *Credit, Currencies, and Culture: African Financial Institutions in Historical Perspective*, Uppsala: Nordiska Afrikainstitutet, 124–51.

Marconi, R. and P. Mosley (2006) 'Bolivia during the global crisis 1998–2004: Towards a "macroeconomics of microfinance"', *Journal of International Development* 18(2):237–61.

Marron, D. (2007) 'Lending by Numbers: Credit Scoring and the Constitution of Risk within American Consumer Credit', *Economy and Society* 36(1):103–33.

Martin, E. (2020) 'Oxfam says IMF loans force spending cuts that exacerbate poverty', *Bloomberg*, 12 October, available: www.bloomberg.com/news/articles/2020-10-12/oxfam-says-imf-loans-force-spending-cuts-that-exacerbate-poverty.

Martin, R. (2002) *The Financialization of Daily Life*, Philadelphia: Temple University Press.

Marx, K. (1990) *Capital: vol. I*, New York: Penguin.

—— (1991) *Capital: vol. III*, New York: Penguin.

Matul, M., M. J. McCord, C. Phily, and J. Harms (2010), *The Landscape of Microinsurance in Africa*, Microinsurance Paper 4, Geneva: International Labour Organization.

Maurer, B. (2012) 'Mobile Money: Communication, Consumption, and Change in the Payments Space', *Journal of Development Studies* 48(5):589–604.

Mawdsley, E. (2018) 'Development Geography II: Financialization', *Progress in Human Geography* 42(2):264–74.

McBride, S. (2016) 'Constitutionalizing austerity: Taking the public out of public policy', *Global Policy* 7(1):5–14.

McClagan, E. D., L. Samaldas, F. F. Lyall, F. W. Johnston, W. Renwick, M. A. Ali, and R. B. Ewbank (1915) *Report of the Committee on Cooperation in India*, Simla: Government Printer.

McCord, M. J., F. Botero, and J. S. McCord (2005) 'AIG Uganda, A member of the American Insurance Group of Companies', *CGAP Working Group on Microinsurance Good and Bad Practices Case Study no. 9*, Washington: World Bank Group.

McFall, L. (2019) 'Personalizing Solidarity? The role of self-tracking in the health insurance industry', *Economy and Society* 48(1):52–76.

McGrath, S. (2013) 'Fuelling global production networks with slave labour? Migrant sugar cane workers in the Brazilian Ethanol GPN', *Geoforum* 44:32–43.

McKinnon, R. I. (1973) *Money and Capital in Economic Development*, Washington: Brookings Institute.

McKinsey & Co. (2016) *Digital Finance for All: Powering Inclusive Growth in Emerging Economies*, San Francisco: McKinsey Global Institute.

Meagher, K. (2016) 'The Scramble for Africans: Demography, Globalisation, and Africa's Informal Labour Markets', *Journal of Development Studies* 52(4):483–97.

Meehan, J. (2004) 'Tapping the financial markets for microfinance: Grameen Foundation USA's promotion of this emerging trend', *Grameen Foundation USA Working Paper Series*, Washington: Grameen Foundation USA.

MIC (2015) *The Landscape of Microinsurance in Latin America and the Caribbean: A Changing Market*, Luxembourg: Microinsurance Network and Munich Re Foundation.

—— (2016) *The Landscape of Microinsurance: Africa 2015*, Luxembourg: Microinsurance Network and Munich Re Foundation.

MicroRate (2008) *The 2007 microfinance investment vehicles survey*, Lima: MicroRate.

—— (2013) *The state of microfinance investment 2013: Survey and analysis of MIVs, 8th edition*, Lima: MicroRate.

Milberg, W. (2008) 'Shifting Sources and Uses of Profits: Sustaining US Financialisation with Global Value Chains', *Economy and Society* 37(3):420–51.

Miller, P. and N. Rose (1991) 'Governing Economic Life', *Economy and Society* 19(1):1–31.

Milliman (2016) *Health Microinsurance Instructional Pricing Tool: User Manual*, Tampa Bay: IAA and Milliman.

Mirowski, P. (2009) 'Postface: Defining Neoliberalism', in P. Mirowski and D. Plehwe (eds.), *The Road From Mont Pellerin: The Making of the Neoliberal Thought Collective*, Cambridge, MA: Harvard University Press.

Moore, J. W. (2015) *Capitalism in the Web of Life*, London: Verso.

Morales, J. A. (1991) 'Structural adjustment and peasant agriculture in Bolivia', *Food Policy* 16(1):58–66.

Morawczynski, O. (2009) 'Exploring the usage and impact of "transformational" mobile financial services: the case of M-Pesa in Kenya', *Journal of Eastern African Studies* 3(3):509–25.

Morris, J. (2016) '"Cultivating the African": Barclays DCO and the decolonisation of business strategy in Kenya, 1950–1978', *The Journal of Imperial and Commonwealth History* 44(4):649–71.

Mosley, P. (2001) 'Microfinance and poverty in Bolivia', *Journal of Development Studies* 37(4):101–32.

Mouton, P. and J-V. Gruat (1989) 'The Extension of Social Security to Self-Employed Persons in Africa', *International Social Security Review* 88(1):40–54.

Mukherjee, P., A. Oza, L. Chassin, and R. Ruschismita (2014) *The Landscape of Microinsurance in Asia and Oceania 2013*, Munich: Munich Re Foundation.

Natarajan, N., K. Brickell, and L. Parsons (2019) 'Climate change adaptation and precarity across the rural-urban divide in Cambodia: Towards a "climate precarity" approach', *Environment and Planning E: Nature and Space* 2(4):899–921.

Natile, S. (2020) *The Exclusionary Politics of Digital Financial Inclusion: Mobile Money, Gendered Walls*, London: Routledge.

National Treasury (2008) *The Future of Microinsurance Regulation in South Africa*, Pretoria: Republic of South Africa.

—— (2011) *The South African Microinsurance Regulatory Framework*, Pretoria: Republic of South Africa.

Navajas, S., J. Conning, and C. Gonzalez-Vega (2003) 'Lending technologies, competition and consolidation in the market for microfinance in Bolivia', *Journal of International Development* 14(4):747–70.

Newlyn, W. T. and D. C. Rowan (1954) *Money and Banking in Colonial Africa: A Study of Monetary and Banking Systems of Eight British African Territories*, Oxford: Clarendon Press.

Nik-Khah, E. and P. Mirowski (2019) 'On going the market one better: Economic market design and the contradictions of building markets for public purposes', *Economy and Society* 48(2):268–94.

Noonan, L. (2019) 'Banks use fintech to make up for lost time on financial inclusion', *Financial Times*, 24 April, available: www.ft.com/content/091c9dd0-4b36-11e9-bde6-79eaea5acb64.

Nowell, W., R. S. Thompson, C. A. L. Irving, and E. Melville (1938) *Report of the Commission on the Marketing of West African Cocoa*, London: His Majesty's Stationary Office.

Ogden, T. (2019) 'Learning from financial inclusion research: what should we expect?' *CGAP*, available: www.cgap.org/blog/learning-financial-inclusion-research-what-should-we-expect.

Patnaik, U. (2017) 'Revisiting the "drain", or transfers from India to Britain in the context of global diffusion of capitalism', in S. Chakrabarti and U. Patnaik (eds.) *Agrarian and Other Histories: Essays for Binay Bhushan Chaudhuri*, New Delhi: Tulika Books, 277–317.

Peck, J. (2010) *Constructions of Neoliberal Reason*, Oxford: Oxford University Press.

—— (2013a) 'Explaining (with) Neoliberalism', *Territory, Politics, Governance* 1(2):132–57.

—— (2013b) 'For Polanyian economic geographies', *Environment and Planning A* 45(7):1545–68.

Phillips, A. (1989) *The Enigma of Colonialism: British Policy in West Africa*, London: James Currey.

Phillips, N. (2011) 'Informality, Global Production Networks, and the Dynamics of "Adverse Incorporation"', *Global Networks* 11(3):380–97.

—— (2013) 'Unfree labour and adverse incorporation in the global economy: Comparative perspectives on Brazil and India', *Economy and Society* 42(2):171–96.

—— (2016) 'Labour in Global Production: Reflections on Coxian Insights in a World of Global Value Chains', *Globalizations* 13(5):594–607.

Platteau, J-P., O. De Bock, and W. Gelade (2017) 'The Demand for Microinsurance: A Literature Review', *World Development* 94:139–56.

Politi, J. (2019) 'No end to poverty without financial inclusion, says World Bank', *Financial Times*, 24 April, available www.ft.com/content/0fb60294-4b36-11e9-bde6-79eaea5acb64.

Pradella, L. and T. Marois (2015) *Polarizing Development: Alternatives to Neoliberalism and the Crisis*, London: Pluto.

Pralahad, C. K. (2005) *The Fortune at the Bottom of the Pyramid: Eradicating Poverty through Profits*, London: Pearson Education.

Price, S. (2019) 'The risks and incentives of disciplinary neoliberal feminism: the case of microfinance', *International Feminist Journal of Politics* 21(1):67–88.

PwC (2016) *Non-Banking Financial Companies: The Changing Landscape*, Delhi: ASSOCHAM and PricewaterhouseCoopers India.

Rahman, R. and S. S. Mohammed (2007) *BRAC Micro-Credit Securitization Series I: Lessons from the world's first micro-credit backed security (MCBS)*, Boston: MF Analytics.

Rankin, K. N. (2001) 'Governing Development: Neoliberalism, Microcredit, and Rational Economic Woman', *Economy and Society* 30(1):18–37.

—— (2013) 'A Critical Geography of Poverty Finance', *Third World Quarterly* 34(4):551–72.

Rao, P. N. and K. C. Suri (2006) 'Dimensions of agrarian distress in Andhra Pradesh', *Economic and Political Weekly* 41(16):1546–52.

RBI (2011) *Report of the Sub-Committee of the Board of Directors of Reserve Bank of India to Study Issues and Concerns in the MFI Sector*, Mumbai: Reserve Bank of India.

Reddy, R. (2007) 'Microfinance cracking the capital markets II', *InSight 22*, Cambridge, MA: Accion International.

Renaud, B. (1984) 'Housing and financial institutions in developing countries: An overview', *World Bank Staff Working Papers, Number 658*, Washington: World Bank Group.

—— (1985) 'Financing shelter', *Water Supply and Urban Development Department Discussion Paper*, Washington: World Bank Group.

Rhyne, E. (2014) 'The PISCES Project: Helping Small Enterprises Swim Upstream', *Center for Financial Inclusion*, available: www.centerforfinancialinclusion.org/the-pisces-project-helping-small-enterprises-swim-upstream.

Roderick, L. (2014) 'Discipline and Power in the Digital Age: The Case of the US Consumer Data-broker Industry', *Critical Sociology* 40(5):729–46.

Rodney, W. (2018) *How Europe Underdeveloped Africa*, London: Verso.

Rolnik, R. (2013) 'Late neoliberalism: The financialization of homeownership and housing rights', *International Journal of Urban and Regional Research* 37(3):1058–66.

Roodman, D. (2012) *Due Diligence: An Impertinent Inquiry into Microfinance*, Washington: Center for Global Development.

Rosenberg, R. (1994) *Beyond self-sufficiency: licensed leverage and microfinance strategy*, Washington: USAID.

—— (2007) *CGAP reflections on the Compartamos initial public offering: A case study on microfinance interest rates and profits*, Washington: World Bank Group.

—— (2010) 'Does microcredit really help poor people?' *CGAP Focus Note no. 59, January 2010*, Washington: CGAP.

Roussi, A. (2020) 'Kenyan borrowers shamed by debt collectors chasing Silicon Valley loans', *The Financial Times*, 10 September, available: www.ft.com/content/16c86479-e88d-4a28-8fa4-cd72bace5104.

Rowan, D. (1952) 'Banking in Nigeria: A study in colonial financial evolution', *Banco Nazionale del Lavoro Quarterly Review* 5:159–75.

Roy, A. (2010) *Poverty Capital: Microfinance and the Making of Development*, London: Routledge.

Ruehll, M. and S. Findlay (2020) 'Indian and SE Asian fintechs braced for coronavirus storm', *Financial Times*, 3 April, available: www.ft.com/content/461abbc2-c73a-466b-aboe-f9619b4d5fa6.

Ruehll, M. and H. Sender (2020) 'Coronavirus chills Indonesia's red hot fintech startups', *Financial Times*, 26 April, available: www.ft.com/content/8992491e-8c83-4b02-81a6-b122a0633918.

Rutkowski, M., A. Garcia Mora, G. L. Bull, B. Guermazi, and C. Grown (2020) 'Responding to crisis with digital payments for social protection: Short term measures for long-term benefits', *World Bank Blogs*, 31 March, available: https://blogs.worldbank.org/voices/responding-crisis-digital-payments-social-protection-short-term-measures-long-term-benefits.

Sachs, J. (1987) 'The Bolivian hyperinflation and stabilization', *American Economic Review* 77(2):279–83.

Sahay, R., U. Erikssen von Allmen, A. Lahreche, P. Khera, S. Ogawa, M. Bazarbash, and K. Beaton (2020) 'The Promise of Fintech: Financial Inclusion in the Post COVID-19 Era', *International Monetary Fund Monetary and Capital Markets Departmental Paper Series, no. 20/09*, Washington: IMF.

Saltzman, S. B. and D. Salinger (1998) *The Accion CAMEL: Technical note*, Washington: USAID.

Scully, B. and A. O. Britwum (2019) 'Labour reserves and surplus populations: Northern Ghana and the Eastern Cape of South Africa', *Journal of Agrarian Change* 19(3):407–26.

Selwyn, B. (2017) *The Struggle for Development*, Cambridge: Polity.

—— (2019) 'Poverty chains in global capitalism', *Competition and Change* 23(1):71–97.

Settle, A. (2020) 'The financial inclusion agenda: for poverty alleviation or monetary control?', *Review of International Political Economy*, DOI: 10.1080/09692290.2020.1844780.

Sharma, S. and S. Soederberg (2020) 'Redesigning the business of development: the case of the World Economic Forum and global risk management', *Review of International Political Economy* 27(4):828–54.

Shaw, E. S. (1973) *Financial Deepening in Economic Development*, Oxford: Oxford University Press.

Shephard, C. Y. (1936) *Report on the Economics of Peasant Agriculture in the Gold Coast*, Accra: Government Printer.

Shipton, P. (1992) 'Debts and trespasses: Land, mortgages and the ancestors in Western Kenya', *Africa* 62(3):357–88.

Sinclair, H. (2012) *Confessions of a Microfinance Heretic: How Microfinance Lost Its Way and Betrayed the Poor*, San Francisco: Berrett-Koëler.

Sinclair, T. (1994) 'Passing judgement: Credit rating processes as regulatory mechanisms of governance in the emerging world order', *Review of International Political Economy* 1(1):133–59.

Singh, A. (2018) 'Regulate digital loans sector to reduce borrowers' risks', *Daily Nation*, available: www.nation.co.ke/kenya/blogs-opinion/opinion/regulate-digital-loans-sector-to-reduce-borrowers-risks-63214.

Sinha, F. (2006) *Social rating and social performance reporting in microfinance: Towards a common framework*, Washington: M-CRIL, The SEEP Network, and Argidius Foundation.

Sinha, S. (2011) 'Initial public offerings: The field's salvation or downfall?', commissioned workshop paper, *2011 Global Microcredit Summit*, November 14–17, Valladolid.

Skees, J. R. and B. J. Barrett (2006) 'Enhancing microfinance using index-based risk transfer products', *Agricultural Finance Review* 66(2):235–50.

SME Finance Forum (2014) *Annual Report 2013*, Washington: International Finance Corporation.

Smith, N. (1990) *Uneven Development: Nature, Capital, and the Production of Space*, Oxford: Basil Blackwell.

Soederberg, S. (2013) 'Universalising Financial Inclusion and the Securitisation of Development', *Third World Quarterly* 34(4):593–612.

—— (2014) *Debtfare States and the Poverty Industry: Money, Discipline, and the Surplus Population*, London: Routledge.

—— (2017) 'Universal access to affordable housing? Interrogating an elusive development goal', *Globalizations* 14(3):343–59.

S&P (2007) *Microfinance: Taking root in the global capital markets*, New York: Standard & Poors.

—— (2009) *Microfinance: Taking root in the global capital markets, Part 2*, New York: Standard & Poors.

Star, S. L. (1999) 'The ethnography of infrastructure', *American Behavioural Scientist*, 43(3): 377–91.

Staritz, C., S. Newman, B. Tröster, and L. Plank (2018) 'Financialization and global commodity chains: Distributional implications for cotton in sub-Saharan Africa', *Development and Change* 49(3):815–42.

Stein, D. (2016) 'Dynamics of Demand for Rainfall Insurance: Evidence from a Commercial Product in India', *World Bank Economic Review* 32(3):692–708.

Stiglitz, J. (1990) 'Peer monitoring and credit markets', *World Bank Economic Review* 4(3):351–66.

Struyk, R., R. Buckley, and M. A. Turner (1985) *Housing finance for LDCs: Developing a systematic approach*, Washington: US Agency for International Development.

Struyk, R. and M. A. Turner (1987) *Guidelines for creating a housing finance system in a developing country*, Washington: US Agency for International Development.

Suri, T. and W. Jack (2016) 'The long-run poverty and gender impacts of mobile money', *Science* 354(6317):1288–92.

Swindell, K. and A. Jeng (2006) *Migrants, Credit and Climate: The Gambian Groundnut Trade 1834–1934*, Leiden: Brill.

Tan, C. (2021) 'Audit as accountability: Technical authority and expertise in the governance of private financing for development', *Social and Legal Studies*, DOI: 10.1177/0964663921992100.

Tarazi, M. (2020) 'What's a donor to do? The financial impact of COVID-19 on the poor', *CGAP Blog*, 12 April, available: www.cgap.org/blog/whats-donor-do-financial-impact-coronavirus-poor.

Taylor, M. (2011) '"Freedom from Poverty is Not for Free": Rural Development and the Microfinance Crisis in Andhra Pradesh, India', *Journal of Agrarian Change* 11(4):484–504.

—— (2012) 'The Antinomies of Financial Inclusion: Debt, Distress, and the Workings of India Microfinance', *Journal of Agrarian Change* 12(4):601–10.

—— (2013) 'Liquid Debts: Credit, Groundwater and the Social Ecology of Agrarian Distress in Andhra Pradesh, India', *Third World Quarterly* 34(4):691–709.

—— (2016) 'Risky Ventures: Financial Inclusion, Risk Management, and the Uncertain Rise of Index-Based Insurance', *Research in Political Economy* 31:237–66.

Thurston, A. (1987) *Smallholder Agriculture in Colonial Kenya: The Official Mind and the Swynnerton Plan*, Cambridge: African Studies Centre.

Tignor, R. (1987) 'Senegal's Cooperative Experience, 1907–1960', in M. Gersovitz and J. Waterbury (eds.), *The Political Economy of Risk and Choice in Senegal*, London: Frank Cass.

Tilley, L. (2020) 'Extractive investibility in historical colonial perspective: the emerging market and its antecedents in Indonesia', *Review of International Political Economy*, DOI: 10.1080/09692290.2020.1763423.

Toye, J. (1993) *Dilemmas of Development: Reflections on the Counter-Revolution in Development Economics*, London: Blackwell.

Tun Wai, U. (1957) 'Interest rates outside the organized money markets of underdeveloped countries', *IMF Staff Papers* 6(1):80–142.

Turner, J. F. C. (1972) *Freedom to Build*, New York: Macmillan.

Uche, C. (1999) 'Foreign banks, Africans, and credit in colonial Nigeria, c. 1890–1912', *Economic History Review* 52:669–91.

UKAP (2012) *An Actuarial Model for Credit-Life Microinsurance*, available: www.microinsurancenetwork.org/groups/credit-life-actuarial-pricing-model-toolkit.

United Nations (2018) *Financing for Development: Progress and Prospects 2018*, New York: United Nations.

Upadhyaya, R. and S. Johnson (2015) 'Transformation in Kenya's banking sector, 2000–2012', in A. Heyer and M. King (eds.), *Kenya's Financial Transformation in the 21ˢᵗ Century*, Nairobi: FSD Kenya, 15–62.

USAID (1983) *Handbook 7: Housing Guarantees*, Washington: Department of State.

—— (1986) *Investment proposal for a US $2,500,000 loan to Accion International Ltd., Micro-lending Guaranty Facility*, Washington: Department of State.

USGAO (1978) *Report to Congress by the Comptroller General of the United States: Agency for International Development's Housing Investment Guaranty Program*, Washington: Government Accounting Office.

—— (1984) *Report to the Administrator, Agency for International Development: AID's Management of the Housing Guaranty Programme*, Washington: Government Accounting Office.

—— (1995) *Foreign Housing Guaranty Program: Financial condition is poor and goals are not achieved*, Washington: Government Accounting Office.

Van Ginneken, W. (1996) 'Social Security for the Informal Sector: Issues, Options, and Tasks Ahead', *Interdepartmental Project on the Urban Informal Sector Working Paper*, Geneva: ILO.

Van Waeyenberge, E. (2018) 'Crisis? What crisis? A critical appraisal of World Bank housing policy in the wake of the global financial crisis', *Environment and Planning A: Economy and Space* 50(2):288–309.

Velasco, C. (2020) 'Monopoly and competition: Kenyan banks at the end of the colonial period (1954–63)', *Business History*, DOI: 10.1080/00076791.2020.1744569.

Von Pischke, J. D. (1978) 'When is smallholder credit necessary?', *Development Digest* 16(3):6–14.

—— (1991) *Finance at the frontier: Debt capacity and the role of credit in the private economy*, Washington: World Bank Group.

Von Pischke, J. D. and D. W. Adams (1980) 'Fungibility and the design and evaluation of agricultural credit projects', *American Journal of Agricultural Economics* 62(4):719–26.

Vyas, M. (2017) '1.5 Million Jobs Lost in First Four Months of 2017', Centre for Monitoring the Indian Economy, available: www.cmie.com/kommon/bin/sr.php?kall=warticle&dt=2017-07-11%2011:07:31&msec=463/.

Watts, M. J. (2013) *Silent Violence: Food, Famine, and Peasantry in Northern Nigeria*, Athens, GA.: University of Georgia Press.

Weber, H. (2002) 'The imposition of a global development architecture: the example of microcredit', *Review of International Studies* 28(3):537–55.

—— (2004) 'The "New Economy" and Social Risk: Banking on the Poor?', *Review of International Political Economy* 11(2):356–86.

Werlin, H. (1999) 'The slum upgrading myth', *Urban Studies* 36(9):1523–34.

Williams, E. (1994) *Capitalism and Slavery*, Chapel Hill: University of North Carolina Press.

Wipf, J., D. Liber, and C. Churchill (2006) 'Product Design and Insurance Risk Management', in Churchill (ed.), *Protecting the Poor: A Microinsurance Compendium*, 146–73. Geneva: ILO.

Wipf, J., E. Kelly, and M. J. McCord (2011) 'Improving Credit Life Insurance', *Microinsurance Innovation Facility Working Paper no. 9*, Geneva: ILO.

Woodhouse, P. (2012) 'New investment, old challenges: land deals and the water constraint in African agriculture', *Journal of Peasant Studies* 39(3–4):777–94.

World Bank (1973) *Appraisal of a site and services project in Senegal*, Washington: World Bank Group.

—— (1974) *Bank policy on agricultural credit*, Washington: World Bank Group.

—— (1975a) *The Assault on World Poverty*, Washington: World Bank Group.

—— (1975b) *Housing: Sector policy paper*, Washington: World Bank Group.

—— (1976a) *Operations evaluation report: Agricultural credit programmes, vol. II, Analytical Report*, Washington: World Bank Group.

—— (1976b) *Project performance audit report: Gujarat agricultural credit project* (Credit 191-IN), Washington: World Bank Group.

—— (1977) *Report and recommendation of the President of the International Bank for Reconstruction and Development to the Executive Directors on a proposed loan to the Republic of Ecuador for an agricultural credit project*, Washington: World Bank Group.

—— (1978) *World Development Report 1978*, Washington: World Bank Group.

—— (1979) *Pakistan: Staff appraisal report, fourth credit for the Agricultural Development Bank,* Washington: World Bank Group.

—— (1980) *Accelerated Development in Sub-Saharan Africa: An Agenda for Action,* Washington: World Bank Group.

——(1983a) *Report and recommendation of the President of the International Bank for Reconstruction and Development to the Executive Directors on a proposed loan in an amount equivalent to US$70 million to the Bank for Agriculture and Agriculture Cooperatives with the guarantee of the Kingdom of Thailand for the second agricultural credit project,* Washington: World Bank Group.

—— (1983b) *Staff appraisal report: Pakistan – fifth agricultural credit project,* Washington: World Bank Group.

——(1985) *Report and recommendation of the President of the International Bank for Reconstruction and Development to the Executive Directors on a proposed loan in an amount equivalent to US $100 million to the Central Bank of the Philippines with the guarantee of the Republic of the Philippines for an agricultural credit project,* Washington: World Bank Group.

—— (1988) *Project completion report: Ecuador, agricultural credit project (Loan 1459-EC),* Washington: World Bank Group.

——(1989a) *Project completion report: India – Fourth Agricultural Refinance and Development Corporation project (ARDC IV) (Loan 2095-IN/Credit 1209-IN),* Washington: World Bank Group.

—— (1989b) *World Development Report 1989: Financial systems and development,* Oxford: Oxford University Press.

—— (1990a) *Project performance audit report: Zimbabwe, small farm credit project (Credit 1291-ZIM),* Washington: World Bank Group.

—— (1990b) *Memorandum and recommendation of the President of the International Bank for Reconstruction and Development to the Executive Directors on a proposed loan in an amount equivalent to US$ 148.5 million and a proposed credit in an amount equivalent to US$ 1.5 million to the Islamic Republic of Pakistan for an agricultural credit project,* Washington: World Bank Group.

—— (1990c) *Staff appraisal report: Pakistan – Agricultural credit project,* Washington: World Bank Group.

—— (1992a) *Performance audit report: Morocco – fifth and sixth agricultural credit projects,* Washington: World Bank Group.

—— (1992b) *Performance audit report: Philippines agricultural credit project (Loan 2570-PH),* Washington: World Bank Group.

——(1993a) *Housing: Enabling markets to work,* Washington: World Bank Group.

——(1993b) *Poverty reduction handbook,* Washington: World Bank Group.

——(1995a) *Project completion report: Honduras – Fourth agricultural credit project (Loan 2991-HO),* Washington: World Bank Group.

——(1995b) *Micro- and small-enterprise finance: Guiding principles for selecting and supporting intermediaries,* Washington: World Bank Group.

—— (1997) *Implementation completion report: Pakistan – Agricultural credit project (Loan 3226-PAK/Credit 2153/PAK),* Washington: World Bank Group.

—— (1999) *The World Bank and micro-enterprise finance: From concept to practice,* Washington: World Bank Group.

—— (2013) *World Development Report 2014: Risk and Opportunity: Managing Risk for Development.* Washington: World Bank Group.

—— (2016) *Doing Business 2017,* Washington, DC: World Bank.

—— (2018a) *Toolkit: Developing and operationalizing a national financial inclusion strategy,* Washington: World Bank Group.

——(2018b) 'Press Release: The Bali Fintech Agenda: A Blueprint for Successfully Harnessing Fintech's Opportunities', 11 October, available: www.worldbank. org/en/news/press-release/2018/10/11/bali-fintech-agenda-a-blueprint-for-successfully-harnessing-fintechs-opportunities.

—— (2019a) *Climate smart agriculture investment plan: Cote d'Ivoire,* Washington: World Bank Group.

——(2019b) *Policy note – Unlocking agriculture finance and insurance in Uganda: the financial sector's role in agricultural transformation,* Washington: World Bank Group.

——(2020a) *Accelerating digital transformation in Zambia: Digital economy diagnostic report,* Washington: World Bank Group.

——(2020b) *Africa's pulse, vol. 21: Assessing the economic impact of Covid-19 and policy responses in sub-Saharan Africa,* Washington: World Bank Group.

World Bank and IMF (2018) *The Bali Fintech Agenda: Chapeau Paper,* Washington: World Bank Group and International Monetary Fund.

Wrede, P. and C. Phily (2015), *Pricing for Microinsurance: A Technical Guide,* Geneva: ILO.

Ye, J., J. D. van der Ploueg, S. Schneider, and T. Shahin (2020) 'The incursions of extractivism: Moving from dispersed places to global capital', *Journal of Peasant Studies* 47(1):155–83.

Young, S. (2010) 'The "Moral Hazards" of Microfinance: Restructuring Rural Credit in India', *Antipode* 42(1):201–23.

Zhao, H., and S. E. Seibert (2006) 'The Big Five Personality Dimensions and Entrepreneurial Status, a Meta-Analytical Review', *Journal of Applied Psychology* 91(2):259–71.

Index

Thanks to our Patreon subscribers:

Andrew Perry
Ciaran Kane

Who have shown generosity and
comradeship in support of our publishing.

Check out the other perks you get by subscribing
to our Patreon – visit patreon.com/plutopress.
Subscriptions start from £3 a month.

The Pluto Press Newsletter

Hello friend of Pluto!

Want to stay on top of the best radical books
we publish?

Then sign up to be the first to hear about our
new books, as well as special events,
podcasts and videos.

You'll also get 50% off your first order with us
when you sign up.

Come and join us!

Go to bit.ly/PlutoNewsletter